NATIONAL UNIVERSITY
LIBRARY   SAN

D0458707

mary
spillane

BRANDING
YOURSELF

how to look, sound and behave

your way to success

PAN BOOKS

First published 2000 by Pan Books
an imprint of Macmillan Publishers Ltd
25 Eccleston Place London SW1W 9NF
Oxford and Basingstoke
Associated companies throughout the world
www.macmillan.com

ISBN 0 330 48148 7

Copyright © Mary Spillane 2000

The right of Mary Spillane to be identified as the
author of this work has been asserted by her in accordance
with the Copyright, Designs and Patents Act 1988.

All rights reserved. No part of this publication may be
reproduced, stored in or introduced into a retrieval system, or
transmitted, in any form, or by any means (electronic, mechanical,
photocopying, recording or otherwise) without the prior written
permission of the publisher. Any person who does any unauthorized
act in relation to this publication may be liable to criminal
prosecution and civil claims for damages.

9 8 7 6 5 4 3 2

A CIP catalogue record for this book is available from
the British Library.

Printed and bound in Great Britain by
Mackays of Chatham plc, Chatham, Kent

This book is sold subject to the condition that it shall not,
by way of trade or otherwise, be lent, re-sold, hired out,
or otherwise circulated without the publisher's prior consent
in any form of binding or cover other than that in which
it is published and without a similar condition including this
condition being imposed on the subsequent purchaser.

Contents

INTRODUCTION

This project has been thrust upon me – not by my publisher but by my clients. I have worked as an image consultant and performance coach for over 15 years and have had the privilege of helping people make more of themselves. In the process, they have helped me make more of me.

I also write this book from the heart, as someone who has branded and rebranded herself a few times and is going through her latest branding exercise as she writes this book, having sold one business and being in the process of establishing a new one.

MUDDLE, MUDDLE, TOIL AND TROUBLE

This book is a challenge to all who muddle along day in and day out, year in and year out. You work hard, try your best but don't seem to get the opportunities that you want and feel you deserve. Why is it so much easier for others? They don't put in half the effort but seem to breeze through. Or do they?

What is it about certain people that bowls us over when we meet them? What do they have that we don't? Are they better-looking, cleverer, more charming or just lucky? Are the successful and confident *born* that way or does money make them appear more of who they really are? Money can't buy you love or charisma. But you can *learn* how to be both more loveable and charismatic, or almost anything you want, whatever you want ... if you understand *your brand*.

GET CREATIVE, ANALYTICAL, PERSONAL

This book asks that you view yourself as a product . . . your most important one. It's the same exercise used by companies for their own products and corporate brands. To succeed, you will have to be both creative and analytical as well as very, very personal. The creativity will come in developing your brand values – what you want others to believe to be true about you. Analysis is required for how well you live your brand – does your voice *sound* the part or does it let you down? If so, how? How well do you handle difficult people, new situations, the opposite sex in business? Does your dress sense jive with your brand or are you sending conflicting messages? If you are really honest, when was the last time you really challenged your communications skills? Have you been cruising along in neutral doing just 'OK' and, hence, missing opportunities?

You won't buy a new brand unless it is *yours*. So, we're going to get personal. It's *your* dream in *your* head that we will be dealing with, not trying to turn you into someone else. As you will learn, a great product has integrity. Think Mont Blanc, think Post-it Notes, think Dunhill, think Jaguar, think Vaseline, think Tiffany, think Play-doh! Think YOU!

Try to be as dispassionate as you can and keep emotions at bay. Past rejections and failures blind us to future possibilities. Learn from some of the case studies, do the questionnaires and audits of your image, get input from people you trust. Together, we'll look at your brand values, define your uniqueness and see how well you are promoting yourself.

THE JOURNEY

I have organized this book much in the way I organize coaching for individuals. Chapter 1 is the sales job as to why you need a brand. If you don't understand why you should be bothered developing your brand the whole process will be muddled and less useful. The next chapter tells you how you will do it, because defining your brand clarifies your thinking about what you want from your job and what you want others to believe about you. There is no right formula for certain jobs or sectors. It is up to you to choose your values and develop *your* personal brand identity (or PBI).

In Chapter 3 you'll learn how sounding the part can help influence the people you need to and be more effective. Acting the part in Chapter 4 adds to the power of your voice by dissecting non-verbal behaviour with suggestions on correcting some idiosyncrasies that you will find out you have (if you don't already know) by getting input from others. And everyone's brand benefits from the occasional reminder on minding your manners if for no other reason than to feel more at ease in testing situations. Besides, your mum will be impressed! The next two chapters – 5 and 6 – are about looking the part. Read what's suggested for your own sex, along with insights for image issues for the opposite sex. Influencing others is discussed in Chapter 7 with practical suggestions for developing rapport quickly and to build lasting relationships. Find out how sharp and effective your communications skills are in Chapter 8, 'Presenting . . . Yourself', and what you need to do to be a more impressive presenter. Sex at work in Chapter 9 isn't the kind of fun you're probably thinking of; rather it covers the dilemmas that men and women sometimes have in understanding and dealing with each other at work. We are creating new terms for male/female partnerships that demand understanding and respect on everyone's part.

VALUE-CENTRED BRANDING

Do you want more out of life, your career and your relationships but don't know where to begin? I will ask you to define *your brand* first, the *values* you want to project to others and learn how to live them by the way you look, sound and act. How you live your brand will emanate from *your* values, not the boss's or your partner's or even mine. *Your values.* The kind of person you want others to know that you are, or that you are capable of being.

In defining your brand and learning how best to project it, you can transform your life. Why do I have confidence in saying this? Because I have seen people learn how to *be* the dream in their heads. You don't need to win the lottery, have cosmetic surgery or a personality transplant to achieve your dreams. It's only a matter of learning techniques used by top performers, business people and, OK, even some politicians and by observing successful, confident people who we meet every day and analysing what they do that we don't. It's also choosing from all the role models, advice and your own experiences the lessons you want to apply to your own life.

You know that you adapt your image and your behaviour to suit different situations. We need to be chameleons in business as well as in our fast-paced, evolving lives, adaptable to our ever-changing world. What has worked well for us over the last 5 or 10 years might not be enough to get us what we want in the future. Become a chameleon, not a charlatan: personal growth and development takes integrity both to work as well as to be sustained. Besides, you know how terrific you really are – it's just the rest of us who don't get it . . . yet.

SPEAKING FROM EXPERIENCE . . .

Like many readers, my career has been a surprise. I had a game plan upon leaving university with a degree in politics: to enter the political fray and make a difference. OK. It was 1972, we were idealistic then and in the US shaping public policy was a very sexy as well as worthwhile sphere which still attracted many of the 'best and brightest' from my generation. In my twenties, I had various jobs in lobbying, public relations and journalism, finally working for both Presidents Carter and Reagan as a crisis manager. Like many who recognize advanced degrees as key to advancement and further opportunities, I did two postgraduate stints. A magical year at Harvard's Kennedy School catapulted me straight into a presidential appointment in Washington DC.

But love and marriage intervened, bringing with it relocation to

Britain (my husband had to return home according to the terms of his fellowship). Did I mind leaving Washington and a terrific career? You bet I did, but he was worth it. But in Britain, neither my education nor experience was understood, let alone valued. After earning handsomely and having highly visible jobs with lots of responsibilities, I found few options for applying my skills. It was also 1981 and we were in the depths of a recession. If there were jobs going, a Brit was first in line (rightly so). The one attractive option, to set up a public affairs operation for one of Europe's largest PR firms, was rescinded once they learned I was pregnant (something illegal even then in the US, and mind-blowing to me).

A married woman expecting her first child is not supposed to feel the despair of unemployment. After all, I was being 'supported' by my husband and being a mother is *a full-time job*. But it wouldn't have worked as a full-time job for me! I had studied hard, worked hard and had every intention of having a career. Like many women, I wanted children and a career and was determined to try both simultaneously. Besides, being the second child in a family of twelve meant that I thought I should be able to do it blindfolded!

Hence, I started my first branding exercise. I was going to find an opportunity that I could manage with a new child, would make the most of my experience and skills, and grow into something for the future.

BEAUTY? YOU'VE GOT TO BE KIDDING

The phone call came out of the blue. A friend from Washington had just taken over this 'crazy colour company' which was a runaway success – Color Me Beautiful. Could I take it on in Britain? Having few options at four months pregnant, I figured I'd check it out. But a beauty business? I had never read a beauty book in my life, wore little make-up and had a personal style typical of most Americans in the early 80s – very preppy and *not* what you'd call fashionable. But after reading the best-selling book by the same name and hearing American friends enthuse about having their 'colours done', I had a hunch it would be worth trying in Britain. Besides, no one I knew from my former life would know what I was doing. I could experiment in something blatantly commercial and seemingly frivolous without my cred being destroyed.

If I was going to succeed, I would have to turn myself into a credible-looking/sounding/projecting 'colour, style, beauty'-person. Cripes! Suffice to say that most rebranding exercises are not so painful (and painfully obvious whilst I was learning). I went to America and absorbed the US Color Me Beautiful culture – a trip into the Twilight Zone with flawless women (indeed 98 per cent women-dominated which was bizarre enough after working for a decade in a mainly male milieu) colour-co-ordinated from their eyeshadow and fingernails to the bows on their shoes! It was fun, more fun than I imagined and very successful. But the American version would not fly in Britain or Europe without serious rethinking.

In the first 5 years, I set about doing a postgraduate equivalent, studying everything I could on fashion, beauty, men's tailoring, communication and public relations whilst shaping this new business. Not only was Color Me Beautiful new, the whole notion of image consulting was new and unknown. My job was not just to market CMB services and products but to establish a new industry on my new side of the Atlantic. That challenge alone was so stimulating that I never looked back to my lost career in politics. Besides, I soon found that politicians would be prime candidates for CMB, and before long I was back in the political world, albeit in a totally new capacity as image maker to current and future leaders.

In the last decade I have branched into personal coaching, covering most aspects of confidence-building including: colour and style consulting, personal shopping, makeovers, presentation and media training, speech-writing, fitness and nutrition advice, business and social etiquette, career coaching (CV preparation, planning for promotion, marketing oneself for a new job, interview techniques, cross-training for a new career) and, more recently, motivating others about ageing successfully and happily.

Performance coaching grew out of the work on dress and style because packaging alone doesn't help people change and become more effective. Drawing on my own background as a management consultant, speech writer, PR person, presenter, fitness/health freak, lobbyist and managing director as well as a chronic advocate of lifelong learning, I said 'yes' to most pleas for help beyond just image.

So after a career in politics, another in business, and now as a performance coach, I have had three major rebranding exercises. That doesn't count the many 'fine-tunings' along the way when marketing myself or my business to different sectors in different countries. So much of the advice in this book is from personal lessons learned along with coaching others and continual learning from gifted, insightful mentors. My clients will have to vouch for whether or not I practise what I preach. Because unlike other American authors, this one simply can't bring herself to include glowing testimonials that boast her 'brilliance'. (I'm becoming more European by the year!)

WHAT'S CHANGING FOR YOU?

I am fascinated with *change* and how it affects us from how we look and feel, to how we think and behave. People generally seek out an image consultant or performance coach when they are going through changes. You were probably attracted to the title *Branding Yourself* because you are perhaps feeling threatened or vulnerable or uncertain about the future.

Image advice is sought for both personal and professional reasons generally to address problems or dilemmas like:

- *I want to get promoted this year and need to do everything possible to ensure that it happens.*
- *I am not being taken seriously in meetings. Why?*

- *I've gained weight and need to look slimmer.*
- *I look older/younger than I am. Can you help?*
- *How can I look more modern? I've been told I'm very out of date.*
- *I need to convey that I am capable of more responsibility.*
- *I am up against tough competition for partnership and need to look like part of it before I get it.*
- *I always get interrupted by others. Why?*
- *I am single once again and need to revive my social life.*
- *My style is dated and needs a revamp.*
- *I turn down chances to give presentations but they are now part of my job. How can I overcome the fear of public speaking?*
- *The company has just declared that 'dress down' reigns supreme. Help! How do I do it?*
- *I am relocating abroad and this look won't cut it.*
- *I have thrown in the towel as corporate woman/man and now will be marketing my own business. How should I look?*
- *I need others to think I am dynamic. How can I convey that?*
- *My boss says my image is a mess. But I don't want to dress like him. Where's the compromise?*
- *I am sick of looking like Power Woman. Help me look more feminine yet businesslike.*

IT TAKES INTEGRITY

The principles, ideas and tips that I share in *Branding Yourself* should help you reassess your own image and give you suggestions for being more effective in convincing others that you are the person that you want them to believe you are. Don't think for a minute that you can dress better, sharpen your speech, develop a winning manner and fool folks. As you will discover, we are all too good at sizing each other up. In fact, within 3 minutes of meeting people we are 90 per cent accurate in assessing their competence! If you aren't true to yourself you can't expect to sustain a false image no matter how great your acting skills.

Successful personal branding comes from within – who you are today as well as the dreams of the kind of person you want to be. As someone who has been able to transform herself quite markedly based on a new vision of who I could become, I know that you, too, will be able to live your dream if you put in the effort. Besides, you'll have fun and be richer for it; figuratively, that is. Your bank balance might be in for a shock!

1

WHY YOU NEED
A BRAND

YOU are your most important product

The notion that you should treat yourself as a product might initially be abhorrent to some. 'I am human. I have integrity. Branding myself as a product is fake, just an attempt to deceive people.' You might think, 'I want to be valued for my capabilities, taken for who I am.'

Working as an image consultant, I have heard similar views from both men and women over the years. But if I asked you why people sometimes don't understand or fully appreciate you, why you don't get the recognition or rewards that you deserve, the reasons are often down to problems with image and communication. How we look, sound and behave, how we handle ourselves and others, are more important in business today than how capable or clever we are. Don't worry, I'll back up this assertion with research and case studies.

Good people have integrity; so too do good brands. A successful brand must be true to itself. If Coca-Cola, McDonald's, Virgin, Amazon, Mercedes-Benz, Microsoft, Nike, and Disney didn't deliver according to their brand messages they wouldn't be global successes – recognized, understood, valued and *bought* by us. In this book you will define your own brand messages and develop your own strategies – to remain *true to yourself* – and convey those messages more effectively to others.

TOP BRANDS DO IT

The best brands *know* who they are and live their values. Their identity is clear and recognizable just as yours should be. We know what we get when we choose these products just as we need to appreciate as much as we can about you, upfront. If you surprise us over time by being even more than we thought initially, all the better.

Fashions come and go, styles change. A good brand adapts itself to change, it does not try to turn itself into something totally different.

How successful would Coke be if it jumped on the bandwagon of alchopop drinks? Would it still be able to boast its wholesome image, appropriate for all ages? What if Nike, the sports apparel specialists, tried its hand at high fashion? Would its core sports products have the same integrity? If McDonald's were to sell its products via supermarkets would they be as successful as those bought 'freshly-fried' at their own golden arches?

Great brands, like these and others, adapt to the times without sacrificing their true identity.

- **Coca-Cola** – *It's the real thing.* Others have tried to copy the most genuine cola drink in the world but manage only to dent the power of the king of colas. Global, fresh, young and the 'classic' American drink for anyone of any age to feel part of the grand old US of A.
- **McDonald's** – *Golden arches: a stamp of universality.* No matter what city, country or square you are in – be it Red, Leicester or Times Square – the golden arches are there offering their trademark product without variation. The fast, friendly, reliable service and products are delivered irrespective of location, nationality or currency.
- **Virgin** – *Bold, modern, honest, fun and RED.* Synonymous with its iconoclastic founder Richard Branson, voted the most trusted businessman in Britain, Virgin businesses have succeeded largely due to Branson's identification with the product or service. He takes a personal role in launching new Virgin companies: from standing atop one of his (former) aeroplanes to promote new routes or offers from Virgin Airlines; dressing in drag to launch Virgin Brides; designing a cola bottle to rival Coke (good try) after Pamela Anderson's physique (and

canoodling with her to promote the brand); to selling us pensions and financial services knowing that if he tells us his deal is the fairest, we'll believe it.

- **Amazon** – *One of the first online shopping services to bring products (books, CDs, etc.) to us with dizzying speed at competitive prices.* A simple message that delivers as promised – the largest selection of books available anywhere; hence, an 'amazon' among e-tailers on the Net as well as the greatest challenge to high-street booksellers.

- **Mercedes-Benz** – *Classic, not flashy, luxury cars.* Arguably, the most desirable car in the world. Keeps modern with subtle innovation rather than following fashion whims. Keeps us buying or aspiring towards its cars because of status and investment values that remain top in the industry.

- **Microsoft** – *A communication tool shared by millions around the world.* In one's lifetime, few brands have succeeded so pervasively in influencing business, education and communication on a global scale. With its founder Bill Gates the most successful businessman in history, we begrudge him little for his massive $95 billion personal fortune – he's young(ish), philanthropic, not as geeky as he looks and keeps delivering superior products.

- **Nike** – *Just do it!* Developing one of the great straplines in advertising history, Nike brought designer status to sports gear yet made it desirable and accessible to all from top athletes to couch potatoes. The dynamic yet chic logo just says it – i.e. just do it – and we do, buying the gear and making the brand worth $8 billion.

- **Disney** – *Wholesome, optimistic family entertainment.* From branded toys, clothes, games and films/videos to leisure resorts, Disney delivers the 'experience'. Where others have tried to emulate their theme parks, none come near Disney's consistency and value. Long after its founder's dream had been realized, Disney's strategic diversifications make sure it remains one of the top 10 most successful brands.

You might be reading this book because you are in the process of looking for a new job and want fresh ideas for selling yourself. To begin with, you need to remind yourself of *what* you are selling – the intangible values that comprise your brand. You will learn how to present yourself the way you want to as well as understand better what potential employers might *really* want from you, i.e. the stuff beyond the job spec. When you agree your own brand values and learn how to assess others' you will see how getting a 'fit' is much easier. Interviewing should be less stressful – even fun! – as a result.

If you are gainfully and happily employed, perhaps you are reading this book with an eye on future opportunities knowing that she/he who is complacent is generally in for a big surprise. No one – be it the boss, the whiz kid, the techy-know-it-all, the long-standing loyal trooper or devoted personal assistant – is indispensable in today's business environment. Let's harness your confidence and explore what you think others believe about you and reconsider what new brand values might be needed for the next stage of your career. If you have been *effective, reliable,* and *knowledgeable* thus far are these values enough to gain new chances of management or leadership? If not, what new brand values do you need to adopt; to look, sound, behave and project?

We don't like to admit it, but it's fascinating to watch how film/TV/ pop stars reinvent themselves when their 'bankability' is wavering. Their brand needs work and so they retool to present us with a new and improved version. The 'resting' actress re-sculpts her body via personal trainers or cosmetic surgeons and wows the world with her new self. A marketing campaign follows and so too do new job offers. Once hard-living rockers go through rehab, are born-again spiritually, take on good causes, schmooze with presidents, prime ministers, even the Pope. But even the new-and-improved rocker image can tire. Is it then time to revert to their nasty/drug-lovin'/infidel selves to sell the package to the next generation?

Perhaps more painful, but equally enjoyable, is to watch politicians try to rebrand themselves when they discover from media feedback that they have a bit of an image problem. They try a new hairstyle plus a new wardrobe, hang out with new 'friends', have a baby/have an affair/get divorced, resign, come back to go through it again and again. Indeed, there comes a point when ill-conceived efforts at rebranding backfire and are far worse than the original 'problem image'. Perhaps the greatest difficulty for politicians is that we do all *watch the process*, and it gets analysed daily. I am proud to say that most of those that I have been involved with have been so subtle that the effects weren't discernible aside from the rise in their approval rating with the public and with the press commenting that so-and-so 'is more commanding by the day'.

Your own 'celebrity' and 'bankability' are also linked to *your personal branding*. By reading this book, you have an opportunity to get yours together before your next important crossroads.

New file needed: C/My Documents: Aha!

Your CV is on file, ready to print, right? Even if you aren't presently hunting, your CV should be fresh and ready to print within 30 minutes of updating. If you are self-employed and unlikely ever to want to work for anyone again, you require a personal biog instead of CV. All entrepreneurs need a succinct, dynamic biog ready for speaking engagements (as introductions) or for media relations (as background). If yours isn't ready or up to scratch, set up your 'Aha!' file.

You know the basics, the background stuff. What needs constant refreshment – every few months – is what you've achieved. This is your **Aha! List** – those Amazing Hits Achieved that reminds you of your own brand values and keeps you projecting them to others.

Think for a few minutes about your achievements in the past year. Scribble down everything that comes to mind. From there, set up an **Aha!** file in My Documents that you can update regularly. Here's what you should include:

Your Amazing Hits Achieved (Aha!) List
1) Key projects completed (business and personal)
2) Commendations and testimonials received about your contributions
3) Expanded horizons – how you really grew this year
   Why you are a bigger and better person as a result
4) New contacts made that you can tap for networking purposes. How have you kept them fresh?
5) A re-definition of personal and professional goals

Refine your CV/biog and **Aha! List** every year and keep them together, ready to be honed for the next performance review, job or media interview. In Chapter 2, when you define your brand, refer to these key achievements and include what you consider to be values that are endemic to them.

As an example, here's mine for this year:

Key projects completed:

Business:
- Sold one business/started ImageWorks
- Published another book

Personal:
- Designed and planted my new garden
- Took mini-breaks with each daughter and my husband as well as enjoyed two family holidays
- Spent a week with my dad
- Celebrated fiftieth birthday without turning into a witch!

Commendations & testimonials:

- E-mails/letters from clients who've won the promotion or got the job after my coaching
- Poems from my daughters about how much I mean to them
- Cards of thanks from elderly, housebound neighbours that I spend time with or do errands for
- Thoughtful notes of appreciation from former staff and consultants
- Glowing letters for conference presentations or company seminars

Expanded horizons . . . how I grew this year:

- Read every issue of the Garden magazine (from the Royal Horticultural Society) and memorize the Latin names of all my new plants so that I could hold my own with horticultural connoisseurs
- Studied Spanish again to converse more fluently on holiday
- Read at least one book of fiction and non-fiction a month to be more interesting company

- Used the Internet for more than just e-mail so I could feel like a hot-shot and say that I'd bought shares on-line

New contacts . . .

- Have followed up eight key leads from a recent conference and have lunches or appointments scheduled to see how we might work together in the future

Re-definition of personal and professional goals for next year:

Personal Goals:
- Accept that my marathoning days are over and become passionate about a new sport
- Have more adventures just with my husband
- Begin part-time study in horticulture

Professional Goals:
- Learn the technology to fully exploit my web site
- Develop two new products to add to what I already offer my clients
- Be more selective about projects so that I use my talents and energies on the ones where I will really make a difference

Your career depends on branding yourself

Let's face it, work simply isn't what it used to be. Forget comparing your career with your dad's or mum's. Just reflect back to your vision of what you would be when you grew up. Think back to when you were 18 or 20. Remember the dreams, the aspirations? It was clear then. You got the job, became the corporate/organizational person. Provided you did your work, didn't offend too many, didn't screw up too much, you could be secure of tenure for some 5, 10, or maybe 20 years.

Ha! Few readers under 40 can relate to this. You've been through seismic changes from the cut and thrust of the entrepreneurial 80s to downsizing in the 90s. You live in a world of flexible, short-term contracts – in other words, sort out your own pension and health benefits. As organizations flatten and shed bureaucracy, job security is gone. You must be 'multi-skilled', assume 'multi-tasks', welcome change as you do the seasons in order to survive in today's job market. But survival is only relative.

Despite the uncertainty of today's job market, the busier you are, the more 'stressed' you feel in your job, is apparently linked to your happiness (Mintel Men 2000). When we are less stretched in our work, happiness declines and our health worries multiply. So getting work right matters to us emotionally as well as economically.

Our careers, the rewards, the satisfaction and, most importantly, their viability, are down to us. You might be reading this from the 'secure' position of a tenure or partnership or might own your business and agree that even from your more privileged position the vision of the future is unknown. Professional firms of accountants, management consultants, architects and lawyers merge at dizzying speed with talented people becoming 'redundant'. Regarded academics find their 'chairs' pulled out from underneath them despite bequests supposedly being for life. Civil servants, once seemingly immune to market forces, find departments closed, programmes cancelled. All modern state bureaucracies are being honed in order to be more responsible and accountable to their 'clients', the citizens and taxpayers.

STOP THE TRAIN, I WANNA GET OFF

Fortunately, the upheaval of work as we know it forces us to think and rethink what we are doing, to ask whether we are fulfilled, well-enough rewarded or should be doing something altogether different. This book assumes you know what you want to do and guides you in convincing others that you can do it. There are several good books to help you rethink your career and your life with some of my favourites listed in Further Reading.

Why you choose a career varies by person and by generation. Many students today who are contemplating their futures would prefer to forego high salaries and long hours in favour of having a home life, friends and developing *themselves*. In a global survey of ten countries, college / university students put a balanced life as their top priority after graduation (Coopers & Lybrand, 1998).

My simple barometer for measuring whether or not you are doing the right job or are in the right career is whether or not you bound out of bed in the morning and look forward to going to work. Honestly, I know no better indicator to guide you in 'stopping the train' and heading somewhere else. The American journalist Studs Terkel, who spent a lifetime talking to working people, said, 'Work is about daily meaning as well as daily bread – it's for recognition as well as cash; for astonishment rather than torpor; in short, for a sort of life rather than a Monday through Friday sort of dying.' Terkel adds, 'We have a right to ask of work that it includes meaning, recognition, astonishment and life.' So, if your current job offers little of any of these perhaps it's time to find one that does.

CH-CH-CH-CHANGES!

Change is a much overused word in business today, meaning anything from a business failing or facing severe competitive challenges to the impact of technology being so pervasive that the nature of most jobs will never be the same. Even for the people who thrive on new challenges and get bored in jobs that are too predictable, the pace at which many of today's companies change is dizzying. Companies embrace new strategic directions, pursue different product lines and markets, transform their methods of operation, uproot and transfer staff around the globe with organizational charts and corporate brochures out of date by the time they are off the press.

According to the Institute of Management/UMIST Quality of Working Life Survey (1998) based on 5,000 managers at all levels, nearly two-thirds said that they had endured major structural change in the last 2 years. As a result, 15 per cent of chairman/chief executives, 48 per cent of senior managers, 60 per cent of middle managers and 58 per cent of junior staff reported decreased loyalty. Job insecurity, unsurprisingly, leads to plummeting job satisfaction. How can you get enthusiastic about helping a company grow if you don't know you'll be around to benefit from the growth next year?

'Change Management', once considered a tangential subject in business schools, is now a core competency. Companies have ever-changing 'change teams' established to implement change, then disperse and be reconstituted when the next wave of change is required (usually right on the heels of the last wave of change). If you aren't involved with designing change, you are implementing it. If doing neither, you are fretting because you know it's needed but don't know what the hell to do to change things for the better. So, in come the 'change consultants' to guide you through until their ideas are proved wrong and the new gurus of change come along.

It sounds mad, of course, but sadly it's what our businesses, education and health systems and governments need if they are going to keep pace with market demands, economic realities and technological innovations. None of us can afford to be change-averse if we want to continue to enjoy careers in business.

Trawl through all the learned reports over the last 5 years and they concur that employment as we know it is waning. Jobs don't exist – *work* exists. In the next decade, most of us will be 'suppliers', not staff. We will have 'clients', not bosses. The Henley Centre predicts that by 2010 *less than 50 per cent of jobs will be full-time.* Self-employment is the fastest growing sector in the job market.

Good companies, aware of business realities, try to make whatever time you work for them rewarding. They know that if you leave happy, you will speak well of them, perhaps become clients of the firm later yourself. Two different perpetrators of this 'boomerang' effect are the Disney Corporation (who wants us all – including former employees – to visit their theme parks and watch their movies) and McKinsey, a leading management consulting firm. They court former employees with regular alumni parties and publish an alumni directory to encourage networking. The effect is that most former McKinsey people speak well of the firm and, indeed, hire them for their new firms.

Even the McKinsey strategists concur that you have to prepare your own strategic plan to have a viable business, in this case *your business.* A good strategy includes a marketing premise for the product (you), and must have clear values for its brand/product if it is going to be able to sell itself.

Rebranding required

Maybe you are a confident character, who's been tooling along in life doing well but have bought this book because you've been hit sideways by something that has you rethinking everything – who you are, the life you live, relationships, your work, how fulfilled or unfulfilled you feel.

Do you find yourself daydreaming about alternative jobs? Trying a different lifestyle? Different partner? Maybe you find you aren't sleeping as soundly as normal and wake up thinking, questioning everything? Even a wonderful job with a great salary, status, perks and prospects is sometimes not enough to hold you when you feel that gnawing away inside. Something must change. You're not sure what, but something must for you to feel more enthusiastic about getting up and living through every day.

You can suffer an identity crisis at any age, with even many in their twenties and thirties questioning life on the daily treadmill. Many jobs force us to work as they 'shelve' those whom they consider have reached some predetermined sell-by date – bankers, journalists, marketing managers, computer programmers, advertising directors, salesmen, teachers. Is it a question of age or attitude?

Despite the prophets of gloom and media hype about mid-life crises, a ten-year study of middle-aged Americans says that the stressed-out and downhearted are the exception not the rule. The MacArthur Foundation found that people actually feel more secure in their jobs particularly between 40 and 60, one supposes those that are lucky enough to hang on to their jobs that long. 'Normal people recognize that lifespan, regardless of age, brings change and that a healthy response to change is to make the necessary adjustments,' said Orville Brim, the social psychologist who directed the study. More than 70 per cent considered themselves to be in excellent health, though they may be deluding themselves as few said that they made much of an effort to stay in shape. The only things that the 8,000 middle-aged working Americans said they could use more of was sex and money!

Our jobs, just like our lives, can continue to have purpose and meaning provided that we feel we are using our talents and capabilities. Being in control of your destiny as much as possible is also proven to being key to both happiness and a sense of fulfilment.

THE YOUNG SIGN UP TO 'ME, INC'

If you are under 30, you probably know that there is one firm to join for life: *Me, Inc*. It will promote you and your potential to others. Your generation has grasped the fact that if you know what *you* are about, and sell it well to others, you will get the opportunities that you want, most of the time.

You know that you can happily get a job, be a loyal trooper and do excellent work but won't be seduced into believing that the organization will look after you any longer that it needs to – a sad reality, but reality it is. I've met superstar dynamos in their twenties, employed by a good firm (in recruitment, advertising, journalism, finance, technology, management consulting), who openly declare their desks and telephones, contacts and clients, *their* business. When they get fed up of where they are working they take these valuables with them. Mercenary, perhaps. But this is the wave of the future for firms that don't do everything possible to keep their people happy, loyal, inspired and rewarded.

Douglas Coupland's acclaimed novel *Generation X: Tales for an Accelerated Culture*, published in 1991, has become a mainstream bible for those burnt-out and bored by the corporate rat race. Preferring to opt out rather than fight it out, 'Xers' pursue success and wealth on their own terms. They start out with a portfolio career in mind, picking up experiences – successes and failures – along the way. Their adaptability, refusal to have the long-term plan, has been misunderstood as laziness and apathy by anyone over 40 (Xers cover those born between 1961 and 1981). But fully cognisant that the world is moving too damn fast to predict little beyond months ahead, Xers have the flexibility to jump on board or jump ship as the economic climate as well as their own priorities shift.

The young, along with others burnt by experience, understand that treating yourself as your 'own business' helps you to market your prospects continually. You don't have to 'do time' in a job unless biding your time is *your* choice. You take advantages on the job to promote yourself so that promotion becomes inevitable. You jump at opportunities to learn more and to explore new possibilities for your career all the time. If you do become a victim of reorganization or corporate retooling, you don't take it personally and are ready with new ideas. *You* are *clearly branded* for new opportunities both inside as well as outside the company.

Be fearless and take risks or you'll never find out what you *love doing* and what you *can do*. As the internationally acclaimed management guru Tom Peters says, 'People who try but make mistakes should be promoted. Those who never try should be fired.' Peters would applaud you trying to brand yourself!

LIFELONG LEARNING ISN'T AN OPTION, IT'S A REQUIREMENT

Believing that you are trained for a career when you complete schooling is naïve whether you have GCSEs, A levels, a degree or even a postgraduate degree like an MBA. In fact, some of the most marketable characters today chucked traditional schooling in favour of online learning with computer skills.

Learning not only keeps you viable in your present job but it enables you to throw in the towel on an unfulfilling career and get into something that you might really enjoy. We all know people who have been 'born again' when they changed careers, either by moving sectors, going from a large corporation to form their own company, or staying in their job but working more from home to get more balance in their lives. It is not a question of *if* you will ever change your career, it's a question of *when*. It's inevitable for all of us – even those who win the lottery! After all, they've got to learn to manage investments and, hopefully, become good philanthropists.

In addition to new skills, we all have to embrace the generally perceived wisdom that skills, even the new and improved ones, won't be enough to succeed if we don't develop our *emotional intelligence* along the way, i.e. how well we handle ourselves and how well we handle others. I've coached many women and men preparing for promotion committees or partner admission panels who had to explain how they had grown as a person – not just in their managerial or technical competencies. Increasingly you are stymied in your career if you can't prove that you have had personal challenges and benefited from them. Products and systems don't grow companies – people do. If you can add value via your people skills – for instance, with your mentoring and coaching of other staff; dealing more effectively with clients; being a better team player or leader, etc. – both you and the organization will be richer!

Continued learning, personal development and new skills add to your brand as well as make the CV more impressive. No better way to sell being 'modern and innovative' than by sharing a new project (outside your normal job spec) that you've been involved with or a discovery/adventure made or personal growth or achievement attained.

BRANDING MAKES YOU VIABLE LONGER

At the beginning of the twentieth century the average life expectancy in the West was 47. Now it is 75 – a 60 per cent increase in a century. But the forecasts are being revised almost every year. Twenty-year-olds today will live to 120, and most of us (like you, reading this book), who have benefited from good medical care and nutrition and increasingly take note of new improvements to postpone ageing, might be working until our eighties and probably celebrate our hundredth birthday if we don't get killed off by stress or additives first! Predictions are that those of us who remain in work into our eighties in this new century won't be doing so wearing incontinence pads, shuffling off to meetings behind Zimmer frames. The survivors will be the characters who keep pace, remain inspired by change, keep learning and current.

Older people are more vital today than ever before and will become even more dynamic and relevant as well as great sources of wisdom and experience in the twenty-first century. Some of us have had fleeting experience of four generations for a time – a great-grandmother, grandparents, parents and children. This could increase to five or six generations for our children and grandchildren. Just think of the potential for more cohesive, extended families as well as for businesses.

My dad set up his own business after 35 years as a corporate man. Like many, the company policy was to send home all achievers from the age of 65. Dad wasn't up for retirement in the traditional sense of it – playing golf, bridge or pottering around the garden for 20 years. So he set up his own business and for 10 years he was still earning money from selling a mixture of past skills and experiences (he was a marketing/promotions consultant within his previous sector) and developing lifelong hobbies. He even honed his amateur dramatics and comic skills to become a part-time actor on TV adverts! But he also recognized new opportunities in advising the over 65s in computer skills as well as in managing their tax affairs. An expert in neither, he took courses and achieved new qualifications that enabled him to add two more services to his portfolio (which he did as a volunteer to local associations and clubs).

My parents-in-law are equally resourceful. For 20 years after their full-time employment ended (at the age of 55) they ran a bed and breakfast from their country home, hired out their car for weddings, and made business introductions on behalf of new ventures with old contacts, earning welcome fees.

If you want to or *need to* remain employable and earning, you must keep reassessing your brand values to make sure that they are relevant

Image-building

When asked to describe the process of building an image, I like to use the 'Johari Window' developed by psychologists Joseph Luft and Harry Ingham (they named it after themselves!). The model is particularly useful in analysing and understanding conflict. It is a vehicle for coming to terms with yourself, especially the inconsistencies inherent in your personality, perception and behaviour. Once you explore your 'windows' you are freer to be open with others. The more you know about yourself, the more you can read and understand others.

Public Self	Blind Spots
Private Self	Unknown Self

The Public Self is what I show to the world – it is the image I have developed so far that I am happy to share with people. It's what everyone sees and understands about me. The Private Self is what I know about myself but others don't. It encompasses my dreams and aspirations. Only those nearest and dearest get a 'look in' to my Private Self, others don't have a clue. Then we all have Blind Spots. These are things that others see about me but I can't see for myself. Finally, there is the unknown dimension of our potential. This is unknown to us and to others.

In personal image-building, we explore the Private Self – try to find out more about your dreams and aspirations. How do you want other people to react to you? How would you like to appear, behave and sound differently? By observing the Public Self we share your Blind

Public Self:	Blind Spots:
- Easy-going	- Lazy speech
- 'Jack the lad'	- Unprofessional behaviour ('street' hand-shake, gum-chewing, bitten nails)
- Approachable	- Casual/inappropriate dress
- Unambitious	
Private Self:	**Unknown self:**
- Entrepreneur	- I can learn how to comport myself better so that people respond differently, i.e. positively, from the start
- Determined	- My accent needs clarity (not changing)
- Confident	- If I just slow down I sound more convincing! I feel so much more confident because people listen to me for longer. As a result I am reading more sector/business journals and stating my views more openly than I did previously
- Admired	- Making more of an effort with my clothes helps me take myself more seriously. When I walk into a room people seem to take more notice of me so that I feel welcome and more at ease in myself rather than playing the comic to break the ice

Spots – these are both *positive* and *negative*. 'Are you aware that you say "you know" as a filler a lot?' 'You have a great body that could be enhanced with different clothes and better posture.' 'Your handshake is very submissive and doesn't convey confidence.' By bringing out more of the person *that you want to be* (the Private Self) and sorting out a few Blind Spots your potential to influence others is increased along with your self-esteem and self-confidence. Finally, there is the Unknown Self – what we don't know about ourselves and our own potential. This is the most frightening and exhilarating dimension.

For image-building to succeed it has to be true to yourself. Trying to become another person (especially someone that you feel you *should* be but don't want to be) is doomed to failure. Successful branding and image development requires integrity.

Opposite is an example of a Johari Window for Darren in Chapter 2 (see page 65):

FIRST IMPRESSIONS – TRUE LIES?

You know how quickly you judge others and appreciate that you are subjected to the same sizing-up every time you meet someone. We make profound judgements in seconds about someone's age, background, how successful they are, their nationality and education – a host of things.

Most people are so worried about saying the right thing upon meeting, with a lot of people in business (particularly men) hating initial small talk. My answer is to worry less about what you do say and more about what you *don't* say, i.e. pay attention to your non-verbal behaviour. We'll get to developing an effective voice and influential language in Chapter 3, 'Sounding the Part'.

But we have all had plenty of experiences when we felt that we judged others wrongly, that someone eventually proved to be more or less than we thought at first. But it is hard to get over a bad or ineffective first impression – a weak handshake, little eye contact, a faltering/apologetic voice, an aggressive manner, or a nondescript dress sense. These factors get in the way, they bother us and block valid attempts by the person to influence us.

YOU'VE GOT 30 SECONDS

If you need convincing that you've only got 30 seconds to transmit to others who you are, what you are about, let me introduce you to Professor Albert Mehrabian. His work (*Silent Messages*, 1971, 1985) is one of the most powerful for proving the point of the importance of image *initially* over substance. Mehrabian found that only 7 per cent of our immediate impact came from what we said (the spoken words), with 38 per cent being from the sound of our voices, but with the bulk of our impression – 55 per cent – coming from signals sent from our behaviour and appearance. Like it or not, 93 per cent of how we come across initially has nothing to do with substance.

Think about the last drinks party or conference you attended where you didn't know many people. You started chatting but really didn't remember a lot, to begin with, about what was being said. Names flew around, you caught some business links but really not much in detail. Without much information, however, you formed a pretty strong opinion about a few people just on intuition, gut feelings. The rest made little or no impact on you mainly due to how they looked and behaved, not because of who they were.

The accuracy of our first impressions is dependent on too many factors, most of them subjective, to be conclusive. In Daniel Goleman's *Working with Emotional Intelligence* he cites studies from Harvard University proving that we can be very shrewd judges of a person with little information. Within 30 seconds we know someone's competence within about 80 per cent of accuracy, i.e. we can tell how capable some-one is by how they look and act. In less than a minute, we will already know what we will think of people 15 minutes later or 6 months down the line. Scary but true.

Credit managers, recruiters and detectives all concur that in less than 3 minutes they have a person 'sussed'. Human resources people and recruitment specialists say that despite having all the instruments necessary to judge a person's character and suitability for a job, when it comes to the crunch they choose the person that they *feel* is the right one. This feeling comes down to the image that we project – how we look and how we handle ourselves and whether that's what others want.

MAKE THAT 3 SECONDS

The time we give someone to impress us is negligible, even shrinking by the day as a result of the meteoric changes in mass communications. Twenty years ago, advertisers selling products to us on television used to spend on average 3 minutes per product. Today, some 30-second adverts appear drawn out, with the newest ads spending just 1 to 3 seconds to stamp an impression on us simply by showing their logo. We see it, flinch, say, 'What was that?' The ad men say that we focus hard on split-second imagery. An indelible icon has *values* and we get them in under 3 seconds! A whole generation has been weaned on MTV and pop videos with its language of flashing new images every 1 to 3 seconds. Any longer now is overkill.

When surfing the Net, brands need to grab us quickly or it's click stop or back . . . we are out of there – our time, attention and money spent on something else. Perhaps even truer on the Net than for us personally, you don't get a second chance to make a first impression.

Online media imagery has trained us all to judge both products *and* people from conscious and subliminal messages. For instance, if you were a 3-second brand, what would we think of you? Imagine a 3-second ad of you, by you. Fortunately, you are more than a simple logo or hologram or film clip; you are multidimensional and multi-faceted. But wonder for a minute if these dimensions and facets are as apparent to others as you want them to be? If not, clear branding will help.

Hopefully, you are now convinced that you should define your brand – the values that you want *everyone* to believe about you. You've got to look them and live them and get them right first time, every time, to get the opportunities you deserve.

As you set about defining your values, remember that you are in for the long haul. You can try to fool some of the people, some of the time, and will. But if true to yourself and to others, your brand will be far more enduring, rewarding and marketable.

2

DEFINING YOUR BRAND

Time to determine what you want for your brand – the values you want others to believe you have from the moment they meet you.

Your own self-image is a montage of personality traits, attitudes, behaviours, habits, values and personal style. Your self-image acts as a monitor of how you act and interact with others. We have a comfort zone or public self that we have shaped and, by and large, live within it.

Of course, your own perceptions of how you come across to others might be accurate but could also be totally unrealistic. Are you someone who is frequently surprised to find that people think something about you that you know to be off the mark (or at least *you think* it is off the mark)? Maybe they say that they find you very confident, shy, older, younger, aggressive, funny, thoughtful – something that surprises you. If so, there will be work to do throughout this book either to recognize yourself more honestly or to discover how you are sending the wrong signals to others and change your image to reflect that.

Branding was once exclusively the purview of the marketing and advertising world. They developed packaging, images, logos and product messages that would encourage us to buy. The rest of business just got down to doing the business – to making the widgets, selling and distributing them.

▩ It's ginger, it's spice

But in the twenty-first century branding is endemic and everyone is in on the act. New ventures with clever branding have investors tripping over themselves to get a piece of their potential e-commerce success. Come up with a clever concept, add '.com' and you are branded for cyberspace.

Personality brands like Richard Branson's Virgin, Chris Evans' Ginger Group or Terence Conran's Conran Group arguably have inflated values due to the endorsement and co-branding of their founders. Try and imagine Virgin without Richard, or Conran without Terence. The jury is out on how well the Ginger Group will survive without Chris. But all great personality brands have to evolve eventually without, and sometimes in spite of, their founding fathers and mothers to be viable in the long term. Many great brands merge with previous competitors and sweat to define an even more powerful brand to conquer their markets, like PricewaterhouseCoopers (formerly Coopers & Lybrand and Price Waterhouse), AOL/Time Warner, Glaxo Wellcome (which dropped the 'Smithkline Beecham').

In the entertainment world, we see individuals brand and rebrand themselves constantly. Cher and Tina Turner do it with enduring magic. Madonna evolved from bad girl to material girl to naughty girl; from being desperate Susan to evocative Evita; her image has been tramp, then vamp, then Earth Mother. Critics suggest that she is still able to top the charts more from shrewd rebranding of her image than from her music. As a result, many pop singers try to follow her lead by reinventing their brands with dizzying speed like the transformations from Spice Girl to UN Ambassador to solo artist Geri Halliwell, or the grunge to glam-rocker to actress Courtney Love.

Branding: more than just a slogan

All companies have to establish an identity – a purpose and statement which defines what they are about. This must be very clear, as branding guru Wally Olins (of Wolfe Olins and author of *Corporate Identity*) states: 'It must be the yardstick against which the companies' products, behaviours and actions are measured. The corporate identity cannot be a simple slogan, a collection of phrases: it must be visible, tangible and all-embracing.'

A branding statement can't be restricted to its products but must cover everything, especially the services that the company gives around the product. All businesses today are about *service*. The products just have to work, be priced appropriately and do what they promise they will do. Few complaints from customers are about products; the complaints are about service, the people – their actions and attitudes.

'If there isn't an alignment between the corporate identity and what service is actually being delivered the company is in trouble,' explains Olins. The main audience for mission statements and corporate branding should be the company's own people. 'If the staff convey the values – how they look and act – and pass that on to the customers, then the company succeeds,' says Olins.

Today we expect companies to deliver what they promise. What thrills us is when they exceed our expectations. A few notables that do are:

- The friendly, efficient teams at Starbucks where your latte never varies nor disappoints.
- The dynamic, young 'chefs' at Prêt A Manger in Britain who both make and sell 'passionate' sandwiches with a passion day after day.
- The energetic ground and flight crews on British Airways cut-price subsidizing Go! Airlines who make business travel feel like going on a holiday.

- The impeccably well-dressed, personable and helpful Nordstrom's department store's sales assistants in the US who make you feel that you, too, can look as stylish as they.
- The Europe-wide Carphone Warehouse 'advisors' who sell you the best mobile phone for your needs – at the cheapest price.
- The casual yet welcoming teams at Gap who make us feel that we can be young and trendy without looking foolish.

When considering your brand, are you confident of always projecting what others expect? If you are going to a meeting, walking into a job interview or meeting people socially are you just what we expect, more so or less so? Are you at a point in your life where meeting expectations *isn't* enough? You feel you need to be (and want to be) more than what others expect. Whatever your goals and ambitions might be it is up to you to decide how far you take your own branding from the minimum of meeting others' expectations to surpassing them.

Your Personal Brand Identity

Imagine yourself as your own company in need of a corporate identity. You are 'Me, Inc' in need of a Personal Brand Identity (PBI).

Your PBI is an amalgamation of your assets (skills, abilities and experiences), your values (the things that matter as well as your passions) and your image (what you project to others). Your PBI is what you measure everything you do against – how you meet new people, nurture relationships, handle colleagues, give presentations, run meetings, have lunch, dress. It's how you look, act and sound. It is what makes you stand out from the crowd, be an individual.

A successful PBI never loses sight of your individuality – you live it with family and friends as well as at work. Strangers 'get it' when they meet you. You exude your PBI. When companies lose sight of their uniqueness (their USP – unique selling points) – they make mistakes and sometimes fail as a result. They make tangential acquisitions not related to their core activity or ruin a brand by taking it mass market when its USP includes exclusivity, or diversify so much that they lose focus. There are countless ways to send the wrong messages, to mask your true values which cause others to doubt or dismiss your abilities.

So too must you remember your PBI is special to you. You can fine-tune it but should never lose sight of what makes you so special. Value your background, what you've achieved, what you know that you are capable of in the future.

▓ 3 steps to your PBI

Your own reflections about how you feel you come across to others coupled with some valued input from people who know you well, can demonstrate the difference between perceptions and reality. To start, let's focus on first impressions. In Step 1 you will describe what impact you feel you have on others. Step 2 involves a conversation with a colleague or two who will then tell you what they felt about you when they first met you and how accurate or false those initial impressions were. You will then reflect on how you might want to build upon your current impact and define the values for your Personal Brand Identity.

Step 1: How I feel I come across initially

Take the following quiz about the impact you feel you have on others when you first meet them. There are no right or wrong answers, so be as honest as you can.

WHAT DO YOU FEEL YOU CONVEY IN UNDER 30 SECONDS?

1   When meeting people socially, I

- ❏   A   Find the host/hostess and make sure I meet the key people
- ❏   B   Hold back, preferring others to make the first move
- ❏   C   Introduce myself and try to engage others in conversation

2   My voice can be described as:

- ❏   A   Confident, even impressive
- ❏   B   Weak, perhaps not my strongest point
- ❏   C   Friendly

3   My handshake is

- ❏   A   Strong and positive
- ❏   B   Considerate towards others: not too strong or too weak
- ❏   C   Firm and direct

4   When it comes to small talk,

- ❏   A   I'm never at a loss and generally have a few good stories up my sleeve
- ❏   B   I hate it and can't wait to get down to the matter at hand
- ❏   C   I look for signals from the surroundings or the weather as general ice-breakers

5   When I walk into a room,

- ❏   A   People know that I've arrived
- ❏   B   I like to wait to follow the lead from the most senior person
- ❏   C   I try to look positive and approachable

6   My physical presence can be described as:

- ❏ A   Large, tall, strong, dark
- ❏ B   Slight, short, delicate
- ❏ C   Average

7   For colours, in business I generally wear:

- ❏ A   Dark or bold colours/striking combinations
- ❏ B   Mid-tone to light colours blended together with nothing too bold
- ❏ C   A variety of colours depending on the day and occasion

8   My most impressive accessory in meetings is:

- ❏ A   My watch – recognizable and expensive
- ❏ B   My pen – good quality
- ❏ C   A personal organizer – the latest, all singing and all dancing

9   My view on using humour when meeting people initially is:

- ❏ A   Nothing better breaks the ice!
- ❏ B   I never use it as it doesn't come naturally
- ❏ C   I try to sense how welcome it would be before trying it out

10   When it comes to remembering people's names,

- ❏ A   I do my best but generally just remember key players
- ❏ B   I try to make a note of names but don't use them until I get to know people better
- ❏ C   I repeat the person's name when I can to aid my memory and to make the conversation more personal

11   If a person seems ill at ease upon meeting I will

- ❏ A   Move on to someone more confident
- ❏ B   Feel just as awkward and tend to keep talking even though I know they aren't interested
- ❏ C   Ask them questions to find out more about them so that I can bounce a discussion off their information

12 I find it easiest to talk with

- ❏ A   Anyone because I do the talking
- ❏ B   People who share my interests
- ❏ C   People with whom I can find a common interest

13 If someone moves away from me when meeting me I

- ❏ A   Move closer so that they feel I am interested in them
- ❏ B   Assume they dislike me
- ❏ C   Watch their movements and give them the space they seem to require

14 My posture is:

- ❏ A   Straight shoulders, straight back
- ❏ B   A bit slouchy, not impressive
- ❏ C   Naturally erect

15 I find direct eye contact,

- ❏ A   A challenge and can give back as good as I get
- ❏ B   Very intimidating
- ❏ C   Useful in establishing rapport

16 When it comes to listening to other people,

- ❏ A   If I am uninterested I jump in to get back on the agenda
- ❏ B   I get bored easily and probably show it but generally wait until they are finished
- ❏ C   I aim to convey that I am interested even when I am not

17 Regardless of age or size, my physical fitness is

- ❏ A   Not bad
- ❏ B   Not good
- ❏ C   Good to excellent

18 In the morning, after showering and getting dressed, for grooming I allow myself:

- ❏ A   Not more than 10 minutes
- ❏ B   Not more than 5 minutes
- ❏ C   More than 10 minutes

19 Regarding my shoes

- ❏ A   They're expensive
- ❏ B   They're comfortable, if not impressive
- ❏ C   I take care of their style, condition and practicality

20 After meeting people, the impression I leave is:

- ❏ A   They won't forget me fast
- ❏ B   Probably not great initially but over time they will value me more
- ❏ C   Positive and that the communication was two-way

ANSWERS

Add the number of times you ticked A, B and C.

A   _____

B   _____

C   _____

Mainly A

Your initial impact on others is very self-confident; where others are timid you are brave. But your confidence might be misperceived as 'overconfidence' or even arrogance. When meeting new people are you more concerned about how you come across rather than showing genuine interest in others? So at ease in most situations, and enjoying being the centre of attention, you can appear a little too slick to people you need to impress. See ideas in Chapters 4 and 7 about how you can relate better by focusing on others rather yourself – getting 'into their heads' and out of your own. Your personal image is sharp but may look too predictable, possibly not modern enough to win you all the opportunities you want. See Chapters 5 or 6 for ideas for maybe softening the 'power look' to win others over more naturally.

Mainly B

Your uncertainty in new situations may leave some people unimpressed upon first meeting you. You will learn that you don't always have the time for people to get to know your true value so you will need to work on making a greater impact initially. Remember that shyness is a problem of 'I'-ness, i.e. worrying too much about yourself and not enough about others. Tell yourself that they will be glad to meet you and show more interest in *them*. Work on a more confident voice, eye contact, handshake and initial greeting to make a stronger impact upfront (see Chapter 4). Also, your image probably needs more time and attention. *It matters!* See Chapters 5 or 6 for ideas on making more of yourself.

Mainly C

You are striking a good balance between projecting yourself and showing interest in others when you first meet. You have also discovered ways to help others through the awkward initial minutes. If you answered B to some questions, you might be sending conflicting signals – self-confident sometimes; uncertain in yourself at others. Note what areas – e.g. voice, dress, behaviour – need improvement and read about new approaches in the relevant chapters.

Mixture of A, B and C

Simply put, you project a confused and inconsistent image. Maybe it works some of the time but it certainly doesn't all of the time. You need to learn to develop the confidence to face new situations, people and environments more enthusiastically as now they throw you off balance and you perform below par when you need to excel. Make sure that your brand values are harmonious. If they don't appear to be so, ask yourself how you can make them work together. For example, if you want to project both friendliness and power how can you convey them without confusing people? Right now you are sending conflicting messages.

Do this quiz again in a month after you have tried some new approaches. See if your initial impression on others has changed.

Step 2: How others feel I come across initially

Invite a colleague, your boss (if your relationship allows), your partner (if she/he is objective as well as subjective about you) or a mentor for a coffee or drink. Choose someone who you feel is observant and a good judge of others. Friends are not good at this as they will probably prevaricate one way or the other – telling you that you are fine in respects where you are not; or telling you that you are hopeless when you are anything but!

Tell them that you are doing some personal development and have to get some feedback on how you come across to others. The process involves self-assessment (i.e. Step 1) and feedback from someone that you admire (e.g. them!) and then input from an image consultant (i.e. me in the rest of this book!). The fact that you are owning up to going through a personal branding exercise will put them in both an empathetic as well as constructive mindset.

Ask them the following questions:

- *If you met me today, for the first time, what kind of woman/man would you say that I am?*
- *What impression did I make on you when we first met?*
- *How has your impression of me changed, if at all?*
- *Overall, how would you describe my image (how I look, sound and behave)?*
- *Is there anything about my image that you would recommend that I change and why?*

If you discover things that you never realized before (i.e. problems), just register them for reflection as you read further. But remember all the good qualities as well. Concentrate on all the wonderful things that you were told and don't lose sight of them. What brand values were apparent from what you've learned so far? Are you happy with them? How will you hone them in the future to create a better impression first time, every time?

■ Step 3: Defining your PBI: your brand values

Having now developed a sense of how you come across initially to others, now you need to decide what you want other people to feel about you when they meet you as well as get to know you. Be as specific as you can, choosing as many of the values as you'd like for each of the four categories of brand projection – the *look*, *sound*, *behaviour* and *feel of your brand*.

Note which values you feel you succeed in projecting already and those that require development. If you have other values not listed, please add them. This is *your* brand, after all! Get branding!

THE LOOK OF MY BRAND

The look of your brand involves your basic packaging – your appearance and personal style. Your physical characteristics – height, build, weight and colouring – plus your age and sex are the basics. The overall look results from what you do with your characteristics in creating your personal style which, ideally, projects your brand values.

The overall impression of your brand image is up to you. There is no mix of values that would be right for any two people even if they were in the same business. There is no formula that is right for all PR managers, no prescription that's perfect for accountants. Some attributes others might also share but how it is interpreted is down to your personality. Note any number of the following values that you would like to describe your image – the look of your brand. Add others that you might feel to be even more on target. Then note which values you feel you already project and which ones need further work.

stylish   expensive   professional   casual   modern young   arty   traditional   international   creative classic   understated   attractive   relaxed   dramatic chic   powerful   cutting-edge   elegant   approachable European   American   British   successful.

Values I want to project:	Already convey:	Need work on looking more:
. . . .	. . . .	. . . .
. . . .	. . . .	. . . .
. . . .	. . . .	. . . .
. . . .	. . . .	. . . .
. . . .	. . . .	. . . .

There are two chapters in the book to give you more details on projecting the look that you want. Women: see Chapter 5; men: see Chapter 6.

THE SOUND OF MY BRAND

The sound of your brand is key to the messages you send about yourself. It involves both the quality of your voice as well as your communication skills – the language you use and how you adapt your communication techniques in different forums. Everyone's voice sends signals. If you know that you convey positive messages already note them along with the values that require more work. Which of the following would you like to convey by how you speak and your use of language?

> *friendly educated amusing urbane articulate mature confident knowledgeable powerful influential youthful colloquial quick driven thoughtful compelling unassuming animated distinctive serious.*

Values I want to project:	Already sound:	Need work on sounding more:
....	....	....
....	....	....
....	....	....
....	....	....
....	....	....

Chapter 3 will give you ideas for developing your voice to project more effectively with Chapter 8 covering effective communication and presentation skills.

THE BEHAVIOUR OF MY BRAND

How you handle yourself speaks volumes about who you are. You, no doubt, feel confident with people that you know. Reflect for a minute how you come across to them and how you would like to come across to others that you meet for the first time. Does your behaviour need to be *different* in business?

You have a natural body personality which may only require a bit of fine-tuning to be more effective if you feel that you don't always have the impact that you want on others. Select from the following list what you would like to convey noting how successful your body language is (in most situations) but where it might require some new techniques.

> *approachable reserved friendly confident energetic assertive considerate easy-going dynamic well-mannered natural formal slick helpful unassuming thoughtful fun trusting reserved sensitive considerate extroverted introverted.*

Values I want to project:	Already convey:	Need work to behave more:
. . . .	. . . .	. . . .
. . . .	. . . .	. . . .
. . . .	. . . .	. . . .
. . . .	. . . .	. . . .
. . . .	. . . .	. . . .

Chapter 4 dissects all aspects of body language for you to discover how you convey more quickly the values that you want to project to others. In Chapter 9 you will learn how to use your behaviour more effectively when dealing across sexes and nationalities.

THE FEEL OF MY BRAND

When we meet someone for the first time we form an opinion about them based upon our *feelings*. These are formed from a person's image (their look, sound and body language) but also from how well they communicate with us. In this section, determine what feelings you want others to have about you when they meet you. These values should not be transient but sustainable – you want others to believe this about you because it matters deeply to you.

Identify the key feelings of your brand (or add others that you feel are better). Which do you already project (having had feedback that it is so) and which need further development?

motivated decisive kind conscientious ethical resilient high-quality influential self-aware impactful sensitive risk-taking generous competitive supportive leadership innovative authoritative refined free-spirited independent opportunistic political sociable driven impulsive optimistic flexible determined authentic integrity focused capable.

Values I want to project:	Already convey:	Need work to convey more:
....	....	....
....	....	....
....	....	....
....	....	....
....	....	....

For others to get the right feel about you, see Chapter 4 on Acting the part (as you might be sending out the wrong signals from your behaviour) as well as Chapter 8 on influencing skills and Chapter 9 on presenting yourself via communication techniques.

Building your PBI: your assets

The cornerstone of your PBI is your assets – your skills, experience (background, work, personal) along with your personal passions. Reminded of these factors of your individuality you will be better equipped to define your brand values.

SKILLS

Here list the skills that you have developed via schooling, experience as well as personally. Too often we distinguish between our professional achievements and personal ones not realizing that the two need to be interwoven to develop an accurate as well as achievable PBI.

Education

Include all learning achievements – formal schooling, additional certificates, qualifications/on the job training. Plus: extra-curricular achievements (formal or informal; academic, recreational, sports, musical, public service, or other).

. . . .
. . . .
. . . .
. . . .
. . . .
. . . .
. . . .
. . . .
. . . .
. . . .
. . . .

Additional skills I want or need in the next 2 years:

. . . .

. . . .

. . . .

. . . .

. . . .

. . . .

. . . .

Brand values apparent from my current/future education and training:

- . . . .

- . . . .

- . . . .

- . . . .

EXPERIENCE

This needs to be a holistic view of your life experiences, noting key experiences of background (e.g. large family / only child; latch-key kid; summer jobs from a young age; lots of travel, etc.); work experience and recent personal experience that will be relevant to your PBI.

Background: family /upbringing

. . . .

. . . .

. . . .

. . . .

. . . .

. . . .

. . . .

. . . .

Brand values apparent from my background:

- ....
- ....
- ....
- ....

Work experience

Use the following format for each job.

Company ....

Dates ....

Position ....

Key job responsibilities:

- ....
- ....
- ....
- ....

Key duties:

- ....
- ....
- ....
- ....

Key achievements:

- ....
- ....
- ....
- ....

Recognition/promotion:

- ....
- ....
- ....
- ....

Brand values proved by this work experience:

- ....
- ....
- ....
- ....

Personal experience

Including: *health* (e.g. fitness freak / was couch potato but got a grip / meditate; sports); *family* (if yes, how central or tangential to your being), *social life* (active / diverse / solitary); nature / clubbing / arts / music / sports / country or city-based.

Key Personal Experiences:

- ....
- ....
- ....
- ....

Additional experiences I look forward to in the next 2 years:

- ....
- ....
- ....
- ....

Brand values apparent from these personal experiences:

- ....
- ....
- ....
- ....

PASSIONS

Successful, compelling people are passionate – about life, people, activities, issues, causes. The things that stir them often stir us as a result of knowing them.

If in cataloguing your skills and experiences thus far you seemed to have omitted your passions, list them here. Ask the special people in your life, who know you best, why they admire, or even love you? You may discover some passions – or new reasons to become passionate – that you hadn't realized until now!

I am passionate about:

- ....
- ....
- ....
- ....

Brand values apparent from my passions or conveyed to me by those closest to me:

- ....
- ....
- ....
- ....

▨ Your Brand Statement

For those readers currently marketing themselves for a new job you should develop a brand statement that in two to four sentences *states who you are and what you are capable of.* You can use your brand statement at the top of your CV to focus people's attention or in a covering letter when targeting yourself to different markets.

You now have a panoply of values that you want to project to others. You've reflected on how well they come across already and where you feel you need further development to project them to the people that matter.

Now see if you can write two to five sentences that describe who you are, the essence of your achievements and what you offer, all in terms that project the kind of person you want to become, assured that by the time you finish this book you will know exactly how to do so.

MY BRAND STATEMENT

. . . .

. . . .

. . . .

. . . .

. . . .

. . . .

. . . .

. . . .

. . . .

. . . .

. . . .

. . . .

. . . .

Case Studies

To see how three different people branded themselves for new career opportunities read the following case studies. First, there's Darren, a former postman desperate for a new job in Web design despite having no training or qualifications for it. Then there is Grayson, a management consultant keen to become a partner in his firm but who has learned that his demeanour is casting question marks with several of the partners. Finally there is Claire, a single mother recovering from breast cancer who learned just prior to returning to work that her department was to be closed. She had to get a new job but who would employ a bald nurse in her mid-forties?

BRANDING FOR A NEW JOB: DARREN

Darren was one of 1,200 hopefuls who answered ads to 'get the job that you want' on the Internet to be part of a new BBC programme on marketing yourself for a chosen career. Darren's personal story won him the chance of a week's worth of career advice and an interview within his chosen field of Web design. Darren's journey would be filmed for a new documentary series.

Darren left school at 16 with a handful of O levels and worked for 10 years as a postman. In his spare time, Darren became a computer addict and dreamed of working in 'something, anything to do with the Net'. Darren got the opportunity to do just that by winning £30,000 in the football pools. He grabbed the money and ran off to Silicon Valley in the US to learn what he could at the seminal epicentre of information technology and e-commerce. Limited to a one-year tourist visa, Darren had to return to Britain after a 'total immersion experience' into state of the art Web work in California. Once home, he was determined to be part of the emerging, booming e-commerce world.

I was asked to coach Darren for his interviews and to get his act together for the competitive world of new media Web design. I began by watching a tape of him discussing his dream to get a job in Web design with a programme researcher. Despite spending a year in the business in California, Darren didn't *look* like a Web designer. Dressed in an old-style leather jacket and a nondescript shirt and tie, Darren looked like a computer programmer, not a Web designer. Web designers dress casually but look both modern and creative. Darren's look was neither innovative nor current.

The tape also projected a young man with great, perhaps too much, confidence. He sat back in his chair, arms stretched out, legs akimbo – very relaxed and self-assured. Sure, Darren had a good story and showed great initiative to take his winnings to learn the business. But the side of the business he was keen to join – Web design – is very competitive, with most jobs going to qualified graphic designers or geeks with some training in design, not a former postman with few qualifications aside from tremendous drive.

The programme makers chose Darren because of his unique story but also because he had an uphill battle to get the job he wanted yet was unaware of how hard it was going to be. His HTML (Hyper Text Mark-up Language) skills needed sharpening and this coupled with his lack of design training would probably mean he would need to work as an 'apprentice', part of a team, to learn design on the job.

But Darren needed more than just sharper computer skills to get himself a job. He had to get his brand statement clear and learn how to sell himself better to a potential employer.

In our first session, Darren watched the videotape and listened to how I interpreted his image, behaviour and approach. He tried not to show his surprise but admitted, 'I never thought about any of these things.' When I asked him to come up with some brand values that he wanted to project he was stymied. 'I just want to do Web design. I don't know what on earth you mean by my brand values. I'm just Darren, who has worked bloody hard to turn his life around. As my CV says, I am creative, have an endless thirst for knowledge and can learn things very quickly. I know I can do this job and would love an opportunity – any opportunity – to get into the business,' he said.

From this outburst, there were a variety of messages coming across that we could work with as Darren's brand values. He was *determined, motivated, hard-working, individualistic* and *creative*. 'Yeah, I'm all of those things. Great. Those are my brand values,' he agreed triumphantly. Any potential employer would want these values but what other values in addition?

Darren had more homework to do in addition to extra tutorials in HTML in case an employer would sit him in front of a screen and say, 'Show us what you'd do for this client.' He also had to glean from corporate web sites for prospective employers *their* brand values so that he could integrate his with theirs.

Over the week while Darren was doing more research and getting more data on companies, we worked on his appearance and coached him in interview techniques. We ditched the leather jacket in favour of a smart casual, zip-fronted number along with a fine-knit V-neck top and a pair of khaki trousers. His black leather shoes were exchanged for a more current pair of suede desert boots. When asked what he planned to bring to the interview, Darren looked perplexed. 'Myself, of course,' he said. Additionally, a designer always carries a case with samples of his work as well as a smart notepad and pen for note-taking. 'Note-taking?' he asked. Indeed. As a prospective employee, the interview is two-way. They want to find out more about you but you need to show that you are interviewing them, that you want to learn more about them in developing yourself to be part of their team.

We practised how to ask open questions of the interviewer and how and when it would be appropriate for Darren to jot down things the interviewer told him about the company. He asked for the names of key staff, about some clients and work that he wanted to look up later on the Net, of awards that they had won. So when Darren would be invited for a second interview he would have plenty of insider-information to discuss with other staff. Doing your homework, finding out more than you have to about a company, shows your enthusiasm to be part of the company.

One additional caveat had to be added to Darren's note-taking routine: his fingernails were appalling and were surely picked up by anyone speaking to him. They needed attention before any interview. A designer's 'tools' are his hands and Darren needed to show that his were instruments to produce quality work. Of course, people don't consciously say 'show me your hands' when offering a Web design job but they will note candidates' if they are unkempt. Any small detail that is negative can have an impact on your candidacy. Hence, we got rid of this distraction with a long overdue manicure.

The day before his interviews with two target Web design companies, Darren agreed to include the following brand statement on his CV.

> I am a highly motivated candidate who is determined
> to produce quality, innovative Web designs as part of the
> XYZ team. I plan to continue to develop first-rate technical
> competencies on the job as well as in my own time in order
> to take on more responsibility for billable projects.

By the time Darren had his interviews, he was more realistic about his short-term goals. At best, he was capable of an entry-level job working as part of a design team. With this clear in his own mind, he now conveyed persistence and enthusiasm for growth and development rather than overconfidence that he could set the Net on fire simply because he had won the pools and hung around Silicon Valley for a year. It was a sobering few days for a fine young man who did get the opportunity he wanted and now is beginning the career of his dreams. 'Next year, my brand values will include successful and highly regarded,' he added as his parting shot. One thing he will never lack is self-belief. Lucky Darren.

Grayson had a proven track record with one of the leading global management consulting firms and was keen to be put forward for partnership. To do so meant preparing for a somewhat gruelling process involving the sponsorship of his business practice leader, endorsement of several other partners, an elaborate application process, interviews with a practice selection panel followed by a firm-wide global selection presentation and interview. During his 6-month candidacy, along with another 50 eligible, Grayson was expected to carry on his own demanding schedule managing a £5-million cost-improvement programme for a big telecoms client and participating in major new business pitches.

Having succeeded in getting promoted consistently during his 9 years with the firm, Grayson approached his candidacy for partnership with some confidence. 'My business case has to be one of the strongest amongst the contenders. My revenue generation has been considerable with two clients buying significant add-on work as a result of the success of my projects. I don't like to tempt fate, but this should be a shoe-in.'

What Grayson was not factoring in, was that making partner is quite unlike going for promotion. It is more akin to getting accepted into a club than being rewarded for one's achievements. 'I'm worried by Grayson's attitude,' confided his sponsoring partner. 'Of course he's smart and capable. But that isn't all that they are looking for. Partners have to be leaders as well as good team players. They need to be motivators of others and have the ability to get on at the most senior levels in business. Grayson thinks he's these things, and I believe he *wants* to be these things. But it is not apparent yet.'

After a few practice interviews with partner colleagues, Grayson had feedback that he came across as arrogant and insensitive. Although he heard people tell him this he didn't believe it until he saw himself presenting and answering questions on camera. 'I know I said those things, but they *sound* awful. I looked awful too – Mr Know-it-all! Help.'

Grayson had to start with his own Personal Branding Identity. He had to define what he was about and how, as a candidate, he brought something special to the partnership. His brand values included: *professional, leadership, innovative* and *trustworthy*. To see how well these values came across to others, I had him interview other partners as well as his own staff to find out directly areas that they felt he was strong in and where he needed to improve. '360-degree feedback is daunting stuff, but boy did I get some priorities defined for me,' he admitted.

Knowing he didn't 'suffer fools gladly', Grayson learned from others that he demotivated people by not listening to them which was always apparent by his behaviour. He would look away after a minute or two of staff trying to discuss an issue or shuffle papers urging them to 'get on with it' whilst he did other tasks. 'I know if a client did that to me I would feel either angry or wounded. Not a nice trait, I admit.'

Together we worked on a Personal Brand Identity to help focus his application and the values that he would want to project to the various interview panels ahead. He scratched through his draft application which listed his laudable achievements and honed the following statement to project himself for partnership:

> *I want to lead others in developing themselves as well as generate profitable business for the firm. This will require a broader leadership role than I currently hold. Additionally, I look forward to working with partners in developing cross-selling opportunities internationally in the CRM [customer relationship management]/e-commerce area.*

The PBI sounded good but Grayson needed to convey his belief in it by how he handled the interviews. In practice sessions, he started to use 'we' rather than 'I' to express his desire to help the business, not just his own career. He developed original ideas for working with other partners to exploit what he saw as great market opportunities. This was to convince others that he could be innovative despite being a former accountant! He stated that he had the confidence to market projects on his own; he felt that by suggesting a 'full-court press' to include others, the partners would recognize both teamwork and leadership.

As a result of some soul-searching, taking honest feedback on board and trying new approaches, Grayson felt a new confidence in approaching the admissions process. 'I have those brand values and my brand statement at the front of my mind, now,' he said. 'I am starting to feel like a partner. Is that dangerous?'

Indeed the partners wanted candidates that they found believable as partners already. Grayson sailed through the admissions panels impressing all he met. 'A process that I was dreading has turned out to be very enjoyable. I'm almost sorry it's over.'

REBRANDING YOURSELF: CLAIRE

'It turned my world upside down,' explained Claire, an American nurse in her mid-forties who was just completing months of chemotherapy for breast cancer. 'Nurses think they are immune from serious illnesses but, of course, we get them just like everyone else.'

Claire came to a seminar on 'Branding Yourself' offered to health-care professionals and stood patiently in a queue of people wanting some specific tips for their situation. Noting her newly sprouting cropped hair, her age and general demeanour, I guessed that all was not well and suggested that she join me for coffee at the break so that we could have a proper chat about her situation. 'I've been a nurse with this hospital for over 20 years. They've been very supportive with my treatment for breast cancer but I've just learned from my staff that our programme will probably close 3 months after I return to my job,' she explained, looking more resigned than frantic with the news. Claire had also shared that she was a single mother and had a 15-year-old son facing expensive college tuition ahead. 'I not only want to continue working but must, for Todd's sake.'

Many people faced with redundancy in their forties do not have the luxury of taking a year off to 'find themselves' or to learn a new skill. The majority, like Claire, have to keep working and remain viable to keep their family and lifestyle intact. Most, however, don't contract a life-threatening disease, undergo difficult treatment *and* have to find a new job simultaneously. 'I would have been crazy with worry about losing my job before the breast cancer. But believe it or not, I feel like I can take it in my stride now. Staring death in the face puts a lot into perspective,' she explained philosophically.

I arranged to see Claire in my hotel the next day to spend some time on her CV and help her to think more broadly about work possibilities rather than just finding another job. Having attended the lecture on developing personal brand values, Claire joined me brimming with enthusiasm for what she worked on overnight prior to our session. 'Here I am: *confident*, *caring*, *capable* and *experienced*,' she announced with a laugh, dressed in a smart suit instead of her loose-fitting casual gear from the day before.

'You are all that and more,' I added. Before we could draft a brand statement for Claire first we needed some 'dream talk'.

'Dream talk' is musing about possibilities and reflecting on lost opportunities, 'If I had to do it all over again, I would . . .' Women in Claire's situation, bearing great responsibility, rarely take the time to dream, let alone articulate their musings to a complete stranger. They just don't dare to dream about a different life or career, thinking those options are for others, not them. They have to keep their nose to the grindstone, carry on in order to survive.

With some prodding, Claire admitted that she would love to leave frontline hospital work and 'not wear a uniform ever again'! 'I'd love to meet new people, different people. Working in business seems so much more glamorous than medicine. Is it too late for me to have a bit of glamour in my career?' she asked only half in jest.

Claire turned out to be a successful manager as well as a nurse and seemed particularly good at operational matters. 'With my seniority, it is cheaper for hospitals and health centres to hire younger staff than myself. I guess I need to be prepared for a cut in salary. But having a job is better than no job,' she explained. Whilst I am all for people being realistic about their prospects, I am an ogre when it comes to selling yourself short as Claire was doing.

We spent what time we had together discussing career possibilities in a broader context of the health-care industry rather than in the delivery of health care. There were many major global pharmaceutical firms in the area but Claire dismissed the escape route that many American nurses take into becoming a sales rep. 'That would give me no joy whatsoever,' she said, now sounding more discriminating than desperate – a good sign. But there were plenty of other jobs that Claire could do and would be qualified for considering her administrative and project-management experience.

I challenged Claire to identify all the key firms that she dealt with in the course of her own job that were based in the area and to research the ones that sounded the most interesting to her, e.g. drugs vs equipment vs research and development. We agreed to stay in contact via e-mail as I planned to rewrite her CV from hospital jargon into business-speak.

'Is that really me?' came the e-message from Claire once she saw how I'd represented her career for business. Having done her homework on target firms, Claire had to work to craft her branding statement. The firms she was interested in were all global entities and market leaders in their fields. Hence, she needed to add the following brand values to her own list which was finally honed into: *confident, professional, experienced* and *adaptable.* The latter value – adaptable – was particularly important to add and to convey as mid-lifers are often wrongly rejected from consideration for not being willing or able to adapt to change. We highlighted all the 'change management' that Claire oversaw and initiatives she implemented to convince potential employers of her adaptability.

One thing that helped Claire accept the polishing of her CV was that we wrote it in the third person as if someone else was presenting Claire and her abilities objectively. Rather than say, 'I am confident and successful' it is more effective to say, 'Claire is confident . . . her proven success in . . . she is resourceful.'

On the CV, try to eliminate the use of 'I' by using incomplete sentences that state your achievements. For example: *developed* new staffing rotas that resulted in a 14 per cent drop in sick days, *chaired* an interdepartmental task group; *increased performance* of a new team by . . .

Claire's brand statement read:

> *Claire is a confident health-care professional looking for the right opportunity to manage change for a leading medical supplier. Her proven success in implementing a variety of technical and operational initiatives for a respected health-care provider verifies that she is resourceful to senior management and motivational to her staff.*

We were in contact every few days as Claire sent through her draft letters to companies and even photos of herself in suggested 'interview outfits'. She had 6 weeks before she had to return to work and wanted to see if she could get the process rolling before she was made redundant.

'What about my bald head?' she enquired. 'I'll have to come clean about my treatment.' Indeed, but since completing the treatment her prognosis was good and she had her doctor verify this in writing. But still, people would question her health and possibly worry about her reliability. Claire had to be the picture of health despite reality to allay their worries.

I sent her off to a good department store for a makeover and told her to practise with her make-up every day. Her hair was sprouting and with it being short and punky it made her look younger than wearing a wig so I urged her to keep it, not to hide it. Her suggested navy suit and court shoes for the interview made her look like a nun who had escaped from a convent, plus the dark colours made her *look* ill. When she learned that all the companies with which she had interviews planned had casual dress policies, she bought a smart new mix of jersey separates in co-ordinating colours that created 'pseudo suits' – that is, relaxed jackets and tunics over skirts and trousers. 'I've even bought some jazzy shoes,' she added with pride. The new look showed a confident, ageless, dynamic woman. I was thrilled for her.

Her letters and CV won Claire several interviews but she frankly felt that her health was a worry for many. She had felt it best to be upfront, as she was clearly still recovering. However, two companies did see her potential and were expanding fast and needed people with Claire's experience and medical background. She ended up with two attractive offers.

Upon returning to her old job, Claire met with the human resources director who gave her formal notice about the closure of her department 3 months hence. Considering her long service to the hospital and her recent health scare, the hospital was going to offer her another position with only a 10 per cent cut in salary. 'I was so thrilled to say "thanks, but no thanks" and to tell them of my new job at almost double my previous salary. I wasn't being vindictive. I was just so proud of myself,' she announced over the telephone, sounding quite unlike the beleaguered senior nurse recovering from cancer that I had met two months previously.

These few case studies show how you can make it easier for others to 'buy' you when you know what you want and define it in terms that are meaningful to others. Hopefully, in this chapter, if you have distilled the person you are today and identified the kind of person that you want to be, jump to the chapters that will be of most help immediately. In the following chapters you will learn how to live your brand values by how you handle yourself – how you sound, behave and look – as well as how you handle others – through influence and rapport.

3

SOUNDING
THE PART

You begin to discover how to project your brand by focusing on your voice first, then body language, before entering the more obvious zone of packaging your brand by how you dress.

38 PER CENT OF YOUR IMPACT

The initial impact of your voice on others is very important – it accounts for 38 per cent of the impression you make on people. In this section, we will deal with the sound of your voice and how to improve it. In Chapter 7 you will learn how to use more effective language. Chapter 8 deals with how your voice can enhance presentations.

LEARN YOUR PARALINGO

You know what languages you speak, but do you know what your *paralanguage* is? This is the 'how' when it comes to your voice. The *how* you speak, arguably, conveys *more* to others than the words that you use. Check the values you noted for your voice in Chapter 2 (page 56) that will be the basis of your paralingo.

How loudly or softly you speak and the degree to which you vary the volume conveys much about your confidence as well as your gravitas. The pace at which you speak sends messages. The lively fast-talker can come across positively as enthusiastic or negatively as nervous. Conversely, the slow speaker can seem either thoughtful or pedantic or, even worse, thick!

The pitch and tone in your speech is very obvious to others after only a matter of minutes, conveying many messages about your confidence, background and personality. Although you might know your voice is fairly constant in tone, to others your monotone is monotonous! Is your accent very distinctive? A discernible accent is fine as long as it's understandable. All these factors together – the volume, pace, pitch, tone and accent – form your paralanguage, which speaks volumes to others.

I HATE MY VOICE!

Everyone who's ever seen themselves on camera or heard themselves on tape cringes. 'Is that really how I sound ?' Yes, it is how you sound to others.

The reason it sounds so different from when we hear ourselves speak 'live' is we have the benefit of quadraphonic sound. All the noise we make as we speak bounces around inside us creating more resonance than it has once it has been projected. Listening to yourself on tape reveals what actually carries to others, and so provides powerful clues to how we need to improve. As I said at the outset, try to be objective and rational about these personal matters.

Many people that I coach are well aware that their voice isn't an asset and state it so as if that's just their bad luck. It is amazing to see just how much you can improve the quality and impact of your voice after just a few sessions. You can by trying some of the tips and techniques described later.

Wanted: a new voice

No problem. We all learn how to speak and can unlearn and learn to speak all over again. Physical impediments need skilled therapy to redress problems (with speech therapists being some of modern medicine's great unsung heroes). But for those of us who have no valid reason for a poor voice aside from bad habits or not having a parent, teacher or colleague to help us, improvement can result in as little as a few hours or trying new techniques.

It's much easier than you would believe. Sure, you will feel like a ninny trying to make your voice more interesting but others won't even be aware of your efforts. When you find you aren't getting interrupted as much or that people are listening for longer you'll know that it's working.

I have consciously changed my voice twice in my life. Reared outside Boston, Massachusetts, I was raised on the broad, flat accent of the area: 'I pahked my caahr in Haavid Yaahid.' (Think of the voice of American *Tonight Show* host Jay Leno; or, Matt Damon, Ben Affleck and Robin Williams in *Good Will Hunting*.) Moving to the New York region in my teens, I was mimicked unmercifully by my peers but, thankfully, rescued by Sister Jeremiah at the Academy of Holy Angels and given elocution lessons to define my 'r's and add more depth to my voice. It worked. I got very good at imitating accents as a result and can still 'do Brooklyn' *priddy good, tawkin' lik dis.*

When I moved to England 20 years ago I soon discovered that the American accent grates on the nerves of the natives. The realization was disappointing at first, but as a confirmed ex-pat now myself I know how ridiculous many American accents can sound abroad. I worked to eliminate most American slang (not street-stuff, necessarily, but business terms not used in Britain) and adopted some British pronunciations to reduce the impact of the American sound. The result is what is described as mid-Atlantic. My goal was not to pass myself off as a Brit (no offence, but heaven forbid), but not to get up the nose of people so immediately upon meeting as Americans can, albeit unwittingly. (It was not only my voice that put folks off. See Chapter 4 for more details on how I cleared rooms with my body language!)

SEPARATE THE WHEAT FROM THE CHAFF – FIND WHAT *REALLY* NEEDS IMPROVEMENT

After years of coaching people on presentation skills and voice projection, I wager you might be hypercritical about your shortcomings – many people are. But maybe you only need to improve one aspect, like slowing down and learning how to employ pauses or discover techniques to project more effectively (not just for formal presentations but even when speaking conversationally). Others (cognisant of the dreaded voice-mail message) see their regional accents as a liability when they are anything but. A great accent reveals both character and personality in the voice. All accents, by the way, are potentially charming. The key is for them to be understandable.

To balance the overly critical are the smugly overconfident who believe that they are either quite effective (usually because they are extrovert and *like* to talk), or perhaps they are just snobs who were 'born into' a posh voice. Many remain blissfully unaware of their ineffective voices because no one has ever told them before. Many senior businessmen, for example, mumble or speak in a monotone and only hold people's attention because of their position or power. Others who listen to them can be unimpressed.

EXERCISE: GET SOME FEEDBACK

If you value your own critiquing skills, speak into a cassette recorder. Describe a recent film that you've seen or a book that moved you. When you play back, complete the following questionnaire and note a few things that need improving. Ask yourself what kind of person you sound like – confident, bored, tentative, inspired? What values do you want others (even those that hear your voice-mail message!) to pick up when they hear you? How might you convey these by changing the way you speak. Read on to learn how.

If you don't feel that you can critique yourself, ask a colleague to complete the following questionnaire, having listened to you speak for 3 to 5 minutes. Choose someone who is a good mentor or coach who has impressed you before with interesting observations on others. Those closest to us know us warts and all and are either likely to be too easy on you or overly critical. Explain that you are working on a presentation and want to get some input on the quality of your voice, not the content of your talk. A good friend or your partner is generally not a smart choice for this exercise.

If you don't want to talk shop for this exercise, *present* what you did for the weekend starting from leaving work on Friday night to hitting the hay on Sunday night. If it was a mundane weekend, describe your ideal weekend or an embarrassing experience that might be amusing.

Stand up when you do your spiel while your colleague sits and listens. When you are finished, have them complete the form and give you more feedback. Tell them you are looking for ways to improve so don't want to be told that you are simply splendid (unless you really are!).

VOICE CRITIQUE

VOICE PRODUCTION

1 **Breathing**

❑ Good   ❑ Needs improvement   ❑ Weak

Comments
. . . .

2 **Vocal quality (e.g. harsh, nasal, breathy)**

❑ Good   ❑ Needs improvement   ❑ Weak

Comments
. . . .

3 **Overall energy**

❏ Good ❏ Needs improvement ❏ Weak

Comments

. . . .

SOUND PRODUCTION

1 Articulation (pronounce words distinctly/ words flow well)

❏ Good ❏ Needs improvement ❏ Weak

Comments

. . . .

2 Physical flexibility (face, lips, jaw, tongue)

❏ Good ❏ Needs improvement ❏ Weak

Comments

. . . .

BODY LANGUAGE

1 Posture and movement

❏ Good ❏ Needs improvement ❏ Weak

Comments

. . . .

2 Gestures

❏ Good ❏ Needs improvement ❏ Weak

Comments

. . . .

3 **Facial expressions**

❏ Good ❏ Needs improvement ❏ Weak

Comments

. . . .

Common voice problems and solutions

TONE

Flat, monotone sound can be improved by adding the three E's – energy, enthusiasm and expression. Monotone sound is often the result of a stifled, introverted personality who, from a young age, was rewarded for not getting overexcited. Business people often develop flat voices from a misconceived notion that the more controlled they sound and behave the more professional they will appear. Years of practice in keeping one's three E's buttoned-up takes commitment to release.

To add energy:

- *Vary the pace*. Monotone flat sounds can appear less so if you work at speeding up, slowing down, adding pauses.
- *Get fit.* Honestly, the fitter you are the more energy you can generate without getting yourself all worked up physically.
- *Check your breathing*. Of course you are breathing, but is the sound nasal because you 'speak through your nose'? A monotone voice is often weak because it uses less wind power (hence, the benefit of being fit).
- *Have a lung capacity test* to see how much of your lungs are actually being used. Standard with many fitness or health screenings, you blow as hard as you can into a valve which monitors your lung power. Many of us only use 50 per cent capacity or even less which attributes both monotone, weedy, or 'breathy' sounds. If your lungs aren't being used to capacity, incorporate deep breathing into your life.

To add enthusiasm:

- *Believe that you are worth listening to* and convey that belief to others.
- *Tune into WIFM* (what's in it for me) to put your message over in a way that is interesting to others, not just to yourself. How can you rephrase things or use words that engage them? When you see you have them hooked, you too will be more enthusiastic.
- *Add variety* however you can – physically moving, changing the pace – it all helps to break up the monotony of a static speaker.

To add expression:

- *Be expressive! Move your facial muscles.* Sure, your lips might move when you speak but many a monotone speaker could easily pass for a ventriloquist simply because they hardly move a facial muscle. Practise in front of the mirror. Of course you will feel like a jerk but you will capture listeners for longer if you are expressive.
- *Smile.* The old chestnut that smiling makes the voice sound lighter and more pleasant is for real. Use your judgement how much you smile as a grin could be seriously out of place during some business discussions. Again, do a mirror test. When you speak, do the corners of your mouth droop? This is an eventuality for most of us as we age. So, when you hit 40 force a grin on your face when you speak. You'll just look pleasant rather than morose! Practise looking pleasant whilst speaking in the mirror to get a feel of what's required.
- *Practise on kids.* If you don't have any, borrow one. If you can keep a child under 10 engaged for 20

minutes you're developing the kind of expressive power you need to be an engaging speaker. If you don't think you are amusing enough yourself or simply out of touch with what kids are interested in (yes, that's you, Dad) try reading them a story.

PACE – LACKS VARIETY

Akin to a monotone voice is one which fails to vary in pace. We all know people who either race along so quickly that we can only digest about half of what they say with others who speak so slowly that we either think that they are mentally slow or being pedantic. Neither extreme is effective.

Most people speak at 120 words per minute (w.p.m.); TV presenters at 150 to 200 w.p.m. The average businessperson can comprehend (reading) over 600 w.p.m.. The goal is not to try to speak at that pace (the *Guinness Book of Records* lists 637 w.p.m. but that would make tedious listening!) but to make it varied and 'pacey' for the average person to hang in there with you.

To check your vocal pace, record yourself reading an article from a newspaper. When you play back, can you comprehend as you listen or do you speak too quickly? If not, is the pace too ponderous and irritating because your brain is ahead of your ears?

The two most consistent requests that I get from clients are how to sound more positive and how to sound more powerful. So here goes:

To sound more positive:

- *Add speed* if you know that you are too slow (do you often get interrupted?) but pause at relevant points so your listeners can absorb what's being said.
- *Be expressive.* Deadpan is never dynamic unless used for comic effect (Jack Dee or Jack Benny style).
- *Visualize the outcome you want.* If you really want the job, want others to keep on schedule to meet the deadline or sell someone a new idea, visualize yourself succeeding in doing just that *whilst speaking.* Your voice will be more compelling, upbeat and, if you know your stuff, result in a self-fulfilling prophecy!
- *Gesture along with your words,* not with every sentence or paragraph but to emphasize key words. Using your body (gesturing and movement) will unconsciously help you to speed up your words. You'll feel more *exposed* and more in *performance mode,* no bad thing for a pedantic speaker.
- *Practise winning wrap-ups.* If you feel you lose your listeners often because you speak slowly or aren't as dynamic or forceful as others, craft your summaries to surprise or impress. You only get good at this by practising when it doesn't matter. Like in a discussion with your partner on the weekends or with your friends just catching up on things.

To sound more powerful:

- *Slow down,* particularly at the important bits that you want others to absorb or remember.
- *Use pauses* for the same reasons. You might be a human dynamo incapable of speaking slowly (we all know 'em) so your best bet is to integrate pauses into your speech – not just when it's important but all the time, in every phone call or when just schmoozing.
- *Emphasize special words or phrases.* 'Do you want to know *why* we can't wait any longer to make this decision? Or, do *you* suggest we wait and see for another quarter when our *backs* will really be against the wall?'
- *Speak softly* when you want to emphasize points. Do this in conjunction with pausing and you'll blow 'em away. But don't overdo it. No one will thank you for having to strain their ears for too long.
- *Speak more deeply.* A deep voice is far more compelling than a high voice, and, yes, you can change the pitch. You do this by using your whole body when you speak, breathing deeply so that you use the full power of your lungs. A squeaky, strident voice enthrals no one.
- *Eliminate fillers* – the 'ums' and 'ahs'. Practice is the cure. Cut them out in every conversation – not just the important ones.
- *Use gestures in moderation.* High-status characters don't flail about.

WHADYA SAY?

If others often ask you to repeat things or to explain what you mean, you either have a problem with articulating your words clearly or have fuzzy thinking. Let's just focus on the former as the latter requires a separate volume itself though Chapters 7 (influential language) and 8 (presentation skills) have some suggestions.

To sound more articulate:

- *Say it clearly.* Is what you say *clear* to others? If you think that your words aren't always understood, speak as if you would to a foreigner – taking time and effort to say your words as they should be said. Use single-syllable words instead of multi-syllabic ones. If you say it clearly, don't repeat unless you are doing so for emphasis. Use active rather than passive words. And try not to babble – bluffing with a bunch of words that say nothing. When in doubt, when developing your concepts, sentences and paragraphs at the end of each say, 'So what?' If you can't find a good answer, cut it.
- *Avoid jargon.* You hate it when you don't get it so avoid using jargon whenever possible. Even in companies where everyone understands the jargon, find clearer words to say the same thing. Jargon is geek-speak – power brokers don't use it.
- *Improve your vocabulary,* not with bombastic words that irritate when simpler ones are far superior but with interesting, better words that you admire others using in writing or speech. Use words and phrases that are evocative – when said we know exactly what is meant. Read at least one well-written trade journal, newspaper or magazine a week (*The Economist, International Herald Tribune, Spectator,*

Management Today, weekend edition of *Financial Times, New Scientist, New Yorker, Atlantic Monthly, Far Eastern Economic Review*).

- *Identify your regular bloopers,* words or sounds that trip you up every time. Either eliminate them altogether with better words you find easier to pronounce or learn to pronounce them correctly.
- *Demonstrate* when you can rather than 'tell' with your words. Keep words active and descriptive. 'Paint a picture' of what you mean. Help them *see what you mean*. Let them *imagine* with you.
- *Get personal.* Take risks, say what *you* think. Use personal pronouns – 'I believe . . . we agree . . .' – rather than impersonal nouns like 'one could say . . . it was agreed . . .'
- *Get emotional.* Men panic when I suggest this but expressing worry, passion, compassion, disappointment, or even anger can be compelling if you don't lose yourself in the emotion. We've all seen the contrived tear-jerker routine, often on the other side of the Atlantic. Bill Clinton is good at expressing both genuine and contrived emotion. We know which is which. And when it's contrived, it is handy to have a sick bag! When it's genuine you can move people beyond your hopes. So, next time you are really, really moved by something (e.g. raising money for charity; wanting to thank your team for going above and beyond the call of duty) take the risk and *get emotional.*
- *Make it compelling.* Imagine presenting your ideas on a TV news programme. How can you hook us upfront to capture our attention? We don't give a hoot about your objectives, we want to know what's of use to, or in it for, us.

- **Resist the urge to think out loud.** Do your thinking in private. Stream of conscious babble is tough for us to follow. If you are prone to do this (yes, you know who you are), watch for quizzical looks and *snap out of it!*
- **Delete Spam.** Related to point 9 is the junk – like all those unwanted e-mails – that you allow yourself to speak. This is beyond thinking out loud, it's just waste of space verbiage. Don't fill the air with nothingness if you want to leave the impression that you are more than hot air.

Influential language

Compare the language of someone you know who is impressive and that of someone who generally fails to do themselves justice. Often it is a combination of *how we speak* (our paralanguage), our *choice of words* and the *clarity* with which we express them that influences others. And just because you don't consider yourself as articulate (yet!) as other colleagues, there are several things you can try today to be a more influential communicator.

DIRECT SPEECH PREFERRED

Modern business-speak should be clear, not convoluted. Your taking the long way round to explain something or wasting others' time with insignificant detail will impress few. The most influential speakers are economical with words. 'But my work is very complicated' is the most common refrain to my plea for speaking plain, conversational language. You will seem even cleverer if you make your subject easily understood. This is not being patronizing; it's about being considerate and making the listener's comprehension a snap. It is very irritating to have to work at understanding a speaker. Most of us just give up – not amused and unimpressed!

YOU SELLS, *I* REPELS

The most compelling speakers and influencers use the 'you' word more than they use the 'I' word. Change the focus of your talk from yourself to others; recognize what *they* succeed at and applaud them for it. Asking, 'What do you think?' is a more influential opener than 'Let me tell you what I think.' Sure, you might be smarter and have a better answer but you won't influence anyone by being Mr or Ms Right all the time. When expressing your opinion, try to put it into the context of *you*, *we* or *us* to build rapport. For example, rather than 'the way *I* see it' or 'according to *me*' try 'it is obvious that *we* will get that contract if . . .'

DON'T ADD FUEL TO FIRE

Word selection can also help mitigate potential negative reactions which increases your influence not only with those you are confronting, but with observers as well.

When you need to confront someone about a failure, weakness or problem, present it as *an issue*. For example, 'Your problem is that you never listen' is more confrontational than 'We seem to have an issue with communication that we need to resolve.' This depersonalizes the potential attack and enables you to hold a more productive discussion about what went wrong or what the person needs to do to rectify things. By sharing ownership of the difficulty you also diffuse the personal nature of an attack . For example, using *we* instead of *you*.

WORD CHOICE

Think of the difference in language used between a civil servant and a politician. The former cares only about being factual or lawful, delivering only what's necessary, while the latter wants to sell his/her message and win our support. The words the two use can contrast markedly. Discussing road congestion, the civil servant might say, 'It is believed that excessive vehicle flow caused this irregular influx into the city centre.' Whilst the politician might say, 'There are simply too many cars on the road creating dreadful traffic jams. We've got to find a workable solution to prevent further inconvenience to everyone.' Obviously, the latter is easier to understand, with neither, notably, taking any blame!

WORDS THAT INFLUENCE, WORDS THAT DON'T

Why qualify or weaken your message with a poor choice of words? I often find that people hold back from using stronger words because they don't want to appear overconfident or arrogant. This is particularly true for individuals who don't sell themselves, who are great team players but resist the limelight. Business today demands that you sell your ideas, your work, your team and yourself with confidence.

From the lists below, which column contains your kind of language?

Influential	*Unimpressive*
Will	Might
Outstanding	Good
Pivotal	Relevant
Endorsement	Agreement
However	But
Leading edge	New
We should	Perhaps we
Massive	Big
Fulfilled	Completed
Achieved	Did
Specifically	What I am trying to say is
Impact	Potential
Immediately	As soon as possible
Global	International
Now	Soon
You'll, no doubt, agree	If you agree
Benefits	Uses

LEARN *THEIR* LINGO

When working with and for clients it is important to learn their culture as well as their language. All organizations have different ways of doing things, as well as what they call their units or departments, how they organize themselves, etc. The sooner you adapt their lingo when working with them the quicker you are welcomed into the organization as an advisor or supplier.

DON'T BE SO BRITISH!

The Brits' natural inclination to be self-deprecating can be charming when it isn't so stupid. 'I am probably not the best person to answer that question but . . .' or 'I don't know much about the problem but what you should do is . . .' Of course, the meaning is the exact opposite: you do know what you are talking about, everyone else knows that you know, so cut the silly, albeit charming, charade. Self-deprecation is fine socially but doesn't help anyone working in a global market. Besides, the Brits have too many international colleagues that take these remarks literally (e.g. Americans and Germans) and will write you off if you qualify your speech.

The other subtlety behind a self-deprecating remark is to avoid ownership and, therefore, potential blame if things don't turn out right. Hence, the overall effect of these comments in business only serves to weaken your influence.

TO EARN THEIR TRUST

The hackneyed expression bandied about at every level in business is 'win-win', we all want to find ways to make deals, doing business that is to everybody's advantage, not just our own. The hard sell is a thing of the past. Few of us in business – or even in our personal lives – will not be *sold to*.

Therefore, the notion of *trust* becomes important in communication, and building trust comes from establishing some kind of relationship with others. You can't do it fleetingly or just with a terrific presentation. It takes more. More of us. How can we convey to others that we are reliable, that they can have faith in our word? Well, a lot depends on how we even speak those words.

Your voice is key in conveying trust. Speaking too high or too low are equally ineffective, as is speaking too quickly or too slowly. When you need to win someone's trust, believe that it matters more to you than to him/her. Earnestness will come through more honestly and convincingly as a result.

WINGING IT

One of the easiest ways to fail to impress others is by not bothering to do your homework about them or the issue at hand. Of course, it is difficult to be well-briefed for every meeting but for the important ones, show respect, interest and intelligence by swotting up on what you would be expected to know. To really influence, know (*and show that you know*) more than they'd expect.

Everyone gets caught out. Hit with the issue you feared might come up but you were not prepared for. The brave will shoot from the hip and sometimes get away with it, able to muster all their wits and know-how for an effective response. But for the topics that really cause you to blank, it is wise to be honest and say that you really can't provide an answer or view but will do so immediately after the meeting by e-mail, phone call (or whatever they prefer).

Talking proper

Many who speak English as a first language are sensitive about their accents and sense ridicule occasionally when they speak. It wasn't until the eighteenth century that different regions of Great Britain became aware that certain accents were 'proper' and others weren't; well, according to the self-appointed, self-righteous arbiters of such things. In the nineteenth century there were dozens of books on the letter 'h' when it was deemed that it was 'social suicide' to drop the 'h' as in the chirpy Cockney greeting of ''Ello, luv.' Some 'educationalists' insisted that dropping the letter 'h' conveyed a defective intelligence!

FIRST POSH, NOW SPICE

For the last two centuries in Britain how you spoke was linked to your social identity. Fortunately, today this is less and less the case. Even the BBC, the twentieth-century arbiter of good speech – Received Pronunciation (RP) – positively try to sound more democratic and not biased towards the London/Home Counties regional accents. Today, among their leading presenters, it is hard to find one with the traditional RP accent.

Even the royal family is not immune from the change. The late Princess Diana, a member of the aristocracy herself before marriage, adopted more modern language and pronunciation that was quite distinctive from Prince Charles. And both young princes William and Harry sound very different from their father – still posh, mind you, but less 'cut-glass'. Harry even described the Spice Girls as 'a bit of all right' – an expression I doubt his dad has ever used.

Twenty-five years ago, the upper classes spoke the same regardless of generation. Watching old films from the 50s and 60s, it is hilarious to see young boys sounding very much like pompous old farts. Even the best-bred kids – especially today's Trustafarians – sound less starchy and more modern than their parents. So, it is only a matter of time that stigmatizing someone by accent should become an anachronism.

Regions with distinctive accents have won huge business investment, as seen in the late twentieth-century birth of the call centre. Friendly, warm, but definitely not posh, Welsh, Glaswegian, Belfast and Geordie accents are the best in the business for winning new business (cold call selling) as well as for manning customer service hotlines.

But if you are sensitive and feel that your accent doesn't impress people, you can take steps to eliminate certain giveaways that you worry might undermine your influence. Like it or not, some accents just don't sound authoritative. They will be fine – charming, engaging, intelligent – in conversation over a beer but just don't have gravitas in a business meeting. Perhaps it's because some of our favourite soap operas or movies make such a parody of certain regions in which people are portrayed as never amounting to more than stall vendors, publicans, farm hands or gangsters. And here you are – a talented, capable manager – and people just poke fun at how you speak. I only raise accents as a concern because I hear from clients *daily* who are worried about theirs.

I am a champion of accents because they distinguish us, add personality and character to people. I only make recommendations to change an accent when certain sounds *jar* or just undermine your effectiveness.

In Britain, I am often asked about accents – which ones score in impressing others and which are liabilities. Without wishing to play Dr Higgins (of *My Fair Lady*), I am happy to pass on key tips about specific regional sounds that can work against you in business. Here are a few examples of regional accents with suggestions on how to improve them for influencing others:

- *Cockney/London.* Practise pronouncing the letters 'r', 'th' and 'l' correctly and any words ending in a hard 't' should be distinct. Avoid endearments when speaking with female colleagues (charming as they are, they are just out of place in the office). And if you can be bothered, use definite 'h's!

- *Liverpool*. Watch the guttural sounds and the use of 'me' instead of 'my'. Along with the Northern Irish, practise ending declarative sentences in a low, not high, pitch which implies a question or underconfidence. A high tone on a declarative sentence makes us think you are asking a question, not stating a fact or viewpoint.
- *Yorkshire*. Add *the* definitive article as used by others using *the* English language. Take it easier on the long 'i' which doesn't require you to stretch your mouth as 'wiiiidely' as possible to pronounce.
- *Manchester*. Soften the letter 'u' – for the word 'bus' try 'bahs' rather than 'boos'. Also watch your lilting when trying to sound definitive. Drop your voice at the end of a sentence when it isn't a question.
- *Newcastle/Geordie*. Watch the speed which is too fast for most outside the region. The musical variation of the Geordies is the opposite of monotone and whilst engaging it is not professional in sound. Slowing down helps in most cases, along with keeping the pitch low when you are enthusiastic. If you tend to use the common Geordie filler 'like', try to eliminate it as it, like, lessens your impact, like.

When speaking a second language most of us have a very distinctive accent simply by incorporating speech patterns we use in our mother tongue. Our native regionalism won't be a problem necessarily but we still can sound oafish when speaking another language to the natives. If you need to work in a second language it is good to get feedback about how you come across and take steps to rectify problems. If the feedback means extra tutorial coaching is required to be more effective, get it. Be observant of how business colleagues speak – including pronunciation, pitch, pace and tone. Mimic as much as possible without becoming a parody.

A few final pointers on making your accent better understood:

- Face people when speaking to them, use eye contact as much as you can.
- Watch not to cover your mouth with your hand as some people do as a matter of course. This makes lip-reading a challenge. Don't laugh. That's what we resort to when struggling to understand an unfamiliar accent. Besides, keeping your hand near your mouth implies deception.
- Speak at a good pace to convey enthusiasm and energy but not too quickly for the rest of us to lose your drift.

All countries have a wealth of regional quirks when it comes to interpreting the national language. America and Australia, Scotland, Ireland, Wales, South Africa, Canada, the Caribbean and elsewhere have rich interpretations of spoken English. Long live the variety. But if your accent is one that has specific words, sounds or tones that undermine your perceived professionalism I'd recommend you do your best to eliminate them while remaining true to your roots.

4

ACTING THE PART

Silent messages

Reflect on how well your behaviour conveys the brand values you want to project, the kind of person you really are. People are often amazed when told what silent messages they emit with their behaviour. After seeing themselves on tape or being observed during a meeting they are surprised at how transparent their feelings are simply by how they sit, from their expressions and gestures, their use or lack of eye contact as well as other things.

Silent messages are more honest then the verbal ones we speak because they are more difficult to control. It is harder to sustain behaviour that is untrue to our feelings but just learning how ineffective bad habits can be sending conflicting signals to others can transform your ability to influence people. A person that is unconscious of the messages that she/he sends is invariably a poor communicator.

▓ Mirror, Mirror

Psychologists, anthropologists and human development specialists have made intensive study of the links between our thinking, language and behaviour for the last 20 years. Neurolinguistic Programming (NLP) is the discipline for this study, and it has been embraced by many people as an overview of effective principles for building relationships and rapport as well as for understanding ourselves better. The *neuro* refers to the brain and how we organize thought; *linguistic* is about the language we use; and *programming* is the behaviour that results or interprets our thoughts and language.

A key concept of NLP known as *mirroring* is about discreetly matching another person's behaviour to build rapport with that person. Think of people whose behaviour irritates you. No doubt it is because they are so different from you. You are composed, they are scatty; you are energized, they are listless; you are impersonal, they are personal. But when we try to behave in a similar style to people that we want to impress or get to know better, it is good to observe their behaviour and give back to them behaviour that makes them comfortable, i.e. like their own, while still being ourselves.

Mirroring someone else is not about deception but about *making others feel comfortable*. When we feel comfortable with other people they are more open in themselves and open towards us – no bad thing when trying to build a compatible relationship.

Back to the brand

List your brand values developed in Chapter 2.

....
....
....
....
....

Now, how obvious are these values are from your behaviour? From how you move and interact with others? As we have seen, every time you speak, you support your words, but even more so your *feelings* with dozens of small signals sent from your gestures, eye movements, posture, body movements, and expressions.

You are already an expert in body language because you constantly pick up messages from other people's and what they are saying by reading their behaviour. 'He didn't say it but I know that he doesn't agree.' 'I hate meetings with her because as soon as she's challenged she gets defensive and can't listen to valid criticism objectively.' 'He's a really smooth operator. I have no reason to feel this way but I simply don't trust him.' These hunches may be valid or may be completely wrong. It doesn't matter. We are *convinced* and it takes a major effort to convince people otherwise when judged wrongly.

Much research has been done in the last 25 years into the importance and meaning of behaviour using various disciplines of psychology, anthropology and linguistics along with new sub-disciplines of kinesics (body movement), proxemics (social distances, 'proximity') and paralinguistics (how you speak). So today there is a body of findings that support what many people know intuitively. Perhaps the greatest value of this work has been to confirm our own instincts and to help us see ourselves more clearly. It is always so much easier to read others than it is to understand how others read us.

Interpreting your values through actions

Without knowing your specific brand values, let me demonstrate how you can *see* the values through behaviour. Here are some common adjectives mentioned by many business people in describing the values they look for in others: *honest, intelligent, approachable, successful, confident.* But how do these values *behave*? Some ways are obvious, others are not.

Honesty is conveyed behaviourally through:

- *Direct eye contact.* Fleeting eye contact conveys uncertainty, stress and lack of confidence all inherent when acting or speaking dishonestly.
- *A positive, expressive face.* Positive (smiling upon meeting/when appropriate) expressions convey inner peace and self-assuredness akin to an honest person.
- *Active listening.* Showing interest in others shows confidence in who you are and your personal integrity.
- *Unhurried/unhesitant speech.* Speaking at a moderate pace, free from stress and anxiety, conveys veracity.
- *A composed body and open gestures.* Looking relaxed and able to communicate with an open body and gestures can only be sustained under stress if we are being truthful. Honest people tend not to cover their mouths when speaking.

You will appear more intelligent when you are:

- *Quiet and composed.* Intelligent people don't have to show off like lesser mortals keen to prove what they are not.
- *More softly spoken.* The words will be so profound that

we'll hang on every one if you speak more softly (yet, still with expression!).

- *Using moderate gestures.* You don't have to paint elaborate pictures for us unless you are inarticulately intelligent!
- *Short on small talk.* But don't expect us to want to buy from you if you are.
- *Not the first to introduce yourself.* The higher the IQ the greater the hesitation in meeting just anyone – you don't suffer fools gladly.
- *A good listener* who makes others sound more intelligent than they are when you feed back or distil what they have said.

You will seem more approachable if you:
- Smile more.
- Introduce yourself immediately.
- Make small talk that seems genuine.
- Stand closer to people.
- Listen with the same enthusiasm that you speak.
- Touch others only when appropriate.
- Show empathy with facial expressions and gestures.

You will look more successful if you:
- Have erect posture and are energetic, yet composed.
- Proffer a firm and direct handshake.
- Don't convey an excess of enthusiasm even when you are brimming over.
- Speak clearly at a moderate pace.
- Don't jump to answer questions.
- Are free of stress – because you've got life under control.
- Use eye contact when speaking and listening.

You will convey confidence when you:

- Do everything to look successful (see above).
- Engage everyone in a discussion.
- Have the courage to tell people what you really think.
- Don't take criticisms personally.
- Use humour appropriately.
- Behave differently from the standard business culture, e.g. be more flamboyant or relaxed if conservative; more mature if young; more youthful if stuffy; more composed if carefree; urbane if parochial; have a broader prospective/be visionary if somewhat limited and narrow.

Reflect now how you can convey the values that you want by your actions. There will be further ways on conveying your brand (that are easier to see) in the next two chapters, 'Looking the Part'.

The eyes have it

The eyes are central to communication. Babies and children read our messages via the eyes long before they understand words. We also learn when growing up (and also later in business) that when we are being looked at we are the centre of attention. Being the subject of someone's eye contact can emote different feelings – like 'threatened' because we *feel* it is aggressive, or 'embarrassed' because the attention is unwanted or important because we value their attention.

You may 'win' eye contact more quickly and for longer periods because of your sex, colouring, age and attractiveness. As a mother of two beautiful teenage girls I know only too well how being blonde, young and pretty wins immediate attention from people regardless of age or sex. I find it amusing to walk with Anna or Lucy and to see men, in particular, not even see me although I am right next to them. They are drawn to the girls because of their colouring (there are fewer blondes than any other hair colour) and beauty. As their mum, I only take delight in basking in their attraction . . . honest!

We are also able to establish and hold eye contact more effectively by how we position ourselves. If you are opposite someone it is obviously easier (though possibly also confrontational) than sitting next to someone. People who are intimate can hold eye contact for far longer than others (though there seems to be a case of diminishing returns to this principle in long-term partnerships/marriages!).

Women use eye contact longer in business the more personal the nature of the meeting; for example, when doing a performance appraisal with their staff versus getting an update on a project. Men are quite the opposite and find when a business meeting gets personal they struggle to maintain eye contact.

Winning eyes: the RADA push/pull technique

The great drama school RADA (Royal Academy of the Dramatic Arts) recognizes that many of the skills that actors develop can usefully be employed by others in business and politics. We are well aware of leading politicians, from the legendary Martin Luther King to the infamous Adolf Hitler learning theatrical techniques for developing their speech-making skills. But modern business people can also learn how to be more effective by studying dramatic techniques.

One of the most effective is the notion of using the eyes to win people over – by *pulling*! When people are angry, negative or confrontational the eyes are blocked, i.e. they will only allow us to talk on the surface to convince them, change their minds internally. Ask someone to look at you in a way that conveys negativity. Tell them to look unimpressed by what you are saying and try to hold this view just by how they look at you.

Now, you try to *pull* them towards you – not by saying anything but just by how you look at them. (If it's been a while since you have done some serious flirting this might take a few go's as it is what we do instinctively when we are flirting.) Look relaxed, think that you really want to try to help them, to understand them. Keep that thought and keep that look *pulling* them. Every time I demonstrate this, the *pusher* relents! Experiment with it the next time you are in a tough negotiation or trying to box yourself out of a jam. Getting *pulled* does not mean that you always score! You will just be able to keep communicating rather than have things breaking down.

It is almost impossible to generalize when and where not to use eye contact. We know when it feels right for us and this is a good guideline. But we also tend to be unaware of how ineffective we are ourselves. For example, many people are very good at using eye contact effectively when speaking, mainly because they want their message to be heard and using eye contact is another way, in addition to effective speech, to driving the message home.

Other people can be quite oblivious to how they turn others off when they speak. A barrister acquaintance of mine was totally unaware that he spoke mainly to the ceiling or to the gods. The effect of looking upwards when you do speak is that you are pontificating which, being a barrister, he did a lot of the time. Doing so socially, or when you aren't aiming to strike fear in the hearts of people, is an unattractive trait to say the least.

Cultural note on eye contact: the advice given above works effectively in most Western or westernized cultures (e.g. those with a strong multinational presence, Western media, etc.) When influencing different nationalities, observe their use of eye contact and follow suit. Scandinavians can seem to stare as listeners but use fleeting eye contact when speaking. Arabs will look at you constantly, while many Asians like the Thais and Malay are intimidated by prolonged direct eye contact.

GUIDELINES FOR MAKING EYES

With the risk of over-generalizing, here are my top 10 guidelines on using eye contact to influence others:

- *Look people in the eye when you're first introduced to them* to show interest in them and approachability. Hold the eye contact for as long as you can naturally for greatest effect.
- When meeting with more than one person, *engage everyone with eye contact* when you are speaking. If you find this difficult, try *planting* one idea per

person. Discuss a paragraph or section of your material per person. If you can 'hit' everyone's eyes during your talk *move* – when standing this is easy; from sitting lean forward, move your chair, *whatever it takes*! (More tips on working large audiences in Chapter 8.)

- As direct eye contact can be intimidating, *lessen the impact of yours by your peripheral vision* as well as looking at your listener's whole face. Try it in your next conversation and note how much you can see other than their eyes. The result is more gentle eye contact – easier for you and easier on them.

- *If you sense a culture finds direct eye contact bad manners*, take a note from the Koreans and converse with people looking at their cheeks – close enough to communicate personally and to sense what's going on without intimidating others.

- *Use eye contact to welcome others into a discussion.* In meetings it is easy for people to struggle to get into the action. As a speaker, you can *invite* participation by using eye contact.

- *Consciously employ eye contact as a listener*, not constantly, but for sustained glances. Accompanied by the occasional head nod, leaning forward and open gestures (not crossed arms) you will convey interest, attention and respect.

- *Make sure your glasses don't compete* and that your eyes are easily seen without the frames cutting across them. Also, non-reflective clear (non-tinted) lenses are best for good eye contact.

- *Make it easy for others to look at you.* If you are nervous and can't look people in the eye they will give up trying to look at you, leading to ineffective communication for both parties.

- *If under attack, don't look down.* This implies submission and underconfidence.
- *Looking away when speaking* at best conveys disinterest in your message, at worst conveys dishonesty. *Looking away when listening* is interpreted as arrogance or shyness – neither being winning traits.

READING EYES

The eyes are very expressive and in many instances you can read a lot by how they are used.

- Wide eyes – attentive, questioning, interested, attracted.
- Narrow eyes – suspicious, angry.
- Dilated pupils – warm, engaged, interested.
- Small pupils – stressed, unconvinced, inattentive.
- Raised brows – inquisitive, startled, amazed.
- Furrowed brows – uncertain, angry, concentration.
- Dull eyes with a glowing smile – untrustworthy, uninterested.
- Bright eyes with a smile – genuine interest, friendliness, warmth, attraction.

A FINAL TIP ON MAKING EYES

The next time you meet with someone you are trying to influence, try using eye contact more definitely. See how comfortable the person is and how they respond to matching your interest with theirs. If they look away, you've got work to do in influencing them. If they respond, take it as a pat on the back.

Facial expressions

We are blessed or challenged with our physiognomy. Like it or not, there is too much research to prove that those who are naturally beautiful have an easier time at winning folks over initially. The rest of us just have to make the most of what we've got (see 'Looking the Part' for beautifying tips) or resort to the surgeon's knife.

Short of taking such drastic measures, we can learn to appreciate that our expressions reveal little or everything to others. We scan each others' faces like radar – in a fraction of a second (150 m/sec). We can rate a person's beauty and stick with that opinion even after further study (*Survival of the Prettiest*, Nancy Etcoff). As those milliseconds tick away we are forming even more profound judgements about personality, ability, background, age, etc. based on our expressions. We can use facial expressions to our advantage (when feeling in control), or reveal more than we want to others which can make us vulnerable.

HOW EXPRESSIVE ARE YOU?

To find out how much you reveal to others do the following quiz:

True	False	
❏	❏	I have a positive, friendly manner that comes naturally.
❏	❏	I enjoy meeting new people.
❏	❏	I love acting out a situation, a game of charades or demonstrating things to others.
❏	❏	After a few beers, I can impersonate people to the amusement of others.
❏	❏	I speak Spanish, Italian, Greek or French like a native.
❏	❏	I find people unlike myself difficult to read.
❏	❏	I don't hold my cards too close to my chest and let people know what I am thinking or feeling.
❏	❏	I love being with children and they respond well to me.

| ❏ | ❏ | I would rather watch the movie than read the book. |
| ❏ | ❏ | In my presentations, I use a lot of visuals to get my message across. |

If you answered true to more than 7 questions you are a very expressive person and no doubt show it on your face. You often risk giving yourself away in situations. Three to 6 true answers reveal that you are a good communicator but probably more expressive with people you know than new acquaintances or in business. Less than 2 true answers means that you are very difficult to read and likely to be putting people off unwittingly on both personal and professional levels.

I CAN READ HIM LIKE A BOOK

Many people feel they are very good at reading others simply by watching their facial expressions. But as someone who has travelled the world and been surprised at how my initial reading of someone was quite inaccurate, I urge you to take on board the information that many expressions reveal but be wary of jumping to conclusions too quickly.

There are six key facial expressions, as determined by Paul Eckman and Wallace Friesen, which we show when we are sad, happy, disgusted, angry, afraid and interested. Every culture has variations of expression and other emotions. Men and women have subtle differences as well but these six are what we recognize and are valid most of the time. These emotions, as well as many others, engage not just all the facial muscles and our features (e.g. the eyes, nose, mouth, chin, etc.) but also the position of the head. All these things together create the expression and they kick in instantaneously with the emotions we feel.

We recognize many expressions in context:
- A smile welcomes us and we respond with a smile.
- Glaring, piercing eyes challenge and we back off.
- A curled, sniffing nose conveys distaste – *a bad smell.*

- An eyebrow flash conveys surprise and/or pleasure at meeting someone.
- A jutting jaw expresses determination, or conviction under stress.

The eyes and our faces express a range of emotions beyond the obvious which we *feel* often before we speak – stress, anxiety, depression, attraction, etc.

SMILE – YOUR HEART AIN'T BREAKIN'

Smiles are one of the most universal expressions of pleasure, delight and self-esteem. We can use a smile to influence others even when we are not feeling any of these emotions but need to express them to others. The air stewardess employs them constantly to reassure the nervous and placate the disgruntled. The losing sportsman uses it to be sportsmanlike even though he feels gutted. Politicians use them to present bad news as really good news!

But we know when a smile isn't genuine. A real smile employs more than the mouth – the eyes and brows, your voice, your whole body is engaged when you truly smile. In business, the higher you rise the more economical you become in smiling – some exceptions might be when you land a big deal, watch a competitor take a knock (then it's a leer), leave your company for a better job or to set up your own new venture.

GEORGE LEARNS TO SMILE

George is senior manager in the health service; talented and hard-working but found wanting in managing his team. I was asked to look at his department because the health trust had a lot of confidence in him and just couldn't understand the high attrition rates among his staff compared to other areas. 'George isn't a very friendly man but is more committed to improving things around here than anyone else,' explained the chief executive. 'Just get him to smile a bit more.'

'This is serious business here. I don't want to look like a goon,' explained George in no uncertain terms. 'My people just burn out, that's all.' The exit interviews from the recently departed staff revealed that George's manner in dealing with them was the reason they left, not the demands of the job. 'He's so brusque and impersonal. Even on his birthday when we delivered him a cake he couldn't manage to look pleased.' 'Life is too short to work for someone so dour.' 'He's talented and right on most things. But he doesn't motivate anyone.'

Before discussing techniques for winning and influencing others, I had to get to the root of George's problem. Did he want others to like him more? What motivated him and how could I convince him that unless he worked on his people skills he wouldn't achieve his goals? I state this in case any readers think that all I do is teach folks some clever tricks of deception to *fool* others. Believe me, it isn't that simple nor is it rocket science. You have to want or need to change for any new behaviours to be sustained. If you don't believe that new approaches can work, are right and better then the coaching fails.

Among several aspects of George's behaviour and personal style that were off-putting was the simple fact that he looked unpleasant. He was decent enough looking but he scowled most of the time which brought out the worst in everyone he met and made him thoroughly unattractive. 'I don't know what they complain about,' he said, 'I am in a perfectly good mood most of the time. I can't help it if I'm not naturally cheerful.'

It took work, many heated discussions and some painful video-feedback sessions, but once George agreed to try smiling *when he was pleased or feeling just fine* he was shocked at how people responded differently. 'This is a joke. All I have to do is smile every time I start a meeting, do so occasionally when I listen to people and try to flash one when I'm not angry about anything.' But it worked and he practised smiling so religiously that it became quite natural after a matter of months. His boss reported, 'The atmosphere around here has changed. George has had a personality transplant!'

Of course not. George is the same complex, committed guy and there were many other things that contributed to his change in behaviour, most of all his becoming aware of his impact on others. But, hand on heart, the best piece of advice he took on board was simply to smile.

If you don't believe me, sourpuss, try smiling more and see how people are more amenable towards you.

Use your head

Your head does a lot of 'talking' – not only through the mouth. How we use our head communicates our thoughts and feelings to others. Learn to read heads when people listen and you will, ahem, be ahead of the game. But like all elements of body language, you can't interpret a nod or a tilt in isolation from other gestures and body movements.

HEAD NODS

Expressing agreement or disagreement via the head is understood around the world. Where other gestures can confuse or get you into trouble, the head nod is what we often revert to when language breaks down. We use the positive head nod with others to encourage them and show agreement. An exaggerated head nod goes further, screaming, 'Yes', 'Right on', or 'Hear, hear.'

To build rapport in others, use the head nod more consciously. Try nodding more in your next conversation and see your partner wax more lyrically or speak for longer. Withdraw the head nod and you signal, non-verbally, you've had enough or you possibly don't agree. They will have to stop to find out what you think/feel in reaction.

Combine the head nod with gentle eye contact, leaning towards the speaker, and they will feel like they have captured you. You can use this technique very effectively to win people over or to shut them off without causing any offence.

The speedy head nod urges others to carry on, to hurry up or to 'get on with it'. Just watch TV interviewers. They always start off an interview with excessive bouts of nods to 'open up' the interviewee. Their signal to wrap up is when they stop nodding, raise their hand, etc. These are recognized by most people except, of course, politicians.

The head is a great indicator when used in combination with the eyes – as a pointer when your finger would be too obvious or rude (e.g. 'no, the one over *there*'). It is effectively used in meetings, like when a chairman wants to signal to someone that their turn to speak is coming.

HEAD TILTS

As with nodding, tilts can be used effectively in communicating messages or unwittingly send screamers that undermine our influence. They work when listening but hurt when speaking.

Effective tilting

Side tilts of the head when listening can mean that we are attentive and processing information. If you want to show really keen interest (to influence), accompany the tilt by leaning forward with your hand supporting your chin. Now, you're really listening! But, carry on for too long and you'll get a crick in your neck. So, do this for only a matter of minutes for effect or just do it when you mean it.

Ineffective tilting

Many women (and most kids when caught being naughty) will combine the head tilt with a head drop, with the eyes looking up to whom is speaking – à la the late Princess Diana. Few behavioural traits undermine women by conveying submission to others more effectively than this move. If you don't know if you do it, ask someone who might and work on holding your head straight and erect when speaking your mind. This is equally important at work and at home!

Gestures

Here we hit a minefield so potentially explosive in misreading and sending signals that a caveat is required at the start. Be aware that your and others' gestures are both fraught with meaning as well as being totally meaningless. I know that body language gurus will take issue with me but after many years of hearing absolute nonsense about what you should and shouldn't do and what different gestures are supposed to mean I have doubts about reading much into gestures *when they are read in isolation*.

Gestures express many things – emotions, personality, background, culture, language – as well as illustrate what we are saying. So, only take them in context with *what is being said, to and by whom, for what purpose*. Just think of how you might describe the following situations / issues differently with your gestures:

- Seeing a purse being snatched outside in the street.
- Meeting the new partner of your boss.
- Speaking in support of the homeless.
- Explaining an embarrassing argument between two colleagues.
- Witnessing the birth of your child.
- Discussing the pros and cons of a new computer system.
- Making one of your staff redundant.

All quite different, with some lending themselves to elaborate gesturing with others demanding minimal gesturing for best effect.

'GESTURING ISN'T PROFESSIONAL'

Too often I have met people fresh from training in presentation skills who have been told not to gesture when speaking. One Italian management consultant was in despair when told that his gestures were over the top. He spent a couple of months trying to keep himself 'under control' only to find that he couldn't think or speak!

As you will read in Chapter 8, effective communication has nothing to do with control, it's about freeing yourself to be yourself, within limits. Gianni spoke with his whole being like many Mediterraneans do. To be told not to express himself was to deny him the ability to communicate naturally. I advised Gianni to be less dramatic in his gestures and to scale them down to the size of his audience. His expressions and gestures were terrific until he got excited, then, even in a small meeting in a small room, he would look like he was directing the evacuation of Piccadilly Circus.

However, some gestures (in the West) weaken our impact by being inappropriate or irritating or both. Here are a few:

Hands down

- *Wringing hands* is done unconsciously by people who are either angry (thinking, 'I'll get him!') or under stress. By doing so you are showing that others are, indeed, getting the better of you. Relaxation techniques can help you chill out when you find yourself heating up. Try sitting down and deep breathing whenever you get the urge to wring your hands together. Of course, a mischievous display of hand-wringing between colleagues when you come up with a clever ploy conveys just what you want!
- *Picking at cuticles, nail biting, ring twiddling, pen tapping* scream STRESS or, in the case of pen tapping, irritation. As our hands are key to communication, if

yours are in a state, and subjected to abuse when you are under stress, others will feel for you in a way that does not enhance your impact. Get a grip by kicking the habit and, again, deploy deep breathing instead of picking your nails to the quick.

- *Pointing* is tiresome and irritating even if you are right about everything. No one likes to be told or a 'told-you-so'.
- *Mouth covering* is not natural and it is awkward to speak with our hands covering our mouths. People do this when they feel stressed about what is coming out of their mouths (e.g. when being untruthful or worried about saying too much). When you cover your mouth as a listener, you convey that you want to interrupt but are resisting the urge. Hence, as a speaker or listener, resist the urge to cover your mouth (even though you will do it unconsciously).

Closed gestures

We know that crossing our arms and legs (when we aren't chilly) conveys a range of negative things to others, ranging from panic (feeling threatened) to distrust ('don't come a step closer'). As a listener, you block out other people who are trying to communicate with you. When it's important, open up within acceptable limits for business. If you want to shut people out, cross everything excluding your eyes!

As a speaker, closed gestures are also negative, expressing a range of things from fear of the situation to arrogance. How often have you felt 'lectured at' by a speaker with crossed arms who conveys 'I don't care what you think, this is the way it is going to be.'

Dancin'

You know what I mean. The twitchers that can't stand still, they are constantly dancin', looking shifty and untrustworthy. Underlings and ex-cons twitch when they speak. Plant yourself on two feet when you speak. Move, by all means, but not like a gnat.

'Come hither' when you don't want them to

Work is filled with people consciously and unconsciously flirting with each other. But I am amused when a woman calls a man a wolf or a man describes a woman as a she-devil because someone *misread* them. Suffice to say, sending 'come hither'/courtship gestures in business is fraught with danger. So you are wise to wager the costs and benefits before you start flirting.

Body-preening, hair-stroking, thigh-rubbing, skirt-tugging, criss-crossing the legs are ways that women convey interest in a man. He, on the other hand, might express interest by *shifting around from the hips down as if revving up his engine*, thumb in belt loops, legs akimbo. If you aren't getting 'return signals', or are at risk of blowing a deal or your job, cool it until after hours.

Posture

When I get to this bit during a presentation everyone sits ramrod in his or her seats. Ask yourself this: do you find Army officers the most engaging company? (Apologies to my former Army officer husband.)

Good posture is about being erect and walking tall but it is also about being and looking natural. The correct posture allows you to move, to gesture, to breathe and speak with comfort. But, wait a minute, not that comfortably! You also want to look impressive, right?

In this era of casual dressing, open-plan offices, collegial management, young men and women running things, many people are taking liberties with their posture – to look cool, and 'with it' you can just be yourself; *they just hang out!* A slovenly, languid, drippy posture impresses no one. Be relaxed, be cool in other ways.

If you know that your posture ain't what it could be, it's time to improve. Just like so many things in this book, posture can be put right. If you don't take measures to get sorted now you are only asking to look older than you are soon (already!), or to develop chronic back and joint problems that will make your life a misery. Here are some simple things that you can do, beginning today, to improve your posture.

Top tips for powerful posture:

- *Carry as little as you can to the office.* Use a backpack (forget its sartorial limitations), it will save your back. Shop around. Leather ones (Mulberry, Tumi, Longchamp, Coach) can be good investments – they will last for years and look smart (well, as smart as a backpack can!).
- *See where you are off-kilter and rectify it.* Many people have drop-right shoulders from carrying briefcases, others have hunched shoulders from hunching over their PCs all day. *Compensate* daily for what you do

against your posture in the gym or at home rolling about on the floor. Yoga-type exercises are the best.

- To 'walk tall' concentrate on the spine between your shoulder blades being straight. Being erect is not about thrusting your chest out.
- Watch your butt. Practise your pelvic tilts, i.e. tilt under and up. Ask a woman to show you how. Imagine an ice-cream scooper action on your tummy muscles, scooping your muscles taut from the lowest part of the pelvis, including your whole tummy. As you 'scoop' your pelvis tilts forward and your butt, under. Add a good butt-squeeze for best effect.
- Your hippy days are over. If you shift your body from hip to hip, you undermine your impact. You might do this quite unconsciously when you speak (ask colleagues for confirmation). When you project a hip your head naturally tilts to the side. Imagine this posture: hip out, head tilted. A tilted head looks like it is questioning or apologizing, both quite undermining when you speak.
- Get back. Leaning forward towards someone is flattering for an instant, then it becomes aggressive. If you want to win people over, step towards them when speaking to them cognisant of how long you can remain in 'their space' (see page 130) without making them feeling uncomfortable. You will know that they are uncomfortable if they step backwards or away from you. Leaning backwards suggests you feel up against a wall ('No, no, don't shoot.') Step back to give others, and yourself, space when you feel threatened. To look on top of things, keep straight.

- *Imagine a string from the top of your head stretching to the North Star* pulling your head out of your shoulders. Our carriage and posture is led from the head – if this is askew so too will your body be.

Remember: an erect posture projects youthfulness, confidence and appeal. Who doesn't want any of that?

Space

We all know how much proximity makes us feel comfortable. But in our crowded, stressed lives more of us seem less tolerant when others invade 'our space'. The American sociologist Edward Hall defined four zones of space that are appropriate when interacting in the West or in most global business settings:

- *The Intimate Zone* from 0 to .5m is the area that allows us to touch those closest to us.
- *The Personal Zone* from .5 to 1.2m is what we enter when meeting people, enabling us to greet each other and shake hands. Holding within the personal zone for too long can be interpreted as a sexual overture.
- *The Social Zone* runs from 1.2 to 3m and is used mostly in business and general social encounters (e.g. when shopping). In business, we are keeping each other at arm's length.
- *The Public Zone* extends beyond 3m where we want to keep the 'unknown' at a distance.

In Chapter 3, I promised to share how I cleared rooms when I first moved to Britain by invading the natives' space. Being of Irish-American extraction, from a large family *and* an extrovert (a triple-whammy), my inclination is to be all over people like a rash when I first meet them. I just love to get close to people quite soon after introductions and get to know them, very 'up close and personal', right in that intimate zone. Well, the Brits aren't crazy about Americans to begin with, nor especially ones that are so damn friendly! To exacerbate things, I am also very touchy-feely by nature, a trait that has got me into all sorts of trouble over the years. Once I got the message and realized that I could shift whole groups of people by getting so close to them when they didn't like it, I pulled back.

Invading others in an unwelcome zone can cause anxiety or even outright hostility. Best to sense what others want from us and give that to them rather than insist on doing what we want and risking an outburst.

GIVE THEM WHAT THEY NEED

Working internationally for the past 20 years has taught me loads about the importance of space and recognizing that to build rapport and to influence others we need to give them what they need, not what we need. In my seminars, I demonstrate this via handshakes. You can read much about a person simply by how they shake your hand and what they do immediately after shaking hands. If a person lingers, typically the Italians, Irish, French, Thai, Malay, Bajan, Arab, they have a small 'bubble' around them and want you to remain close to get to know you. If they jump back after breaking off from shaking your hand, as the Dutch, Scandinavians, Swiss, Japanese and Russians tend to, they can only begin to get to know you from a distance, between the social and public zone. To a 'small bubble' person it can feel very off-putting being thrust away initially, but it is the only way to show respect and to have a chance of getting to know the other person – in *their* comfort zone.

▨ Body language at work

Effective use of body language at work depends on the nature of the work, the situation and your objectives when interacting with others. Use of space, eye contact, gestures and facial expressions will be very different for a software designer, a nurse, a judge and a policeman. Hence it is more useful to look at techniques to employ in situations when you know what you want to achieve in communicating with and influencing others.

Interviewing

Interviews cover a huge spectrum of possibilities. A journalist or TV presenter is trying to encourage their guests to speak, a personnel manager need to probe candidates to discern suitability for a job, a therapist needs their patient to 'open up' with words or actions. But certain techniques will be effective for all interviewers to employ.

To encourage others:

- *Facial expression* conveys interest even if you aren't interested, to put people at ease and encourage them to speak. The eyes need to be 'alive', not glazed, so you will need to consciously enliven them from time to time.
- *Head-nodding* confirms what they are saying even if you don't agree with them.
- *A raised eyebrow* will indicate you might question what they are saying or need more information. Most people pick up on a quizzical brow and can ask you about your concern without you having to interrupt them.
- *Lean forward* when you need to express interest; *lean to the side* to put others at ease (to take the edge off a possible confrontation).
- To help people feel more comfortable and to be able to read their non-verbal behaviour more effectively, *sit away from a table* rather than on opposite sides.
- *Smile.*

To unsettle others:

- Deny eye contact or use a penetrating gaze.
- Keep expressions to a minimum.
- Fidget (i.e. be more occupied with other things than

the speaker, e.g. shuffling papers, looking at your watch, etc.).

- Sit 'side saddle'.
- Interrupt the person when they are in full flow.

Meetings

Effective body language is very important in meetings from start to finish.

ARRIVAL AND GREETINGS

External meetings (e.g. with clients, not on your own turf): be aware of the impression you are making from the reception area through to the meeting room. Walk tall, be energetic, proffer your handshake to all you meet, it will convey you are interested to be there and keen about the meeting ahead. Be prepared for small talk (e.g. the weather, last night's big match, some news that just 'broke', etc.) waiting for others to lead you into the meeting agenda. To the ready: get your papers out, pen ready, mobile switched off. Take direction to where you are to sit rather than race ahead and grab a 'power seat' . If others are more casual in approaching the table, let a few sit ahead of you to see what might be the most opportunistic seat you can take in relation to the key people you need to influence. As a guest, let them take the lead in stating the purpose of the meeting, this is just good manners. If they don't take the initiative to open discussions, ease into it gently, e.g. 'Thank you for making the time to meet with me today to discuss . . .' 'I think it is important that we have this meeting today because . . .' Avoid: 'Today I want to talk to you about . . .' which many salesmen use. No one wants to be 'sold to' but as we know in most meetings we are all selling something. So make it a 'soft sell' with a discussion rather than an obvious pitch. Confirm how much time is available, another courtesy that is much appreciated by busy people. Besides, this always lets you know how you are doing. If you get more than the allotted time, you are winning.

PRINCIPALS ONLY?

An area of some uncertainty in business is about what size 'cast' you bring to meetings. Should you always bring your assistant or team or a heavyweight partner to impress others? Think first: what does the client or the person who you are meeting with need? By *need*, I don't mean what will impress people, rather what will add value to the session. Nothing is more stupid and a greater waste of everyone's time than a parade of characters that add nothing to the proceedings. The larger the number, the more formal the meeting. Even bringing one assistant can hinder communication because you can't probe or challenge as directly as you would like or need to because 'face' can be lost when there is an audience.

Bring the boss?

There is both risk and benefit in bringing a more senior heavyweight to a meeting. But if this colleague has a tendency to dominate you will have greater difficulty in wrestling the relationship with the client who will henceforth want confirmation or input from the more senior partner. Only involve added heavyweight when they can help selling-in a proposal, sorting out conflict when an impasse has been reached, or for more social occasions to convey how important a client/customer is to your business.

Bring the underling?

Junior staff, of course, only learn how to deal better in meetings by being exposed to them. It is important to clarify their role upfront so that they don't overstep boundaries and say something either inappropriate or wrong. If you want them there purely as a note-taker, state this as the case which is perfectly legitimate in many situations. If they are there because they are really involved with the project, find a way for them to be involved in the meeting, to make some contribution to build both their confidence as well as the client's confidence in dealing with them.

The most dangerous scenario is not to brief your assistant on the meeting's objectives and what you want from them at the session. Always discuss how things went, noting what you liked about their contribution as well has how they could have performed better. Otherwise, you have only yourself to blame if they keep getting things wrong.

BE A PLAYER

If you attend a meeting and don't contribute you are wasting your time and everyone else's. Contribute as soon as you can in the meeting to show that you will be a player today. Women tend to hold back longer than men and often find it difficult, once the scene has been set, to get involved. (This is because women in business, generally, wait until they have something useful to contribute or are invited to make a point.) If this makes you nervous, particularly with more senior people (and women, when outnumbered by men), be active in the preliminary chat ('Are the marketing team coming today?' 'Did you see the news of X?').

Use eye contact to get recognition to speak. Hone in on the speaker or the chair to convey you have something to say; signal with your index finger, a polite but assertive gesture that says you want to speak. Lean forward rather than sit back and you will be more likely to be recognized.

DEALING WITH INTERRUPTIONS

It is rude and aggressive to interrupt people intentionally but it is commonplace in meetings, particularly when business gets heated. When confronted with a challenger who is patently trying to under-mine us by interrupting, we can often show our discomfiture very quickly. In doing so, we can become aggressive or submissive which only works to undermine us and let the other guy 'win'.

Hackneyed though it might be, remind yourself that a 'win-win' outcome is always the better, and easier, mentality to assume in negotiations and when challenged in business. Rather than sticking to your guns and fighting your corner take a deep breath and ask yourself, 'How have I provoked this?' Of course, we are not always responsible ourselves, people do challenge us with their own hidden agendas (or simply because they don't like us). But you might easily diffuse a challenge if you clarify a misunderstanding. By probing and finding out more *why* they are interrupting and challenging you can usually resolve things quicker. However, not every meeting is appropriate nor has the time for probing. Hence, you need to use effective non-verbal behaviour to maintain your confidence and the validity of your own views.

Generally, you will look more confident if you accept an interruption and take issue with the concern as it is raised. If you sense that the person isn't really interested in getting something clarified but is on a campaign to unsettle you, look at them directly, lean forward, let your eyes pull them towards you (see page 81), smile (or look engaged if you can't smile) and depersonalize the attack by saying something like, 'We all know what you think about this plan, Bob. And when I'm finished we'll want to hear how your information might be reinforcing this view.' This will convey that he will get an opportunity to rebut your position. If he is churlish enough to continue he becomes the obvious aggressor (who impresses few).

If and when you feel yourself 'losing it' when under attack, concentrate less on the substance of the attack and more on how you appear. Do some discreet deep breathing, look at the challenger fleetingly, then engage supportive eyes, keep still, lean forward, shake your head in disagreement as if you can take issue without resorting to their tactics. When you do reply, speak firmly, more slowly, reiterating your key points without being led off course by the interruption. If they persist, look to the most senior person/the chair to get affirmation to carry on, and thank the challenger for their comments (whether or not this comes across sarcastically is your prerogative!).

WHEN YOU ARE BORING THEM RIGID

We have all had the uninterested audience – the guy whom you wanted to see but didn't reciprocate the sentiment. Maybe he spared the time to humour you or was told to by someone. You are getting nowhere. The signs are there – glazed eyes, expressionless face – and he refuses to accept your bait of open questions and shuts you off cold. Neither of you are enjoying yourself and it's up to you to end the misery.

When you have tried your best to engage someone but failed to do so, you will feel heaps better if you find an angle to end the meeting positively. He also wants an escape route and is more than willing to pass the buck – YOU – on to someone else. You don't want to leave empty-handed so see if you can get a referral to a colleague who might benefit more from your suggestion. When you take the pressure off an unwilling party, they become more animated and even more helpful once they sense that they are off the hook.

But if you are up a blind alley with a very unwilling party, have enough respect for yourself to recognize this as a lost cause, cut your losses and depart as gracefully as possible. Getting over a rejection that lasted only 10 minutes is a lot easier than one that took an hour. Staying way beyond your welcome exacerbates the negativity and will only ensure that you leave a dreadful lasting impression. We are all thankful when others have the intelligence and poise to respect a no-win situation and cut everyone's losses. You will be remembered well for it even though your mission, this time, wasn't accomplished.

DEPARTURES

Gather up your papers when the business is finished, not as the final speaker is wrapping up. Conversely, if someone is taking up too much of your time, 'shutting down' – looking at your watch, papers in folder, top back on pen into pocket, etc. – will get them to see that you've had enough.

When meetings are over, resort to being personable. Even if the meeting was difficult you will look more professional if you leave the business on the table and re-establish rapport as best you can. Always shake hands, except with work colleagues, when leaving and try not to be the first one out the door (unless you are nearest), which can look as if you are trying to escape.

It is near impossible to generalize about exiting. But here are a few tips:

- Do leave staff meetings with energy and pace as if you have a pressed schedule and another meeting – this conveys to others that your time is valuable.
- With clients, however, it is important to leave at *their* pace. A director may want a leisurely stroll to the elevator during which time she/he might share an important insight that didn't come out in the meeting. It is also good manners to leave their premises showing pleasure in having been there.
- Thank those who played a supporting role: the analyst that raced out for copies of your report, the manager who played 'mother' and poured the tea, the assistant who rearranged all the arrangements for the third time.

Minding your manners

Have you ever known business colleagues, held them in fairly high regard and then had lunch with them? Wham! Your opinion of them drops through the floor just because of how they comport themselves over a meal. Here are some examples of ways that we can ruin our image just over a lunch:

- Rushing to grab a seat without consideration of others.
- Diving into the bread basket upon sitting down.
- Ordering a carbonated soft drink (rather than juice or water if not alcohol) at any restaurant with tablecloths.
- Ordering first when not guided to do so by the host.
- Eating noisily (unless in the Far East to show appreciation!).
- Talking loudly, using excessive gestures.
- Talking whilst chewing.
- Using your fingers to eat when the food isn't finger food.
- Grabbing rather than asking for things (e.g. salt and pepper) to be passed.
- Not using a napkin when you should.
- Creating a bib with a napkin aside from when eating lobster.
- Scraping a bowl or plate to get every last bit.
- Using bread to mop up food or juices (unless in southern Europe or countries where this is customary).
- Taking up excessive space at the table.
- Putting your arm across a neighbour's chair, leaning into their space.

- Leaving the table mid-meal to use the lavatory.
- Accepting a telephone call on your mobile.
- Having more courses than anyone else.
- Asking to taste someone else's food.
- Asking for a doggie bag (Americans please note).
- Eating too quickly, drinking too much (alcohol).
- Making inappropriate conversation (rude jokes, gossip).
- Making no effort to be interesting.
- Discussing business in detail when inappropriate.

Being well-mannered, understanding etiquette, showing respect for age and cultural differences are part of your brand and, when used properly and consistently, enhance both your impact and reputation. Good manners are not about being prissy or elitist or making others feel inferior. The well-mannered person excels at making others feel even better about themselves. They ignore our ignorance when we might get things wrong and do everything to put us at our ease when we feel underconfident. Indeed, the best way to learn good manners is to emulate others who have them rather than swot over etiquette guides (although they can be helpful references for new situations).

Business today presents a minefield of possibilities to either impress or offend others and it is the wise professional who reflects before making a hasty decision. Should you call your client at home or on the weekend to clarify an important point or would you destroy your relationship by invading his private time? How widely should you copy business e-mails? Will a client be amenable or angry if you suggest a breakfast or dinner meeting? Will requesting a vegetarian option be acceptable or incomprehensible in certain cultures? How familiar should you be with senior colleagues and/or clients?

It pays to understand the rules for different occasions and for different cultures and there are many helpful guides available today (see Further Reading). But it is near impossible to appreciate all nuances for every culture or situation and we all must learn how to 'wing it' with grace when we don't know what on earth is going on or what is expected of us.

He who finds fault with people who use a fork instead of a spoon for dessert or who unwittingly place their glass on the wrong side of the plate (bless you, lefties) or who fold their napkins rather than leave them at their place is a tedious prat. You want to be well-mannered but just as important is being yourself so that you have the confidence to express yourself rather than be twitchy about which fork or knife might be appropriate at the minute. When in doubt, observe others and act accordingly.

Bad manners is about gauche behaviour and sheer lack of consideration for other people. It is gauche for a man to take his jacket off when dining without asking others if they mind. It is gauche for a woman to put her make-up on at the end of the meal in front of others. It is gauche to create a scene, to grab the first available taxi, to hold back when settling a restaurant bill (if you aren't clearly the guest). There are endless examples of ways that others – and, hopefully, not yourself – can at best bemuse or at worst offend others.

Sadly, bad manners are evident daily, from the irritating bores who use their mobile phones on trains, in restaurants, even on elevators to the louts who get drunk at social functions with clients. Then there are the ungracious hosts who don't introduce guests to each other as well as some arrogant young people who refer to newly-introduced older clients by their first names. Tasteless jokes, gossip and chronic lateness are all examples of bad manners in business.

MANNERS MAKETH THE BRAND

There is no escaping the fact that manners, courtesy and etiquette are part of your brand. Go back to your brand values. Let's say that both professional and reliable are two of your brand values. So far we've discussed what these look like, what they sound like and we've touched upon behaviour like handshakes and gestures. But you also reflect these values through your awareness of occasion, how you treat others and how you behave in the social arena.

A professional person doesn't drink excessively when on business even if the occasion is social. Nor is it professional to try to 'pull' an associate at the Christmas party. You are professional when you send handwritten thank you notes to clients and even more so when you not only remember their partners' names but also what they do. You convey reliability through time-keeping. Always being late or making others wait undermines a reliable brand value faster than anything. The reliable person organizes taxis unprompted for guests, ensures a thoughtful seating plan and doesn't cc everyone in the company when he sends an e-mail to the boss.

Let's face it. Bad manners are bad for business. If a company's staff are awkward or inconsiderate, or don't know how to handle themselves in different situations, it reflects poorly on the company, particularly on senior management, both for not recruiting better as well as not making good manners intrinsic to the corporate culture.

Being an image consultant means that I perform a role often akin to a therapist. I can't count the times that a despairing chief executive or human resources director has told me about a key member of staff who hadn't a clue as to how to handle themselves socially. 'Kevin is your proverbial rough diamond. He's talented and bright but I can't bear to see him with clients. I watch their faces and see them wince just by the way he eats. Then he'll have a couple of beers and gets so loud. Sure, he's a funny guy but he never knows where and when to roll out his routines,' confided a sales director recently about a new manager who was doing stellar business whilst shooting himself in the foot. 'I don't quite know how to raise the subject. He's getting the sales, actually surpassing his targets, but I won't promote him to regional manager until he gets his act together.'

There are many business people who haven't been lucky enough to get etiquette coaching at home. Perhaps their parents had less exposure than they do to the variety of social interactions now so integral to business. There's the business breakfast, lunch or business dinner. There are receptions where you play host or are a guest with attendant etiquette. Sporting events, cultural events, corporate cruises and conferences all have 'form'. If you don't get the form you look underconfident, like an outsider rather than a player and are less likely to enjoy yourself.

Teaching manners and etiquette at school, sadly, has been dropped, considered politically incorrect, in favour of 'diversity'. The theory goes that any form of rules or guidelines are probably offensive to someone else from a different background so don't impose any. Good manners are not about being or acting superior to others. They are about showing respect for others and recognizing when the rules are different and acting accordingly.

So, if your mother didn't teach you what you need to know it is high time you sorted it out for yourself. Of course you can learn by observing others but to look confident you must learn the rules of the game for different situations and different cultures.

Good manners should not be exclusive to the senior team or the client-facing staff; they should permeate the culture from the mailroom to the boardroom. If your team are rough around the edges why not organize a few 'trial events' with someone coaching people through the etiquette minefield, encouraging staff to ask questions and learn from past mistakes.

THE RULES ARE CHANGING

Even if mummy was a gem and taught you decent table manners the rules are constantly evolving in our modern business world. Business social etiquette is different from normal social etiquette in small as well as big ways. For example, socially, women should hold back in offering their handshake first to men, but should not hold back in business. Men are expected to pull chairs out and rise when women leave and enter socially but not for business events.

When travelling abroad, the smart business person checks ahead about an acceptable gift for a client. In one country, like Italy, it should be a gift for the clients' child/children. While in another, like China, a car for the CEO might clinch the deal (we're talking big deals here, don't sweat it). Just knowing when and how to meet socially is vital. You won't be thanked for impinging on the much revered private time of colleagues in Germany, Switzerland and Scandinavia and would be smarter to meet for lunch rather than dinner.

There are guidelines on what and how to eat in every country but sometimes your own integrity, and stomach, can be severely tested in trying to accommodate culture. Western business people doing joint ventures or selling in Eastern Europe have discovered that heavy drinking sessions, sometimes lasting for 2 or 3 days, are a necessary way to clinch a deal. In Saudi Arabia, you will offend if you don't eat sheeps' eyeballs when offered and you'd better use your right hand when you do! Your normal bedtime (if early) must be sacrificed when working in Italy as they will be insulted if you don't last until at least 1 a.m. Don't even ask people if they mind if you smoke in America because the mere fact that you are a smoker may be reason enough for Americans to not want to do business with you.

Globalization means that we are becoming more and more familiar with our cultural differences and, as a result, are more willing to understand someone's hesitation, even refusal, to participate in certain activities. When challenged by any situation that makes you uncomfortable – or at worst, potentially sick – you must find a way to explain yourself whilst showing respect and gratitude to your host. I suggested to a management consultant working in Khaskastan who was desperate to get out of a forthcoming 'booze cruise' with clients that he send a case of vodka ahead of time with his apologies. He wished them a great celebration but said that he could not join them because of a medical condition. Other colleagues willingly prevailed in his place with one needing a week to recuperate afterwards. The hosts understood his 'regrets' and were grateful for his gift.

As a vegetarian I am often in a situation of being served meat that I simply can't/won't eat. Rather than cause upset on the night, I try to alert my hosts ahead of time suggesting a bowl of soup or vegetables whenever they have a meat course. Not long ago I was speaking in northern Finland (yes, the North Pole) as a guest of the government. An elaborate banquet of ten courses was arranged in my honour. About halfway through came the main course of reindeer that was so fresh and rare that it was still twitching (I swear!). It is bad manners in any culture to allow good food to go bad so I had to go through an elaborate and effusive refusal (asking for some soup instead). I proceeded to ask them everything about reindeer and its importance to the economy and culture to show my appreciation of their cherished beast. I was so convincing in my interest to learn about reindeers that we had spontaneous poetry and songs about reindeers from the other guests that extended the meal for an extra hour. After dessert I was given a guided tour of the sheds where the reindeer had been butchered and were hanging! I was delighted as long as I didn't have to eat any and my Finnish hosts were thrilled by my new-found understanding of their national delicacy.

▨ Office etiquette

It is difficult to generalize about manners at work as we all work in very different environments. A very informal company might not mind if staff barge into someone else's meeting or if you perch yourself on the corner of someone's desk or eat your lunch as you walk around the office. But there are some dos and don'ts that are general enough to stand you in good stead when in doubt.

Do:
- Say thank you for small things like someone holding the door for you.
- Introduce yourself when you don't know everyone.
- Use Mr or Ms when introduced if someone is introduced to you that formally (even though you know their first name).
- Use someone's title – Dr, Sir, Baroness – until they correct you to use a name more familiar.
- Present others by way of introduction according to status, lower to higher; client to provider. For example, 'Baroness Thatcher, let me introduce to you our finance director.' 'Martin [the client] let me introduce our chief executive, David Jones.'
- Allow others to go first (getting into an elevator, taking seats, approaching a buffet).
- Offer any visitor to the office a drink (water or tea/coffee). Also, sort out their coats, direct them to the ladies/gents, etc.
- Ask permission when in doubt. 'Do you mind if we reschedule?' Rather than: 'Can't do Tuesday now, it has to be Wednesday.'
- Excuse yourself from a meeting if you have a bad cold rather than spew your germs all over everyone

else. No one will thank you for being a hero.

- Turn your mobile phone off before you go into a meeting. Ask permission to take an important call outside a meeting room.
- Speak softly on your mobile (we all up the volume). Using a headphone enables you to speak more directly into a microphone. Tilt your head down to avoid further projecting your voice to others who don't need to hear.
- Express concern or regrets when a colleague is having a personal crisis or has experienced a loss. Listen rather than be too inquisitive for details. If they don't respond, leave it.
- Share and give credit where it is due.
- Ensure that you smell fresh daily and brush your teeth after lunch.
- If organizing a working lunch of sandwiches, provide plates, napkins and glasses.
- Eat small, manageable portions of food resting your knife and fork in the '20 to 4' position every so often during the meal.
- Ask if people want to drink alcohol with a meal rather than assume it.
- If you are having lunch with one or two people and don't want to drink, encourage them to feel free to have some wine if they would like.
- Accept a glass of wine at a meal, even if you don't want any, to put others at ease and not make an issue of your not drinking whilst they are. You don't actually have to drink it. The only exception would be if the wine was very expensive and you would be wasting a portion others would appreciate.

Don't:

- Invade someone's office without being invited. Hang in the doorway and ask, 'Do you have 2 minutes to take a look at this e-mail?'
- Inspect others' personal things in their office without their permission, especially if they are not in the office.
- Go into someone's files without them knowing.
- Take excessive space at a meeting table. If you have a lot of gear/exhibits store what isn't needed behind you on a shelf. Don't clutter up underneath your chair or on the floor around you as you will look oafish and sloppy.
- Turn your glass upside down to signal you don't want any wine. Either accept a glass and don't drink it or indicate to the waiter, discreetly, with a raised hand by your glass that you will pass.
- Drink as much as you'd like at a business/social occasion. It is still business.
- Cut a bread roll, always break it with your fingers.
- Lower your head excessively towards your plate when eating in the West. Aim to bring the food up to your mouth.
- Put stray bits of unwanted food on the table; always use the edge of your plate.
- Eat directly from a serving bowl. Put a portion on to your plate first, then eat.
- Assume a 'significant other' in the lives of colleagues and clients. Find out status first before any exploration.
- Ask very personal questions in business. If you know that the other person is married, 'Do you have any children?' is a safer bet than 'So, are you on wife number 2 or 3?'

- Share details of bodily functions that might be out of sorts.
- Send verbose or unnecessary emails.

Ain't misbehavin'

When it comes to acting the part, remember that your behaviour is on show, sending signals all the time, in the wide variety of arenas in which you perform. Be conscious of how you come across to others even when you think it might not matter, like when arriving for a meeting, being introduced at a cocktail party or over a working lunch. Actions speak louder than words so remember that your behaviour can say everything you want even before you open your mouth.

5

LOOKING THE PART: WOMEN

Is your image up for a tweak?

Having written five books on women's image (*The Complete Style Guide*; *Presenting Yourself: A Personal Image Guide for Women*; *Bigger Ideas*; *The Makeover Manual*; and *Look and Feel the Age You Want to Be*) my passion for the subject never wanes, it only grows. I find few things more rewarding than helping to boost a woman's confidence, her self-belief, and to see her life change for the better just from some judicious retooling of her personal image.

Some might think that doing makeovers is a pretty silly business. But there is nothing silly about women not getting what they deserve out of a career, a relationship or life just because their image isn't as good as it could be. Change the image, improve it to suit *her*, and she writes a new script for the way ahead. I have seen it happen with thousands of women over the years and it can happen for you if you feel that you aren't understood or, more importantly, *valued* just because of how you look.

You can change your look in baby steps or take a quantum leap. If you are at a real crossroads in your career (or personal life) and feel a total revamp is the order of the day, then roll up your sleeves and get cracking. You might be worried about the reaction of others to your new image – don't be. The transformation is in your own hands, or it should be. Perhaps you feel that your look is pretty well together and want only to 'tweak' it to feel differently or to have some fun. The choice is yours.

The brand revisited

To help you visualize yourself in terms of your brand values, make a note of them again here. As we work through the concepts and suggestions keep reminding yourself of these values, questioning, 'If I gave that a try would others believe I am . . . ?'

My image needs to reflect:

- ....
- ....
- ....
- ....
- ....
- ....
- ....
- ....
- ....

ENVISION THE VALUES

With those values in your head, sit back, close your eyes and imagine *what they look like*. I know that they are descriptive values, possibly intangible ones, but just try to think how you could express them by how you look. In turn, take each of your values and dress them. Work on everything from your hairstyle, your glasses, formal and casual clothes, your watch, your pen, your carrying gear and on until you've covered all the bases, top to toe.

If one of your values is *quality* how do you convey it in your dress? Is it classic or fashionable? To project a quality image you don't need to spend an exorbitant amount money, or only wear designer labels. You convey *quality* through your grooming and attention to detail. Your accessories require more investment than your clothes – a great handbag or leather carrier, smart organizer, great shoes and jewellery convey quality better than flashy outfits.

If another one of your values is to look *urbane, sophisticated* or *global*, ask yourself if your image is too traditional or too British, American or German, whatever? Looking urbane is also to appear worldly. By incorporating some interesting different bits to your look you can achieve this: an interesting Mexican necklace, a sleek Italian jersey dress, shoes from New York, a handbag from Germany. The easy part of looking urbane, sophisticated or global is that these days you can combine many elements of international style in your own country or find them on the Net.

See if you can envision a composite image that embodies all your brand values collectively.

THE CORPORATE IMAGE

If you are currently employed or if you have your eye on a new business opportunity, write down the buzz words that comprise the corporate identity. What messages are you trying to get across to your customers about the company? What messages are loud and clear from their advertising, their corporate literature? List, in no particular order, the corporate values under which you currently (or hope to) work:

. . . .

. . . .

. . . .

. . . .

. . . .

. . . .

. . . .

. . . .

. . . .

. . . .

Now measure your current dress sense, personal style and overall image against these corporate values. How does your image compare with your peers' – about the same? Better? Worse?

DRESS FOR THE COMPANY AS WELL AS THE JOB

If you are in the market for a new job, part of your research should include the corporate culture. Smart people do their homework prior to a job interview. They get a good brief on the company and the key people they will be meeting and have prepared answers to likely questions. But the focus is generally more on selling your background and skills than conveying how you will fit into the corporate culture. An important way to do this is to dress the part; to look like the person that they want.

In Chapter 1, we discussed the importance of first impressions. Nowhere is this more important than in a job interview. Research that I conducted with the financial recruitment consultants Robert Half International confirmed that recruiters and personnel/human resources directors are very subjective in initial interviews. 'I know that I should look at all the data, the CV, the psychometric tests that we use and I do to a large extent. But if I am honest, in the end I go with my gut,' said one senior HR director, who reiterated the views of most involved in making hiring decisions. And recruiters had their particular bugbears for women applicants: 40 per cent mentioned too much make-up as off-putting, but so too was no make-up for 33 per cent. If the woman didn't look 'smart' she was considered less capable than those who did. Attractive hair also came up with 35 per cent of those we interviewed, not just neat and tidy hair but *attractive* hair being a plus. Hands-down, the greatest image hurdle for men is facial hair – over 70 per cent of recruiters said that they 'had a problem' with it, especially beards!

The fact that you get an interview means that you are capable of doing the job – otherwise they wouldn't waste their time. The interview will determine, among other things, whether or not you will fit into the culture. For women this can be challenging, especially if the culture is male-dominated. Female role models can be few and far between but you can still get a lot of signals about what they will be looking for, in terms of image, by doing a bit of surveillance.

INTERVIEW INTELLIGENCE

Prior to any job interview, if you don't already know someone who works at the company who can give you some insider information, go to the offices. Lunchtime is good for seeing a cross section of staff coming and going. How do they dress? Can you differentiate the senior people from the more junior staff or are they interchangeable? What *does* distinguish people? How do they comport themselves? Do staff seem informal, very friendly or are they more reserved?

The building and office design also shape the corporate culture. How open plan is the office or does everyone have his or her personal cubbyhole? Are there comfortable areas where staff can congregate? How accessible are the offices, are they 'sealed-off' with many layers of security protecting the inner sanctum? Physical structures can shape the corporate culture as much as the people. Watch how people interact within the environment to get a feel for the corporate behaviour and style. Some powerful signals, about how you can influence and fit into an organization where you want to work, are there in the corporate lobbies and reception areas.

Women are smart to play safe when dressing for a job interview – but safe does *not* mean a navy suit, white blouse and court shoes. By safe I mean *appropriate*, which doesn't preclude your looking *interesting*. If a suit is the best bet, ask yourself if a skirted suit would look old-fashioned? Would a trouser suit be too challenging or spot-on? You want to fit in, yet stand out as a woman. By the end of this chapter you will understand how to do this.

YOUR PERSONAL IMAGE AUDIT

Rate yourself against your peers to determine the state of your personal style. Try to be as honest as possible. If you are British, Japanese, Dutch or Finnish don't play down your strengths if you know you are first rate at something. If French, Italian, Brazilian or American resist your cultural predilection to think that you excel at these things – there might just be some room for improvement.

Give yourself 1 point for every tick that is on par with peers, 2 points for everything that is above average, and 3 points for everything that is first rate.

Image factor	a liability	on par with peers	above average	first rate
Body basics				
fitness	❑	❑	❑	❑
posture	❑	❑	❑	❑
weight/figure	❑	❑	❑	❑
Grooming				
skin	❑	❑	❑	❑
make-up	❑	❑	❑	❑
hands/nails	❑	❑	❑	❑
hairstyle	❑	❑	❑	❑
teeth	❑	❑	❑	❑
hygiene	❑	❑	❑	❑
Personal style				
colour sense	❑	❑	❑	❑
style/fashion sense	❑	❑	❑	❑
fit	❑	❑	❑	❑
quality	❑	❑	❑	❑
overall look	❑	❑	❑	❑

Accessories

glasses	❏	❏	❏	❏
watch	❏	❏	❏	❏
shoes	❏	❏	❏	❏
carry case/handbag	❏	❏	❏	❏
diary/organizer	❏	❏	❏	❏
jewellery	❏	❏	❏	❏

Less than 15 points

This book was a smart purchase. Not pulling any punches, you need all the advice in this chapter. If you feel unable to put the advice into action yourself, call an image consultant to give you some personal advice or take you shopping until you get the hang of things yourself. Or, book into your diary (mid-week) an hour or two to go 'check out what's in'. Carousing the shops when they aren't crowded can give you a feel for how fashions have changed. Treat yourself to a coffee in a smart area of town with a mission just to note how people are dressed. Observe hair and make-up, shoes, bags as well as clothes. What three new things could you try tomorrow to update your look?

16 to 35 points

Your image is struggling for one of two reasons: you don't care or you are really, really pressed for time. If you are a mother, the latter is more likely. Don't assume that you don't look fine, even terrific, if you only have milliseconds available each day for putting your look together. Ask your colleagues what you think you are doing well and what might be a priority for attention. You'll feel heaps better learning that you aren't as bad as you think! Read this chapter and you will discover many practical solutions to make getting it together a snap.

36 to 50 points

You know that personal presentation is important, and over the years have taken steps to improve your image. Some aspects need updating.

Perhaps you've worn your hair the same way for the last 5 (or maybe 10) years. Or, are your bags and shoes all the same? It might just be time to take some risks to have greater influence as well as to enjoy your image more.

Over 51 points

OK, you are a star. But don't let it go to your head. You've got your act well and truly together and are, no doubt, the envy of many you work with. You are already dressed for your next promotion but read this chapter carefully to ensure that it is in the bag.

Looking the business

At this point in *Branding Yourself*, we are entering a minefield, combining all the possibilities for *looking the part* and projecting your brand values. Coaching woman-to-woman, this isn't always easy. You have preconceived notions from your own experience, you've made assumptions (even without reading any further) about what an image consultant is likely to think. Your hackles might be raised in anticipation. It's OK to be defensive – women always are. Men, I have to admit, are pussycats by comparison. Go on, have a peek at their chapter for ideas on how to nudge your male colleagues or partner into a revamp.

This chapter contains guidelines not formulas. A good image is many things. Whether your work environment is formal or informal here are the guiding principles for the look of your brand:

- The look is *yours*, not someone else's.
- At the very least, you're what we expect.
- At best, you are more.
- You look comfortable.
- Your grooming is impeccable but seemingly effortless.
- Nothing jars.
- Nothing's contrived.
- The fine touches are just that, *fine*.
- It looks like you've chosen your things with care. But, once on, you don't fuss about them.
- You look *now*, not yesterday. But you also look timeless.
- We want to know you *because of how you look* even before you open your mouth.

Let's get serious

Despite wonderful stories in the media about how informal, even sexy (!), business is today compared with a decade ago, supposedly relaxed, fun, entrepreneurial and women-friendly with no dress codes or hierarchies, most of us still go to work in offices where serious business takes place. We still need to make an impact, influence tough characters, sell our ideas as well as ourselves. Even though many businesses *are* re-evaluating what we should look like in our new business world which is, and increasingly will be, driven by high technology and e-commerce, smart women know that they need a range of 'armour' in the wardrobe. We require serious power suits that aren't necessarily black or pinstriped, uncomfortable or masculine. The millennial power suit enables you to walk into a room and make others take note – here she is! Additionally, we require 'pseudo suits' – not all tailored, but relaxed separates that together create a 'suit'. Finally, there are suggestions for developing a business casual look that is, indeed, smart.

DID YOU SAY 'POWER DRESSING'?

The notion of *power dressing* sounds like a real hangover from the 80s and 90s. Power dressers were those horrid women who wore stilettos and shoulder pads, had big hair and scary lipstick – aaaaargh! Powerful women can be threatening because of their success, and, however they can be parodied by others – by women as well as men – they will be targeted. But women doing serious jobs – needing to hold their own, to look authoritative and get things done – require an image that *helps* them achieve their objectives, be they a personal assistant, support manager, management consultant, dealer, advisor, company director, CEO or chairperson.

So, I am going out on a limb here for you women *knowing* that you need advice on strutting your stuff to be taken for the serious, capable and *powerful* woman that you are. But, it's up to you how and when you use the gear to get the job done. Power suiting full-time can be exhausting. But if the rewards are worth it, more power to you!

WHAT WORKS

It's difficult for busy women to get a fix on where things are heading with acceptable (and desirable!) power dressing. You don't have time to cruise the shops endlessly and occasionally might turn to magazines or look online for guidance. Some fashion editors spout 'interesting' suggestions about how we should dress for work. I recall a recent summer when one urged that we attend meetings in floral dresses with cardigans; another argued that billowy skirts and mule sandals were the 'new power dressing'. Viable suggestions for holiday, but not advisable for women in offices trying to get a fair deal in today's business world (where many still don't get equal pay for equal work).

Then there are the paragons of power – the few women in the boardrooms or in public office who look smart all right, but whom you may not want to emulate. Many senior women insist that the only way to make it alongside men in the boardroom is to dress like 'pseudomen'. 'I have stuck to the same formula for years. Dark-coloured, matched suits, always skirts and never trousers. That's the female version of man's power suit and one that never fails,' insists one of Britain's top female directors.

But a new generation of women entering the portals of power want to rewrite the rulebook and change the face of senior management with a modern, more varied style. Just as the nature of our offices and doing business are changing beyond recognition from just 10 or 20 years ago, so too is it time to reinvent power dressing for the twenty-first century.

Professional is a four-letter word – suit

For both women and men the suit remains the armour for doing serious business. As much as I might like to say otherwise – Internet revolution or not – this remains the case at the highest levels in global business. You might not need to wear it every day, but on the days that count, you'd better.

As many women have discovered, however, a uniform is not what's required. In fact, uninspired dressing can undermine a woman's influence, conveying a lack of confidence in taking risks. Seas of navy- or black-skirted suits on women in a very male-dominated business in traditional sectors like law or banking are slowly evaporating. Even in these male bastions, times are a changin', with Arthur Anderson, Barclays Bank, IBM and others declaring the suit defunct and unnecessary in the new business age. Fortunately for me, casual dress policies have been great for business. Once companies see the chaos that results when they say that formal dressing is no longer required, they are on the telephone within weeks to ask for 'guidance'. So, the jury is still out on how smart going casual-smart really is. In the meantime, you are wise to play it safe when in doubt and opt for a suit, choosing between the more powerful options for the heavy-hitter sessions or the 'pseudo suit' for everyday wear.

THE RIGHT STUFF

Finding a new suit can be challenging when fashion decides that suits are anything but fashionable or that we have wardrobes full of them and want some relief with other clothes. The late 90s saw the wane of the suit with less and less floor space in ladies fashions given over to tailored clothes and suits. This forced a serious rethinking of what a suit should and could be. The result was women daring to interpret the suit in new ways that were often more comfortable (softer fabrics) and fun (colours and styles).

Your choice of power suit will depend on the following factors:

1) The image you want to project
2) Your body shape
3) Your colouring
4) Your personality

THE IMAGE

The most *serious, high-powered* suit look remains the skirted suit. Trouser suits are more modern, comfortable and very credible. But nothing coveys status more than a modern version of the traditional woman's suit. Fortunately, it is now up to us, not the corporate dress code, if we *choose* to wear skirted suits as forcing us to is no longer legal. And it is up to you how formal or relaxed, modern or traditional, the suit should be.

I urge all women at the highest of echelons to champion more relaxed alternatives to the super-duper power suiter. It is these women who already have the power to prove that women don't have to be all tailored and trussed up to do business at board level. But alas, most women at the top wear skirted suits much of the time, the reason being: they know that nothing influences men more! Call that sexist, call it politically incorrect, scream, 'Something should be done about it' if you will. But it is the way it is. These suits make *their* lives easier.

Many senior men are uncomfortable (unhinged?) by a female colleague in a trouser suit. They won't say so directly to the woman but will feel that she is trying to be too masculine; or, worse, they question her sexuality! No joke. I have heard this too often by senior men, but mainly those over 45. So it is just a matter of time until women don't have to deal with such attitudes but to deny that they still exist is naive.

At a recent all-male seminar for partners of a global management consulting firm, a participant actually burst out, objecting to my wearing a trouser suit to run the session. 'What are you trying to prove?' he asked. 'I just hate it when you women strut around in those things. Skirts are much *nicer*, less *offensive*.' An honest to goodness quote, that. To be sure, I was getting close to the mark in challenging him on a substantive point, so he lashed out on a personal level. But isn't that what women are up against in many male-dominated situations? The good news is that many younger men do come to our defence, which is what happened to me when this chap went on the attack. They have partners who work and wear trouser suits and they admire and support their female colleagues when dumb objections about their appearance are raised. (More on dealing with men in Chapter 9.)

The power suit is meant for business, not to feel sexy, although it can look downright sexy provided that the fabric and cut flatter you. It should be attractive without being provocative. So when people meet you they have only business on their mind.

To make your power suit high-octane:

- Choose good quality fabric that *looks* expensive.
- Use neutral colours; the darker the more serious.
- Wear a fine or indistinguishable pattern in suit fabric.
- Select a style that is not overly-tailored or figure-hugging, you'll be more comfortable and look more powerful too.
- Ensure nothing is tight: jacket remains buttoned (easily) and skirt doesn't require tugging to stay in place.
- Select the best skirt length – just above or just below the knee.
- If your legs are an asset, enjoy the challenge of taking it shorter.
- Avoid thigh (or more) revealing slits in skirts.

- Team it with a simple blouse, minimum collar details.
- Emphasize the neck with a stunning necklace (not an insignificant chain).
- Always wear earrings to complete the effect.
- Keep rings to three maximum; genuine metals and stones, not junk.
- Tone hosiery with colour of suit and shoes; the sheerer the better and plain.
- Wear elegant, modern shoes (neither funky nor frumpy); never boots, sandals or flats.
- Always be well-groomed.
- Add a lovely scent – it's unsettlingly powerful!

ALTERNATIVE POWER SUITS

For women who mean business but ('Hey give me a break!') would not return to wearing skirted suits no matter what bonus was on the table, there are plenty of alternatives. Your personality, confidence and abilities can blow others away so you have found that pulling back on the power suit itself makes for a more effective package. Indeed, most women concur that since their jobs occupy much of their lives, they are going to enjoy the clothes that they wear.

So, still in serious business mode, let's look at the alternatives that will do the job but offer more variety.

The trouser suit

Perhaps the majority of working women in the last decade have opted for the more comfortable trouser suit for work. Trousers are more practical (long days, commuting, working at a PC) and comfortable than skirts. Of course, women of every size and shape can wear trouser suits provided that the cut and fit is flattering. Always, but always do a check in a three-way mirror to assess how the look works. If in doubt, choose a different style, cut or fabric.

To look your most powerful, follow these tips:

Cut and fit

- The fit should be easy, not baggy. It must look perfect when the jacket is buttoned.
- Clever albeit expensive undergarments can transform your figure. Nancy Ganz body slimmers deserve a medal!
- A fit, not necessarily slim, body makes an inexpensive suit look twice the price.

Style

- Any old jacket and trousers do not make a power suit. 'Pseudo suit': yes; power suit: no. Wear matching jacket and trousers for elegance *and* power.
- Trouser suits require better grooming to look as professional as a skirted suit.
- Brighter jackets help you to stand out but might not be as powerful as neutral colours for sober discussions.
- Invest in simple, quality knitwear, shell tops and blouses to wear underneath jackets so when caught without a jacket you look 'complete'.
- Be ruthless in wearing the right weight clothes at the right time of year.

Accessories

- Make sure your jewellery is as modern as your suit, especially brooches, as classic styles are ageing.
- Keep the neckline simple but add a striking necklace.
- Choose a watch to work a 24/7 schedule (24 hours a day, 7 days a week) – look good for work, play and dressing up.

- Good quality, interesting oblong scarves are more versatile and easier to manage than squares.
- Always wear a quality belt on the trousers.

To complete the look
- Wear quality modern shoes. Flat shoes aren't as elegant as a slight heel but don't wear court shoes or those meant to be worn with skirts or dresses.
- Make sure your hairstyle is as modern as your suit.

A final word on trouser suits: cognisant that being a woman is an asset in business, ask yourself if your femininity is apparent with this look. A sharp black trouser suit is stunning but can challenge both women and men. If a look is too strong and you need to win friends and influence people, then ask yourself how you can soften the look. The choice of earrings, colour of lipstick, or some perfume might be all that's needed along with open, approachable behaviour. Because in a sharp, black trouser suit you will have to do all the running!

PRIME ITEM: THE JACKET

Women with years of experience wearing suits have discovered the pros and cons of different styles for them. The key to getting the suit right rests with the style of jacket, the image it creates, how flattering it is on you and how versatile it might be for teaming with other wardrobe items. Skirts and trousers can be altered easily for a good fit. The wrong cut jacket can't. Hence, if you love the jacket you buy the suit.

Single-breasted (SB) jacket:
- Looks great on all women.
- Flexible to wear with trousers, skirts, dresses.
- Goes from work to play over casual trousers.

- Have three in plain colours before getting a patterned one (then keep it subtle).
- Slashed pockets are best (don't add bulges on hips).

Double-breasted (DB) jacket:
- More buttoned-up and serious than SB jackets.
- Good on average to tall women.
- Good on thin women – adds bulk to the thin or flat-chested.
- 4-button DB makes everyone look chubby.
- 6-button DB is stunning; only button middle button.
- Blazers are for Wrens or women with no imagination.

Collarless jacket:
- Offers endless potential for using scarves and different collars.
- Makes full-busted appear less so.
- Chic when long, a bit cute if short.
- Not stunning if your hair is too cropped.

Mandarin jacket:
- Striking but inflexible.
- Must keep buttoned up or looks silly.
- Not for short or thick necks.
- Long length is smart with trousers or skirts but less so over dresses.
- Accentuates a fuller bust.

Short jacket:
- Good on the short-legged, makes your bottom half much longer.
- Exposes the hips, thighs and bottom so be prepared.

- Can date quickly, but if you're petite it's your best bet.
- Big gals look gormless in these.

Longer jacket – set-in sleeves/tailored:
- Covers the tummy, hips and butt. Yippee!
- Some $\frac{7}{8}$ or $\frac{9}{10}$ lengths even hide thighs!!!
- Keep trousers as narrow as possible.
- Keep skirts short but showing an elegant 10cm (at least) below jackets.
- Long skirts possible provided they're not too full.
- Add a slight shoulder pad for slimming effect if shoulders are narrow.

Raglan jacket:
- Easy, comfy deconstructed style.
- Never looks powerful, too relaxed.
- Great on women with good shoulders but not if yours slope.

Sleeve lengths:
- Best on 'break' of the wrist.
- If too short, the suit looks cheap and you look gormless.
- If too long, the suit looks borrowed and you look lost.
- Three-quarter-length or short-sleeves great for spring/summer to look more relaxed and sexy. But not for the full-busted who look even fuller in them.

THE PSEUDO SUIT

The alternative to these heavy-duty power numbers is to create your own suit effect with separates. This is achieved by realizing that you need an extra layer on top to work as a jacket so that the outfit is, indeed, a *pseudo suit*. Any woman in a company with a casual dress policy should use pseudo suits for meetings and presentations.

The pseudo suit is professional, modern, yet relaxed. It enables you to get the job done but lay down the law when necessary because of the 'jacket'. Of course, this is best achieved if you don't use flimsy, silly fabrics, patterns or colours. Rather, put the pseudo suit together with as much care as you would a more formal suit using quality pieces that work together.

Do:

- Put a jersey dress with matching jersey jacket/coat/ cardigan.
- Wear a shift dress with jacket or shacket (i.e. substantial shirt in summer).
- Team neutral trousers with a stunning jacket or substantial cardigan.
- Match a long skirt with flattering, deconstructed jacket.
- Accessorize with care; get flair.
- Ensure your grooming is immaculate.

Avoid:

- Patterned skirts or trousers.
- Anything floral.
- Loud jewellery.
- Flouncey scarves.
- Casual, unstructured handbags.
- Inappropriate shoes (funky or frumpy).
- Pairing styles that don't mix, e.g. a classic blouse with an ethnic skirt, silk and corduroy, cotton with knits.

BUYING YOUR POWER WARDROBE

Of course, you wish money wasn't an issue when it comes to dressing for success. If you had plenty of time to hunt for bargains, cruise the shops regularly to suss out better deals or spend time online shopping for yourself rather than for priorities like groceries, then you would be able to save money and look like a million bucks.

This book is not aimed at women with loads of time on their hands. You've got your hands full. So, to cut to the chase, here are some investment guidelines:

- A quality suit starts at £350.
- It's smarter to buy one £400 suit than two at £200. Ask any woman who looks wonderful all the time. Better to wear something terrific many times than wear a lot of indifferent stuff infrequently.
- Pay extra to get the fit spot-on. Otherwise the suit will look like a bad bargain.
- Quality suits look good for 3 years max. Then items can be worn as separates but not for anything very important.
- Invest in at least one dynamo suit every autumn and spring if you wear suits almost exclusively.
- Buy suits in September and February in 'transitional' weights. These are wearable most of the year.
- Edit your working wardrobe at the beginning of each season to determine your investment priorities and get rid of the dross.
- Buy for *today's weight* and size not for your *goal weight* for the most flattering effect.
- You always look slimmer in an easier fit/larger size.
- Comfort is a major consideration. 'Test drive' possibilities by sitting, crossing legs, walking,

squatting before buying. When in doubt on the comfort front, forget it.

- Don't buy any skirt or trousers that can't be worn with confidence without a jacket.
- Quality hosiery is a good investment in both effect and durability.
- Repair shoes before they need it, that goes for buttons and hems too.

A final word on investing in your working wardrobe: spend as much as you can remembering that it is no less than you deserve. Stuff guilt! You are dressing for your next pay rise.

Smart casual dressing

OK, OK. Anita Roddick never wears suits and look at how successful she's been! I've heard it a million times. And look: even global consultants – Andersen's, PWC, KPMG, Bain, et al are ditching their suits. Surely, you can do business dressed casually?

Smart casual – an incongruous juxtaposition, but we get the point. Being 'casual' means to be comfortable, not sloppy. Interpreting *smart* is the challenging bit. You've seen how many staff look decidedly *unsmart*, especially in the summertime.

When you have a company that looks like it's filled with shoddy people you question the quality of work that's getting done. Any company that invites clients and customers in must take this on board. A smart casual dress policy *can* work if the company makes clear just what it should look like and what it definitely shouldn't look like.

I am going out on a limb here in giving you some guidelines on interpreting the smart casual thing. Suffice to say that I have seen it done brilliantly about 30 per cent of the time. The remaining 70 per cent put little thought into their image which can and has proven to be undermining in terms of both performance and impact on clients.

THE WHO, WHAT, WHERE, WHEN, WHY AND HOW OF SMART CASUAL DRESSING

Who

Anyone, at any level, can be businesslike dressed in casual clothes. It will depend on the nature of your work, your role and what you consider appropriate casual clothes.

Newer industries like the high-tech and e-commerce sectors are more natural habitats for casual dressing than traditional ones because both the nature of their work and their interaction with clients are different. If you rarely actually see your clients face to face and market your services and products mainly via computer then how you dress is less of an issue.

When advising companies who are considering 'going casual', I force them to revisit their corporate values and see if jeans and T-shirts convey them because *all* casual dress codes invariably result in just that – the lowest common denominator of modern casual dress. This is why many companies start out liberating the troops of their suits only to find that such havoc results that they have to reinstate guidelines on dressing appropriately.

Sometimes dressing down makes great sense in certain sectors (like creative ones) and for many business situations such as for brainstorming work or programme development sessions. In publishing it has helped staff appear more modern, less stuffy. Management consultants seem more like team players than aloof company doctors when working alongside client teams. In telecoms, where customers communicate mainly online or on the phone, it doesn't really matter. In other businesses, there are many days a month when staff are just grinding away in the office and not meeting with clients. Why shouldn't they be more comfortable? The key is always to have 'spare armour' for the unscheduled client meeting or update with the chairman.

If in any doubt about the appropriateness of dressing down, go back to your corporate identity and your own personal brand. Take those values, in relation to the nature of your work, and ask yourself if your clients will have more or less or equal confidence in your abilities (and charges!) if you dress down? If in any doubt, don't risk it.

Many self-employed women enjoy working from home but sometimes look inappropriate when meeting with clients or customers. Because you can beaver away most of the time electronically without needing to be seen, when you do meet other professionals in their offices you can sometimes look like you landed from another planet.

Often because you schedule many appointments, plus personal errands, on your *days out*, you can look as though you are going on a trip rather than attending a meeting because of all the gear you schlep around. It is important for the self-employed to look anything but self-employed. Meaning you don't want to look or behave out of the business norm. Even though you might work out of your spare bedroom, remember the need to up the ante and look like other professionals who work together in offices. Be sure to plan your image as well as you plan your day aware that you have to convey that you are part of it, *not out of it*, in your behaviour and dress.

What

Let's see if you agree with my guidelines on what works and what doesn't as smart casual dress in modern business.

Smart casual is . . .
- Fresh, clean, tidy
- Immaculate grooming
- Substantial enough for your assets not to jiggle
- A spare jacket *in case*
- Trousers, culottes; short or long skirts
- Any fabric except evening fabrics like chiffon, satin or lace
- Leather not PVC
- Loose or figure-hugging, not skin-tight
- Covered backs, armpits, midriffs and cleavages
- Dresses but not sundresses
- Skirts not sarongs
- Blouses worn in or out
- Boots, loafers, deck shoes, flats
- Sandals in summer only if you pedicure tootsies weekly
- Hosiery-free in summer only
- Accessorized well: belts, hosiery (except summer), jewellery
- A complete, not thrown-together, look

Smart casual is not . . .

- Cheap-looking gear
- Body piercing (ears only)
- Shorts
- Clubbing gear
- Sports/exercise gear
- Beach gear
- T-shirts that you would run in
- T-shirts with dumb slogans
- See-through anything
- Underwear worn as a top
- Tops worn without underwear
- Visible panty lines
- Torn anything
- Stained anything
- Wrinkled unless it's meant to be, e. g. linen
- Chewing gum

Obviously, you can ignore all of the above if you don't really care about increasing your job prospects . . . but, then again, you wouldn't be reading this book if you did!

Where and when

Smart casual is best in the office and when mainly colleagues and staff will see you. Think twice about dressing this way with clients and/or suppliers. Better on your turf than on theirs; unless you know that they, too, dress down. If in doubt, dress up.

If meeting with a man or a mainly male group and you are in the firing line, add an extra layer, a jacket or something (cardigan, scarf, etc.). One layer leaves you exposed and vulnerable – there's just too much for them to concentrate on besides your message!

Unless you make real efforts for your smart casual look to be just that, don't take it from the office out into the evening. Make sure the shoes don't look too comfortable and worn. Add a scarf for panache. Freshen your make-up before you leave the office.

You'll have less luck getting an upgrade when flying if you are dressed casually. Why not wear your suit to check in then change before take-off?

Dressing down is more acceptable and prevalent in the summer months so test reactions before launching into it full-time. It can be embarrassing to revert to the suits.

To influence someone who's older, show respect and dress more formally. Many over 50s, bless them, just don't get it.

Why

There are many reasons to choose a casual style over a formal one. If you are a woman who juggles family commitments with work or, perhaps, work from home, much of the time a relaxed style is more sensible. But my advice is to *put together a look rather than throw one together*. No offence meant, but you have seen it. So, no matter how comfortable you would like to be, pull back, aware that your earning potential is at stake.

But in looking relaxed, you can appear more approachable and, potentially, more creative. If you facilitate brainstorming sessions, engage in problem-solving or work at a PC a good deal of the time, then relaxed dressing makes good sense. If you have a very practical job and life, dash about on public transport, walk a lot, fix things, then clothes that 'move' and are comfortable are the order of the day.

The major consideration is this: who do you need and want to influence and will they 'buy' you without any 'armour', i.e. a suit or pseudo suit? If 'no problem' is the answer, then have fun. If you question things, play it safe by looking smarter. I'll have to leave that ball in *your* court.

How

A smart casual wardrobe is challenging (but more fun!) to pull together. You can be more adventurous with both colours and styles. So here's advice on choosing them to suit you.

Selecting colours

Having run Color Me Beautiful for 15 years, I am a bit evangelical about colours and getting them right. If you are part of the 99.9 per cent of women who prefer to look healthy, attractive and younger most of the time then you might want to note a few tips for yourself.

Colour can help enormously. As you may know, when we colour-analyse a woman it takes about 90 minutes and covers her clothing, hair and make-up. Here, I give you a simple guide to selecting colours – year round.

Your dominant colouring type (Deep, Light, Cool, Warm, Clear or Soft) is based on the combination and overall effect of your skin tone, eye and hair colour. See if you can identify yourself below and agree with this basic advice. If you don't 'get it' or want to change your colouring (with your hair colour) then see my book *The Makeover Manual* or check for details at the back of this book about having a personal consultation.

DEEP COLOURING

- Dark hair; strong eyes; rich (not pale) skin tone
- e.g. Paloma Picasso, Cherie Blair, Diana Ross, Cher

Great in strong, deep neutrals: black, navy, charcoal, pewter, rich purple. Your whites should be bright. Pastels: almost white, not sugary. Colours like red, royal, emerald and forest green, plum and turquoise are great with neutrals or on their own. Test to see if rust or burgundy are better on you and adjust your make-up into either a warm (rust) or cool (burgundy) direction.

LIGHT COLOURING

- Blonde or grey hair; pale eyes (blue, grey or green); fair skin

e.g.   Tipper Gore, Mia Farrow, Claudia Schiffer

Light colours (obviously) are elegant on you, boring on everyone else. Pastels near your face are very flattering. Tone medium colours like soft navys, greys and berry shades with pastels or lighter versions of themselves for a stunning monochromatic look. Test to see if warm pinks (e.g. peach) are better than cool pinks (rose) and adjust your make-up in a cool (rose) or warm (peach) direction. You know that very dark or very muddy shades aren't successful near your face so use them elsewhere.

A caveat: if you are a large woman you might look even larger in this palette. See the 'Cool' or 'Soft' palettes as alternatives.

COOL COLOURING

- Ash blonde or grey, white or greying hair (uncoloured!); blue, grey or brown eyes; medium skin tone, no freckles

e.g.   Betty Boothroyd, Germaine Greer, Joan Baez

How light or dark your colours are matters less than the undertone which should be a pink or blue tinge, never yellow or yellow-green. All blues, greys, pinks, and berry shades are terrific. Also jade, aqua, turquoise, lilac and plum. Avoid peach, rust, orange, moss or olive green in particular.

A caveat: if your hair is white or greying it is an asset to you (not to all women). Make it even more so by wearing your best colours near your face.

WARM COLOURING

- Golden blonde, red or auburn hair; any eye colour; skin has freckles or is golden brown
- e.g. Nicole Kidman, Emma Thompson, Jennifer Saunders, Geri Halliwell

It's easy for you to look ill in the wrong colour – and you know it. Never white, always ivory. Use blue only if your eyes are blue; any shade of green or brown depending on your preference – just check if muted versions are better than brighter ones. Grey is less successful than brown. For you, black is only for funerals – 'coz you will look ready for yours if you wear it otherwise.

CLEAR COLOURING

- Medium to dark hair; bright blue, green or hazel eyes; fresh, unmarked or freckled skin
- e.g. Catherine Zeta-Jones, Andrea Corr, Pauline Collins, Oprah Winfrey

Bright, crisp colours are your best, nothing sludgy or muddy. Your whites can be pure or a fresh ivory (cream isn't interesting). Your best navy is ink; best black is jet; best grey is charcoal; best brown is a black-brown. Forget middling colours in favour of true ones: red, royal blue, purple, lemon yellow, turquoise. Black denim is better than blue; stone is your alternative to khaki.

SOFT COLOURING

- Medium, mousey hair; soft brown, blue or hazel eyes; skin – medium tone

e.g.   Macy Gray, Greta Scacchi, Madeline Albright, Cindy
        Crawford

Think elegant, think Armani, not the prices, just the colours. Your palette is muted not loud: pewter, soft moss, olive, khaki and turquoise. Test to see if plum is better than rust which will depend on your skin tone and adjust your make-up to suit a cool (plum) or warm (brown or terracotta) direction. Monochromatic dressing (tone on tone) is better than bold contrasts like black and white. Patterns are best if indistinguishable.

Putting the look together

Here's a checklist to make sure that your casual wardrobe really means business.

NECKLINES

Open necklines draw attention to your face and can make you look slimmer and younger. Don't hide the neck due to ageing or fullness. Better to keep open and distract with interesting collars, oblong scarves, long necklaces. Being 'all buttoned up' can be matronly. Convey maturity and power with the confidence to 'open up'.

- *Polo necks:* wear indoors only when heating is on the blink. Attractive only on young men.
- *Scoop necks:* consider the state of your chest and if the skin is lovely enough to show. If not, try a jewel neckline.
- *V-necks:* slimming and lovely on every woman aside from she with a pointed chin or a long neck.
- *Standard collars:* more interesting and chic worn open, collar up in back, points down in front.
- *Mandarin collars:* wear alone, no necklace or scarf.

Final note: a shirt collar should complement, not compete with, jacket collar. Don't be blasé on this one.

BLOUSES

Spend your money on tops and blouses as they are nearest to your face and are your 'pseudo jacket' in your casual business wardrobe.

- Don't skimp: tops should be substantial, not revealing or skin-tight.
- Ample coverage is essential over the bust, long enough to cover midriff or lower if lumpy. Buttons should never show strain.
- Good foundations are necessary. Underwear must be smooth, the right size and prevent excessive movement when you're active.

TROUSERS/PANTS

Require the three-way mirror test to be sure that you have the right cut, fabric and size.

- Cover up for comfort: if you honestly aren't proud of the look of your waist, tummy and hips in your trousers, wear your tops long enough to cover up. You will be happy, but not as much as your co-workers.
- Straining's a pain: if your thighs or bottom are ample they will look thinner, and you will feel more comfortable, in a more generously-cut size or a fabric that drapes rather than constricts.
- Medium to lightweight fabrics: in trousers these are more slimming than thick or stiff fabrics.
- Medium to dark plain colours: these are more slimming than light or patterned trousers.

SKIRTS

Are a nice alternative to trousers and help a woman in a dressed-down office stand out.

- Soft A-lines (bias-cut and feminine) are comfortable and flattering but not good on the ample-bottomed.
- Long skirts can be great if they allow movement, i.e. pleats, slits.
- Full skirts are for picnics, not working, even in a dressed-down environment.
- Team with appropriate tops: not T-shirts, or classic man-tailored shirt. Twinsets are nice and give that extra layer for extra confidence with the cardigan working as a pseudo-jacket.

Finishing touches for looking the part

You've made the effort to get some great looks together so must finish the job to ensure that you really look the business. Your brand values will guide you here in selecting the right look and quality to project what you want.

BAGS

One of your key accessories is the bag you use to schlep your gear to and from the office. Depending on how you travel (car, public transport, on foot) you should choose an appropriate fabric and shape. If it needs to *work hard* by carrying a laptop, change of clothes, lunch, then consider having another bag in the office for you to go to meetings in style.

I recommend that if you commute to work on foot or by public transport that you use a backpack to save the strain on your back. Sartorially elegant? No. Smart? Yes! Get a decent style and replace it when it starts to look tattered. Alternatives to backpacks are hard-wearing nylon carriers that are no weight in themselves but have the strength to be loaded. Longchamps are noted for theirs which have smart leather handles and trims and come in an array of sizes and colours. Remember: don't take a backpack to important meetings unless you don't mind being asked to get coffee or do photocopying.

Women also tend to carry around so much that we look disorganized and unprofessional – the bulging handbag, the Filofax bursting with Post-it Notes, or the extra bag containing tonight's dinner! OK, we may be organizing more people than ourselves but we look like we have so much on our plates that we aren't focused on what's important in business.

Edit your handbag *weekly* – it's required and you know it! Choose the smallest bag that you can practically live with and you will be less likely to overload it (and look more elegant and in control as a result).

See if you could get away with one of these combinations for carrying around what you need to daily:

- Shopper style bag: carries a folder/small laptop/purse
- Neat, elegant handbag plus an attaché
- Leather folder and neat handbag
- Elegant, neat backpack with handle to double as a proper handbag
- Attaché with small envelope/clutch bag inside with personal bits

As you need to replace your daily handbag every 12 to 18 months spend good – but not stupid – money. Investment items should be your folder and/or attaché – both of which can last for years. Many designer bags and those made of fabric don't go the distance and look tatty after a month or two especially if you commute by foot or public transport. If you carry two pieces, e.g. a folder and a handbag, it is elegant if they co-ordinate (they don't need to match). Being the same colour is a safe, if boring, bet.

PERSONAL ORGANIZER

Anyone's choice of diary is very personal. With today's electronic personal organizers they also become a major investment. Before you switch from what you are using, ask people about their experiences with them. Get the pros and cons of particular brands and models. Ask yourself what features you require. Do you really need e-mail at your fingertips if you have easy access to your PC most of the day? Will a typing format (e.g. Psion) be preferable to tapping or scribbling with a stylus (Palm-tops)? Or will an old-fashioned fountain pen and leather bound diary be even more stylish?

Keeping your 'toys' (organizer, mobile, laptop, etc.) up to date is important if you work with men. They are toy-obsessed and like to show off when they have their latest gadget. 'Send me your business card,' he will request across the table. When you actually hand it over to him (bemused by why he asked you to *send* it) he smirks and says, 'To my Palm-Top, woman!' He meant for you to zap it across the table, diary to diary via infra-red signal. You can either play 'keeping up with the boy-toys' and master the damn things better than they do (now that's fun) or stick to your guns with your own method. Just be sure it is an efficient one and looks professional.

Grooming your brand

Your hair and make-up are key to the overall effect of your brand. Give them short shrift and you short-change yourself. Women who wear make-up earn up to 25 per cent more and are promoted faster. It's not fair, it's just the way it is. If that raises your feminist hackles, see the grooming section for the men in Chapter 6, *it includes make-up*!

HAIR

Short or long? High, medium or no maintenance? Natural or unnatural colour? The choices are endless but can have a dramatic effect on your overall image.

Your choice of hairstyle is contingent on many things – your personality, the texture of your hair, the effort required and the effort you are prepared to make, *and what actually suits you*. Most of us have several possibilities. Here's what you need to consider in choosing yours:

- If you are a tidy woman, then a fussy hairstyle (no matter how attractive on you) shouldn't be considered. You know how you like balance and order in your dress. If your hair is wild you will feel unkempt. So, forget that suggestion for every day.
- If you are very relaxed and natural, a style that requires fiddling with products and special brushes to look good is not a wise one. Save the 'wow' effect for when you visit the hairdresser but be sure the cut is one you can easily manage (in 5 minutes) yourself.
- The texture of your natural hair will dictate both possibilities and limits. But most hair textures can be changed effectively with special shampoos,

conditioners, styling products and waxes, as well as perms and straightening techniques. Don't wince at the suggestion of a perm – today's versions are indiscernible and really do give body to limp, lifeless hair.

Tell the hair stylist how much time you are prepared to put in, every day, to create the look that you want. If you bring a picture, use it as a guideline. Don't expect the stylist to replicate it.

Face shapes

These need consideration. If yours isn't a perfect oval you need to add balance. If you have other challenging features, consider these suggestions:

- *Long face:* soft fringe, no longer than shoulders, fullness on side.
- *Round face:* sharp angles rather than fluffy layers best, height at crown.
- *Square face:* minimal width on sides, softening at neck, height at crown.
- *Full face:* cut with wisps on the face, minimal width on the sides and neck.
- *Narrow forehead:* no fringe; keep open.
- *Long forehead:* soften and balance with fringe.
- *Strong jawline:* soft layers on the face.

Long versus short

You can look professional with your hair at any length. The goal is to keep it tidy. If you must keep touching it, to keep it out of your eyes, it is a distraction. Watch if you have long hair (or a long fringe) that you don't hide behind it. Many women do so unconsciously which conveys lack of confidence. When tying your hair back, use quality clips (not scrunches or plain bands) to *finish* your hair. The more substantial the hair clip the smaller your earrings should be. Ditto with regards to hairbands; the thinner and plainer the better. When choosing a length consider your body size:

- Small-boned/petite women: too much volume will swamp you; cropped will be 'cute' but short with some fullness is most elegant.
- Big women (size or height) need hair. Closely cropped cuts make you look larger; but too much volume adds bulk, so, something in between. But not longer than shoulders.

Hair colouring

Today this can add lustre, sheen and texture to hair in addition to colour. It is fun and not as risky as it once was to experiment with hair colouring. For business you can change your colouring for dramatic or subtle effect provided that *you go with nature*. If you have a cool skin tone and choose red you will look quite ill. So too, if you go much darker or very much lighter than you are naturally. For advice, see the chapter 'Change your Colouring' in my book *The Makeover Manual*.

SKINCARE

You know that the better condition your skin is in the less make-up you will need to look polished. Your skin might not be in tip-top condition now but you can improve if with some attention morning and night and with a judicious selection of products that work for you.

Stress can also take its toll on your skin causing spots and dryness. When stressed your body is depleted of B vitamins as well as vitamin C and zinc, all of which are needed for healthy skin. Taking supplements of these helps.

If you are using the same skincare routine you were 5 years ago you aren't doing your skin justice. Sorry, but technology has changed so much with wonderful new products *that really make a difference* and they don't all cost a fortune. But beware of trying a new routine when you are stressed, unwell or have your period as your skin is more likely to be acting up during these upsets. If your skin is sensitive, try one new product at a time so that you can pinpoint any problems which might result.

Despite time pressures, try not to shortcut your daily skincare. Both morning and evening routines are important to develop and to maintain. In the morning, you need to get all the dead skin cells off your face before you apply make-up. As your face is pretty clean, a quick cleanse with a good cream or gel cleanser washed off with the aid of a flannel means you don't need to use a toner as well. Remember sunscreen is necessary year round if you want to keep lines and blemishes generated by harmful sun rays at bay. Moisturiser is important to keep moisture in your skin and pollutants out. But you only need a little of the right stuff for your skin type. You will need to vary your moisturiser throughout the year, using a richer formula in wintertime when cold wind and indoor heating dries out the skin and a lighter cream in summertime when the skin can be more balanced.

Take special care of the eye area which is comprised of thinner, more sensitive skin and requires special eye formulations for treatment. UVB rays from PCs, working under fluorescent lights and general eye strain from doing close work like reading all put extra stress on your eyes and the skin around them. A cooling eye gel is a welcome, restorative treat in the morning as well as at the end of the day.

If in doubt about your skincare needs get advice, plenty of which is available for free. Ask for trial-size samples or travel-size products so you can test how well products work for you.

MAKE-UP

Don't wince at the suggestion that you should *wear make-up every day to work*. I do know that many working women bristle at the assertion that make-up is fundamental to a successful image. But that's the way it is. We are part of a very visual world and women are judged, in part, on their grooming. You can ignore this fact on principle or you can put in a little effort every day that will make your job influencing others all that much easier.

10 minutes for 8 hours' impact

If you haven't learned what suits you, how to apply it and achieve a lasting effect in less than 10 minutes then it is time that you did. You owe it to yourself.

Everyone is individual when it comes to a make-up routine. Colour choice is key but if you work with your natural colouring and build a wardrobe that interchanges easily then certain shades of make-up should work with everything – that's if you don't enjoy perusing the beauty counters and experimenting.

But few of us aren't dazzled when we see the effects of a great makeover. Often, it is hard to believe that it is the same woman. After years of doing makeovers, working with colours and fashion, revamping hairstyles – it is the make-up that makes the real difference. A new hairstyle has little impact on a bare face. Ditto for a great new outfit. Are you cheating your image, raising questions about your brand values because you take short cuts or are inconsistent with your grooming?

If you are in any doubt about your make-up, book an appointment with a beauty advisor for a fresh approach to how you are doing things. Bring along your current cosmetics and check the colours against what they have used. Only purchase new bits that you like and don't duplicate what you already own. But a beauty counter makeover washes off at the end of the day. For best results, visit a beautician or image consultant who can teach you how to do the techniques yourself.

Insider tips for long-lasting make-up

A few products and techniques are worth mentioning here for women who despair with their make-up 'evaporating' after a few hours. Here are my top 5 tips:

- *Apply make-up after moisturiser has settled.* Your make-up will smear and not last unless your moisturiser and/or sunscreen is totally absorbed. After you put it on, get dressed, then start your colour cosmetics for best effects.
- *Use a make-up base for a perfect complexion* for up to 8 hours. Apply specially formulated make-up bases (Boots, Laura Mercier) after moisturiser before your foundation. Used sparingly, a make-up base holds the foundation for hours. Don't fear a mask-like effect. Your foundation just looks as fresh late in the day as it did in the morning.
- *Use a cream blush (or lipstick as a blush) over foundation,* under powder to brighten the face. Use high on the cheekbones to bring the attention towards your eyes.
- *Eye base is as effective as make-up base* and prevents shadows from streaking or fading, plus you use far less eyeshadow. Try Color Me Beautiful, Body Shop or Laura Mercier.
- *Use lip pencil as a lip base.* Use all over the mouth (not just as an outline), then apply lipstick or lip gloss.

Make-up drawer feng shui

Uncluttering your make-up drawer not only makes you feel more organized and able to *find* what you want much more quickly in the morning but it also protects you from getting infections that harbour in old, stale cosmetics. Throw out anything that you haven't used for 6 months as you are unlikely to again. Sniff all lipsticks for freshness. If they smell of anything they are probably well-past their use-by date. Wash make-up sponges after use and puffs inside your compacts every week. Sharpen pencils before use to scrape off any developing bacteria and toss out mascara over 3 months old (these are real breeding grounds for germs).

Handbag grooming essentials:
- Powder/foundation compact with mirror
- Natural lip pencil + gloss + lipstick
- Styling comb
- Cuticle/hand cream/emery board
- Tissues/hankie
- Spare tights

These are all that you really need to carry around. The powder foundation is best for touching up or for a total refresh of the face later in the day (e.g. when you are going to an evening event straight from work). If you apply a good mascara in the morning it should last all day. If you look pale, use your lipstick as a crème blush for some colour. Lip pencils and lipsticks can be worn alone or together; gloss is great for adding oomph, or can be worn just over pencil for a fresh, natural look. A styling comb is better than a brush for short to medium hair; longer hair requires a brush. Finally, a cuticle and/or hand cream plus emery board are important because you invariably notice nails, cuticles and hands in desperate condition during the day. At night, you are too busy with other things. So, keep these tools handy!

P.S. On grooming – never do so in public. Few things are sillier than a woman putting on make-up in a meeting or at the end of a meal in a restaurant. Always try to sort yourself out ahead of time. If you hate your lips looking bare after a meal, use lip liner all over as a base prior to putting on lipstick, this way your lips retain lipstick and colour for longer. But if you do need to do some urgent repairs, retreat to the ladies' and return looking and feeling refreshed, back on centre stage.

HANDS AND NAILS

Your hands are central to communication so if yours aren't well groomed we tend to focus on the chipped varnish, bitten nails and rough skin.

Some women are blessed with good nails whilst others have to make more of an effort just to keep them in shape. Keep an emery board, nail oil and hand cream in your desk drawer for last-minute repairs. If you are prepared to put in the effort, wearing coloured nail varnish can be attractive, particularly in more relaxed sectors. In male-dominated companies, however, women might want to negate the potential distraction of coloured talons by using a French manicure which is timeless and professional.

FRAGRANCE

Fragrance is both a personal and, nowadays, political issue. We have all been both repulsed and charmed by different scents in our lives and what we consider lovely can be awful to another. However, how you smell – whether it be fresh, stale, pleasant or off-putting – is part of your image.

Suffice to say that being clean every day – free of odours – is the minimum requirement. Body odour can result from not washing (of course) but also from perspiring afresh on to stale clothes. New sweat on old sweat produces the stink! So your clothes need to be as fresh as you are for you to be pleasant company.

Beyond cleanliness comes fragrance. Here's where things can get political. There are women who are offended at the suggestion of masking their body smell. Fair enough. Just make sure that your natural odour isn't odorous!

For the rest of you, who enjoy a lovely smell on others as well as yourself, I commend you for bothering for a great fragrance can enhance your image with both sexes. The guideline should be that the fragrance is a 'daytime' scent . . . not one meant to seduce! Musky, very heavy floral scents are just as beautiful but the smell can be inappropriate for business (it's hard to concentrate when they are wafting around) and can put others off . Examples are many of the beautiful Guerlain scents like Shalimar, Mitsouko and L'Heure Bleue as well as the more obvious ones like Passion, Giorgio, White Diamonds and Rive Gauche. Opt instead for light, citrus-based or floral fragrances that are refreshing and you will be a pleasure in everyone's company. Try Eternity, Allure, Hermes 24 Faubourg as well as most scents from Floris and Antonia's Flowers.

TEETH

Teeth, we notice. They are a focus when you communicate and can interfere with your message if they are problematic.

Dental care is basic hygiene. You need to brush *at least* twice daily; three times (i.e. after lunch) if you have an important meeting. If you brush your teeth unconscious of any methodology, it's time to invest in an electric toothbrush. These gadgets do the work for you and improve the state of your teeth as well as your gums within 2 months.

We all know that we should use floss but few of us are dedicated to the task. Put your pack of floss by the sink and then do it every time you wash. Flossing in bed, when accompanied, is not nice; nor is doing so in the car or anywhere you can be seen.

Breath fresheners and mouthwash should be kept handy for emergencies (like encounters after you've had several cups of coffee or after a spicy lunch). Bad breath makes for bad deals.

A fit brand

You don't need a lecture on the importance of being fit and healthy. You know that it is vital to, well, your vitality. But so too is your fitness vital to your brand.

We have all worked with people who have lost the edge in business sometimes because they have lost the edge with their fitness. Keeping yourself in good condition not only affects your self-confidence (go on, admit it. You feel a million times better when you are your target weight and active). Being fit conveys that you are also sharp, able to go the distance, firing on all cylinders.

Assumptions are rife about the overweight and the unfit. I hear them every day in my seminars when the issue of health and fitness comes up – totally erroneous opinions much of the time and certainly unfair. But, none the less, people assume that if you move slowly you think slowly. If you can't discipline yourself with food and drink, you aren't a disciplined worker who can keep to schedules and deliver. If others are worried about your health and your being able to cope with pressures they start to make excuses for you. Once that happens, you can be marginalized out of the power-loop.

If you feel that your fitness is letting your image down it *must* be a priority for sorting. Follow my tips on dress, making sure that the fit of your clothes is right for your size *now*, not your ideal size. Reflect on how you can energize your behaviour in the short term until you really are able to *be* more energetic once you get on a fitness regime and eat more sensibly.

The right image for the right occasion can help you achieve your desired impact – not to mention basic objectives – faster. Don't be complacent because no one has criticized your appearance. Be pro-active to ensure it projects the third, not the second, millennium.

6

LOOKING THE PART: MEN

Let's get personal

Working as an image consultant has innumerable rewards; one of the chief being that we get to advise men on very personal subjects. Hands down, the subject men are most vulnerable about is how they look. Don't ask me why. We can tackle issues like aggressive behaviour or inept presentation skills with minimal emotion but nothing seems to unsettle a guy faster than discussing how he looks – how to deal with his receding hairline, what to do about weak shoulders, short legs, a double-chin, blotchy skin, etc.

Image issues aren't discussed in locker rooms, at the pub or in small talk before a meeting unless there are women around. If women are present, it's OK to banter about John's new haircut or admire another man's suit or tie. But in a group of guys on their own, it won't be *you* that says anything first. You can't be seen to notice these things let alone want to discuss them.

There are certain image subjects that are safe – like shirts, ties, glasses – and others that are *your deep dark secret* causing real concern, even turmoil. You've been dying to talk about it to someone but the hairdresser, sales assistant or your boyfriend/girlfriend – the ones closest to the problem – you don't consult. Or, if you do, you don't believe them. Too often I've heard, 'My wife suggested I try that, but I didn't take any notice.' Or, 'A sales assistant once said the same thing but he was only interested in selling me a suit.' Whatever the reason, you always assume an ulterior motive.

With an image consultant, you get straight-shooting. We tell you honestly what we see as issues and challenges and give you the options for sorting them out. An initial consultation in one of our studios takes about 3 hours, then we schedule a shopping trip. The purpose of taking you shopping is to: show you how to interpret our advice so that you can shop with more confidence in future; introduce you to the best brands and services available near you and within your budget; and, ensure you return a 'new and improved' model. The process is efficient and fun and, usually, doesn't require remortgaging your home!

WHAT IT TAKES

You like formulas, right? 'Just tell me what to wear, what to do,' is a familiar request. A male request. Sorry, but in this chapter there are no formulas: wear this suit with this shirt and tie; or, chuck the suits and dazzle 'em in this smart casual number. *It is your brand you are working on.* And as with developing every other aspect of your influencing skills – your behaviour, your voice, your presentation skills, etc. – you have to develop *your own* image.

A good image requires a bunch of things to work well. Here are a few:

- The look is *you*, not someone else.
- You are what we expect, at minimum.
- At best, you are *more* than what we expect.
- You look comfortable.
- Your grooming is impeccable, but seemingly effortless.
- Nothing jars.
- Nothing's contrived.
- The fine touches are just that, *fine*.
- Looks like the gear has been chosen with care. But, once on, forgotten (not fussed) about.
- You look now, not yesterday. But you also look timeless.
- We want to know you *because* of how you look, before you open your mouth.

The brand revisited

To help you visualize yourself in terms of your brand values, make a note of them again here. As we work through the concepts and suggestions keep reminding yourself of these values, questioning how they might project what you want.

My image needs to reflect:

- ....
- ....
- ....
- ....
- ....
- ....
- ....
- ....

ENVISION THE VALUES

With those values in your head, sit back, close your eyes and now imagine *what they look like*. I know that they are descriptive values, possibly intangible ones, but just try to think how you could express them by how you look.

If one of your brand values is *intelligent*, how can you dress *intelligently*? This won't require looking like the absent-minded professor, rather looking *interesting*; perhaps paying attention to fine details like your personal organizer or the bag in which you carry your papers, or your tie being unlike any of your colleagues'. If a brand value is to look *global*, ask yourself what about your image is too traditional or too British, or German or American, whatever? A global look is easy to achieve. It means taking some interesting bits from many cultures and putting them together well. We're not talking national costume stuff here. Envision this: an Armani raincoat over a Boss sports jacket, Gap jeans and T-shirt with Paraboot boots, Tag-Heuler watch, Tumi laptop-backpack, Mont Blanc pen – you catch my drift.

In turn, take each of your values and dress them. Work on everything from your hairstyle, your glasses, formal or casual clothes, your watch, pen, carrying gear, etc. See if you can see a composite image that embodies all the values collectively.

The corporate image

Now, back to reality with a bump. For readers who are currently
employed or if you have your eye on a new business opportunity, write
down the buzz words that comprise the corporate identity. What messages are you trying to get across to your customers about the company? What comes across loud and clear from company advertising,
the corporate literature? List, in no particular order, the corporate
values under which you currently (or hope to) work:

- ....
- ....
- ....
- ....
- ....
- ....
- ....
- ....

Measure your current dress sense, personal style and overall image
against these corporate values. How do you compare your image
against your peers – about the same? Better? Worse?

DRESS FOR THE COMPANY AS WELL AS THE JOB

The globe-trotting investment banker has a different image to project
to the e-commerce pioneer working from a cabin in the woods. Just
as internal marketing teams dress differently to the IT staff or directors
dress differently to managers, there is a *need for difference*. Hence, your
job is to fit in while standing out!

If you are in the market for a new job, part of your research should
include the corporate culture. Smart people do their homework prior
to a job interview. They get a good brief on the company and the

key people they will be meeting and have prepared answers to likely questions. But the focus is generally more on selling your background and skills than conveying how you will fit into the corporate culture. An important way to do this is to dress the part, look like the person that they want.

In Chapter 1, we discussed the importance of first impressions. Nowhere is this more important than in a job interview. Research that I did with the financial recruitment consultants Robert Half International confirms that recruiters and personnel directors are very subjective in initial interviews. 'I know that I should look at all the data, the CV, the psychometric tests that we use and I do to a larg extent. But if I am honest, in the end I go with my gut,' said one director of human resources who reiterated the views of most involved in making hiring decisions. And recruiters all have their particular bugbear. For many it is facial hair, i.e. nasty moustaches and beards, for others it is the colour of the suit or the pattern on the tie. It is extraordinary how recruiters 'type' people. They deny it, of course. It's not politically correct or fair. But they do.

The fact that you get an interview means that you are capable of doing the job. The interview will determine, among other things, whether or not you will fit into the culture. A main indicator that you will fit in is that you 'look like one of us' already.

Hence, prior to any job interview, go to the offices (in disguise if you want or send a proxy to suss the look of the people). Lunchtime is good to see a cross section of staff coming and going. How do they dress? Can you differentiate the senior people from the more junior staff or are they all interchangeable? What *does* distinguish people? How well-groomed are the men? How do they comport themselves? Do staff seem informal, very friendly or are they more traditional and reserved?

The building and office design also shape the corporate culture. How open plan are the offices? Does everyone have their personal cubbyhole? Are there comfortable areas where staff can congregate? How accessible are the offices? Are they 'sealed-off', with many layers of security protecting the inner sanctum? Physical structures can shape the corporate culture as much as the people. Watch how people interact within the environment to get a feel for the corporate behaviour and style.

Some powerful signals, about how you can influence and fit into an organization where you want to work, are there in the corporate lobbies and reception areas.

Don't follow standard advice to wear a dark suit, white shirt and blue tie to any job interview! You can look boring, inappropriate, overdressed or underdressed (if not the same quality as everyone else!). Tailor the image to suit the company. You can ignore this advice only if you have three things:

- A dazzling personality
- Glowing references
- Rare skills in high demand

Otherwise, do your lobby surveillance before any job interview.

Your personal image audit

Rate yourself against your peers to determine the state of your personal style. Try to be as honest as possible. If British, don't play down your strengths if you know you are first rate at something. If French, Italian or American, ask yourself if you really are really *that* good.

Give yourself 1 point for every tick that is on par with peers, 2 points for everything that is above average, and 3 points for everything that is first rate.

Image factor	a liability	on par with peers	above average	first rate
Body basics				
fitness	❏	❏	❏	❏
posture	❏	❏	❏	❏
weight/figure	❏	❏	❏	❏
Grooming				
skin	❏	❏	❏	❏
make-up	❏	❏	❏	❏
hands/nails	❏	❏	❏	❏
hairstyle	❏	❏	❏	❏
teeth	❏	❏	❏	❏
hygiene	❏	❏	❏	❏
Personal style				
colour sense	❏	❏	❏	❏
style/fashion sense	❏	❏	❏	❏
fit	❏	❏	❏	❏
quality	❏	❏	❏	❏
overall look	❏	❏	❏	❏
Accessories				
glasses	❏	❏	❏	❏
watch	❏	❏	❏	❏

shoes	❑	❑	❑	❑
briefcase	❑	❑	❑	❑
diary/organizer	❑	❑	❑	❑
pen	❑	❑	❑	❑

Less than 15 points

This book was a smart purchase. You need advice and are on the road creating a more credible image by reading this and, hopefully, every chapter in the book. If you feel unable to put the advice into action yourself, please call an image consultant to take you shopping until you get the hang of things yourself.

16 to 35 points

Your image is letting you down mainly because you don't care enough. Don't fear losing your masculinity by reading this chapter carefully and taking on board valid suggestions to get your act together because, dear reader, it is anything but!

36 to 50 points

You know that personal presentation is important and, over the years, have taken steps to improve your look. However, time pressures and other reasons have meant that you've let yourself slide in some respects. Read carefully, noting where you are slipping off course and get back on track to do yourself justice.

Over 51 points

OK, you are a star. But, don't let it go to your head. You've got your act well and truly together and are, no doubt, the envy of all the guys you work with. Don't lower your standards to their level. You are already dressed for your next promotion. Read this chapter thoroughly to ensure that it is in the bag.

Looking the business

In this wild and woolly, high-tech, entrepreneurial era many of us still go off to formal offices where the bosses wear suits and you risk your job if you dress down. Big business know that they aren't as sexy or often as much fun as start-up enterprises but they don't care – they are big, multi-million/billion/trillion operations with global networks and anyone who wants to be in on the action had better look the part, according to the big power guns. That accepted, let's get down to the basics in looking like serious business.

But dress codes are relaxing. So the goal is to *dress for today* – the situation, the audience, the people you need to influence. Your wardrobe needs different armour for different battles. You need power suits to knock 'em dead when meeting with other 'suits'. A 'soft' modern suit is the bee's knees at an industry conference or for a smart lunch. Sports jackets and trousers – the smart casual thing – are equally important to your power suits and need to be chosen with equal care. The really dressed-down stuff for office-bound days should not be scruffy and so present an inconsistent image with what you project on other days.

Professional is a four-letter word – suit

No, it's not old-fashioned. Even at the beginning of the twenty-first century to look professional requires a suit. Don't flip. It doesn't mean overly tailored, pin-striped, tie-throttling collared numbers – not necessarily. The suit has changed. If you didn't realize it and have pretty much been wearing the dull, dark numbers with only white shirts then, surely, retirement must be round the corner. Because that look is well past its sell-by date.

SO, WHAT SUITS?

The good news is that you have many options in choosing a power suit – different styles, different prices, different effects. Considerations for selection are based on the following:

- *The raw material:* that's you – your build, height, size, and challenges.
- *The desired effect:* how classic/modern/ fashionable; how sharp or laid-back a look.
- *Durability:* how demanding you will you be on it. How much recovery it requires, and you are prepared to give it, between wearings.
- *Price:* we all have a budget but your notion of a good investment might need reconsideration.

THE RAW MATERIAL: YOUR VITALS

If your raw material is in good shape – you are fit, average to tall, Mr 42R – then shopping can be a snap. Your choice of suit will come down to personal taste and price.

If, however, you are not an easy fit here are a few things to be mindful of when choosing suits.

Style

- *English suits*, while more classic and traditional, compensate more for 'figure-faults' than any other cut. More formal than modern suits.
- *Euro-style/modern suits* vary in style (and, therefore, can confuse) more than English suits. Some seasons they are big and baggy, then they are figure-hugging. Soft and deconstructed, i.e. less tailored than traditional suits and a must for every modern guy's wardrobe.
- *Double-breasted suits* can be stylish but not on the portly or the short. The button configuration over the midriff creates extra bulk and width. Hence, if this is where you carry your extra kilos, single-breasted will be a better choice.
- *Single-breasted suits* make you look taller and leaner so great on all guys with exceptions being those already tall and lean (who look like beanpoles in SB suits). Three-buttoned styles make you look taller and are more modern than the two-button jobs which are more classic.

Jackets

- *Six-button DB jackets:* leave the bottom button undone (when you button-up).
- *Three-button SB jackets:* button the middle or top two buttons (never all three).
- *Ventless jackets:* best on neat, not protruding butts.
- *Double-vented jackets:* more considerate on ample derrières; dapper on neat ones. Very English.
- *Sloping shoulders* need help. Hence, choose a naturally

padded shoulder and one not cut too neatly (e.g. extending 1–2 cms off the shoulder).

- *Short men* must watch the jacket length – just a centimetre or two below the buttocks; any longer can make you appear shorter (not the objective). Also, forget turn-ups on your trousers.
- *Full-figured fellas* can wear DB suits open to cover the girth (but only old farts do this). Better to find a good cut/label in SB to look slimmer. Discard any jacket that buttons at your fullest point.
- *Centre vents* should never be taxed, i.e. spread open when buttoned. They accommodate ample backsides best.
- *Collars* should fit neatly around the neck. Sit down when trying the suit on; if it gapes it needs adjustment. Turn the collar over and check to see if sewn by hand. It should look slightly uneven which proves it has been sewn across someone's lap to hug your neck. A straight seam is machine-made and doesn't hug.

Trousers
- *Pleated suit trousers:* allow ample thigh movement but add bulk. The choice is yours.
- *Flat-fronted trousers* are for the young and trim.

For a suit to look its best, follow my top 10 tips:

- *Forget the size, concentrate on the fit.* The jacket should be comfortable when buttoned. If your weight fluctuates get re-measured every time you buy a suit, or be realistic and be sure you have clothes that actually fit for both your fuller and trimmer times.
- *Carry the minimum inside the jacket;* nothing in the

external pockets (aside from the breast pocket (silk hankie or glasses). Internal jacket pockets are for a slim billfold wallet and/or organizer.

- *Wear your trousers at your waist* which is a cm or two below the navel (not near the hips). Keep them there with a belt or braces, but never both.
- *Sleeve and trouser lengths make or break the effect of the suit.* If you aren't perfect, spend the extra money to make sure that they are.
- *The width of the lapel should suit the width of the tie.*
- *Power suits are only variations of blues or greys* or colours that pass as one of them. Brown, green and plum suits are dodgy. Black suits are for funerals or dudes who are both minimalists and very cool.
- *Lace up shoes are the most formal way to complete a suit.* That said, you can take the edge off a formal look with smart, more modern alternatives like slip-ons, the half-boot or side-buckled styles. Trainers are only acceptable as a mode of transport and should be changed when at the office.
- *Rest your suits between wearing.* Store in a trouser press at the end of the day then rehouse in the wardrobe on a wooden hanger. Hang trousers waist down (the weight of the waist uses gravity to pull out wrinkles). Decant all pockets of receipts, stubs, coins daily.
- *Air suits a couple of times a year* (outdoors/in the shower room: steam always helps to relax the wrinkles in the fabric). Dry clean only 3 times a year to extend the suit's life.
- *A new suit deserves new shirts and ties.* Link colours but vary the scale in the patterns when mixing them (i.e. not all skinny, small designs or a bunch of big patterns competing).

The desired effect

Try to define a classic suit and you get a variety of explanations depending upon the country that you are in, the age of the man, and the sector in which he might work. To an American, the Ralph Lauren label typifies the best of their classic look (although originally modelled on the English suit). In Britain, the classic suit is best typified by Savile Row offerings (or Marks & Spencer knock-offs); in Italy the answer is really contingent on the generation – D'venza, Brioni or Canali for the over 40, Armani for the under 40.

Whatever look you desire, be it classic or modern or fashionable, the goal is to complete the look. If you are going to risk having both classic and modern style clothes be prepared to spend serious money in getting the right stuff to go with the right look. Nothing jars more than a mishmash of styles. Throwing odd bits together only works on fashion shoots and is laughable to consider for wearing to work. Chances are that you spend milliseconds getting up, dressed and out in the morning. So, it is probably wise to get a sense of what goes with what and stick to it for a consistent and well-dressed image.

CLASSIC/TRADITIONAL EFFECTS

A classic look starts with fit and ends with finish. Classic clothes are well-tailored, fit the body neatly (not snugly or loosely) and look formal, i.e. a 'buttoned-up', sharp effect.

Suiting fabric for a classic look has less strength and fewer wrinkles than less formal or even European-style suits. The cloth itself is sterner stuff – worsted wool, super 100s or 120s – but the weight doesn't have to be heavy. Indeed, even in the northern Hemisphere a suit heavier than 10oz is too much for most offices.

Mr Classic doesn't like wrinkles. Therefore, a decent internal suit 'chassis' made of horsehair will give him the smoothness he requires. To look modern, however, choose classic tailoring that has been updated and has some drape to the fabric. If it looks too sharp it will look militaristic.

CLASSIC SHIRTS

It is important to choose traditional shirts when wearing a classic suit. Labels like Pink, Turnbull & Asser, Charles Thyrwitt, Hathaway, Ralph Lauren, Stephens Brothers do the job nicely. Best quality Egyptian cotton will impress your CEO but is expensive and not as hard-wearing as basic poplin. Easycare shirts are fine provided you don't take wash and wear instructions literally (always iron!).

Further tips for choosing shirts to complete a classic look:

Colours and patterns
- When in doubt choose white. If you have red hair or freckles your white is ivory.
- Plain blue shirts are the second safe choice.
- Pink, lilac and yellow are the only pastel alternatives to blue for classic suits (green, peach, grey, etc. are Euro-suit options).
- Classic suits look modern with patterned blue shirts (fine checks, herringbone, pin-dots, etc.).
- Monograms on shirts require forgiveness and understanding (oh, he's American).

Cut and fit
- Standard fit shirts are looser and longer and better with a classic suit.
- Plackets (the strip of fabric on which buttons are sewn) should have a seam either side of the buttons. One seam is a cheap shortcut.

- The yoke (across the shoulders) should be a double panel, hence sewn in the middle. A single yoke is another cheap shortcut.

Sleeves and cuffs

- Short-sleeved shirts should never be considered with a classic suit – any time of the year. Cotton shirts breathe, 10oz suits are light and also breathe; hence, forget the excuse that you wear them to be cool. You'll be anything but if you do.
- Rolling up your sleeves to be cooler is cool.
- Double cuffs are dapper with a classic suit. Make sure 2cm of cuff show out of suit sleeve.
- Single cuffs that try to be cute and have buttons and holes (for cufflinks) are sad.
- If your cufflinks try to be too witty we know that they are making up for your own personality. (The same is true for red or funny socks.)

Collars

- Button-down collars don't work with DB suits.
- Button-downs are easier on full, thick or short necks.
- Button-downs never have a 'wow' effect.
- Cutaway/spread collars cut a dash but best on average to long (not short) necks.
- Band (grandad) collars take the formal edge off a suit. Don't button top button.
- Collars with stays require them to prevent points from curling (so don't throw them away and get spares in case they get lost).

Care

- Wrinkles in a shirt are acceptable at the end, not the beginning, of the day.

- Shirts should be worn once and then laundered.
- Frayed collars, intransigent stains and grey discolouration suggest it is shirt burial time.

TIES

Your tie is the first indication of your personality before you open your mouth. Hence, choose yours with care and consider the messages that they send and to whom. What percentage of your tie collection has not been chosen by you? That's frightening! OK, fewer women are colour-blind (30 per cent of men are) but we chose ties for really silly reasons:

- *Pierce Brosnan wore a tie like this in . . .*
- *I've been looking for curtains just like that.*
- *Oh, I remember having a sundress/scarf/blouse like that 10 years ago. I loved it.*
- *That's pretty!*

Do you really want to wear something chosen for you on these grounds? Floral ties, so popular in the late 90s, were fashionable because women bought them and men were stupid enough to wear them! A man who wears daisies all day probably cries on the way home from work. Sorry, that's what a daisy tie screams.

Think of the messages your ties send. If you can't 'read' them, get someone to help you. You might not get it, but the rest of us do.

Further tips on choosing ties to complete a classic look:

Width and knot
- The width of the tie should be consistent with your lapels.
- Half-Windsor knot does the job for most collars.

- Full-Windsor is the business with spread collars and DB suits (but not full, short necks).
- Bow ties require personality and an extrovert nature.

Colour and pattern
- Link the colours in your tie to your shirt, suit or both.
- If the pattern in your suit is bold the tie should be plain or an almost indistinguishable pattern.
- If your suit and/or shirt are plain or have fine patterns a bold tie is interesting.
- Stripes *can* be worn with stripes if they are of a different size.
- Vertical and bold horizontal stripes are silly with a classic suit (again, they belong on Euro-man); but subtle, horizontal stripes just pass.

Fabric and make
- Woven silk ties are more formal and good for evening; plain silk is for daytime.
- Designer silk ties can be striking (to women, 'pretty') but don't hold a knot well.
- Pretty, designer ties are more for Euro-man.
- Your tie wardrobe needs variety. All Hermés or Gucci is unimpressive despite the dent in your bank balance.
- Don't save ties after 5 years. They will never look great again.

POCKET HANKIES

Very British, indeed, and when done well add great panache to a classic suit. The American version of the crisply folded white hankie does not count and should be avoided unless you want to do TV commercials for denture adhesives.

The great Jermyn Street tailors Turnbull & Asser have won me over with the advantages of the pocket hankie. Don't think that you have to be middle-aged and portly to wear them. They are dapper on men who like to stand out from the crowd and want a dash of extra style and personality.

Tips on wearing a pocket hankie:

- Never match to the tie or buy in a set.
- Co-ordinate colours with the tie (which should link with shirt and suit).
- If patterned, should be different scale (larger or smaller) than tie pattern.
- Tails sticking out is OTT; make a 'poof' with tails in, centre sticking out.
- Don't fuss with it.
- Don't blow your nose with it!

Modern/European-style suits

Twenty-five years ago, it was easy to distinguish the Euro-style suit from both the British and American styles. Mr Armani took all the lining out of his jackets, let them drape like a cardigan and other men's wear designers took note. The French would only go so far in looking relaxed and eased their designs to end up somewhere between the English and the Italians. The Germans did things their own way – perhaps in the need of new 'architecture' altogether to accommodate their more amply-proportioned, 'baby-boomer' men.

But today presents a confused picture for the average bloke to decipher. You have British labels doing Euro-suits (Next, Austin Reed, Marks & Spencer), Italians doing English suits (Brioni, D'venza) even the Swedes are into the English look (Oscar Jacobson) along with the Americans (Ralph Lauren). Then Italian labels like Canali and Valentino do French-style suits!

So rather than try to guess what a label is by the sound of it, learn what to look for and chose a suit for what it does for you. You might grow to like a certain label, finding that the cut and tailoring suit well and you like the quality. Then the next time you go shopping the collection looks foreign. You think, 'What the hell has happened?' Well, fashion happens and without warning your loose-fitting, comfy-cut suit is now all tight and fitted. You grew to like double-breasted suits but can't find them any more. Or, there are now so many more buttons to contend with, then before you know there are only one or two on jackets.

THAT'S MODERN, MATE!

The difference between a classic business suit and others is that the latter change – they are more fashionable and reflect how many businessmen of today want to dress. In recent years, with many companies adopting dress-down Fridays, if not going the full hog with casual dress codes, men who still wanted to impress hung on to their suits but changed the style from buttoned-up, tailored, classic styles to more modern, deconstructed suits.

Many readers are getting savvy about fashion changes and have learned a lot about different labels and how to put looks together that work, for work. Others are still confused and feel great frustration when shopping. The following advice is for you, my friend. Because shopping should be fun, satisfying and productive. If you haven't experienced 'Shopping Nirvana', a good personal shopper or image consultant can show you how.

Tips for choosing modern suits:

Fit and cut

- Find a label that suits your size and scale. Some suit smaller guys, some big chaps.
- Short guys always get a short-fitting; don't buy a suit if you can't. Shortening sleeves and trouser cuffs does not make a suit fit on a short guy.
- The fit should be comfortable but tailored; look good buttoned or unbuttoned. If you look like a sack of potatoes in the suit you need more tailoring. As you will wear with sports as well as T-shirts, a neater fit will be more useful than one that is overly generous.
- Experiment with new fabrics avoiding those that shine or cling – silky suits are for clubbing, not business.

Jacket

- Jackets might be quite long. Even if you aren't short, try on a short-fit jacket to see if the scale is better on you.
- Whatever your height, the button (you should

actually button) had better not be at your fullest point or you will look fatter than you are. If it is, get another style or label.

- If the jacket is ventless, check out your butt in a 3-way mirror. If you could carry a tray of drinks there, find a vented option.
- Sleeves are longer on modern suits but knuckle-dusters are not effective.
- High-buttoning SB jackets make a guy look taller but might be too cute for business.
- Low buttoning is best on tall chaps.

Trousers
- Voluminous trousers can make you look short and chubby.
- The trousers require a belt if there are loops. But never wear braces with a modern suit.

CHOOSING SHIRTS, TIES AND SHOES FOR MODERN SUITS

You can make your suit look very sharp and professional if you team it with a business, albeit not too classic, shirt. If in doubt about what goes with it, get advice when buying the suit. Often the designer/label have a selection of shirts that are supposed to go with the suit. If you like the suit but the shirts are over the top, here's some advice:

Cut and fit
- Shirt collars for modern suits can have a looser fit than with a classic suit. Not so loose, though, that you look like you have a wasting disease.
- Longer, pointed collars look great. As do many button-down, band collars and relaxed shirts.
- As to sports, T-shirts and fine knitwear, only wear

knits and T-shirts (for work) if your chest is toned. Sadly, many guys don't appreciate this.

- If wearing a tie, it should be soft silk, weave, knit, linen, etc. if the suit and shirt are soft. If the suit is more substantial (e.g. moleskin/corduroy in winter) you need a heavier tie. Classic ties won't work.
- Slip-on shoes, boots, suede or leather, sandals or sneakers are all viable with many modern suits. The only shoes that aren't are brogues.

Colour
- Buy a range of colours (flattering and appropriate) when you buy the suit to change the look.
- The same colour in your trousers and shirts/tops will make you look smarter, taller and thinner.
- You'll get the same effect wearing colours tone-on-tone, i.e. varying tones of the same colour.
- Wearing the same colour all the time (e.g. black, beige) has been done. Make that overdone.

Durability

How long a suit will serve you is dependent on a few things:

- The fabric and construction
- How you use and/or abuse it
- How you take care of it

Be as shrewd about the choice of fabric, tailoring and detailing when you buy a suit as you are about the colour and the style. The fabric choice should depend upon the feel and drape of it as well as to its look and performance.

Put the fabric through its paces *before* you buy it. Scrunch up the sleeve and see how easily it bounces back. Load up the jacket pockets with your usual gear and check the drape of the suit. If the fabric just can't handle your wallet, consider a lighter wallet (edited down to essentials) or choose a more substantial fabric. Sit down, cross your legs, see how the trousers will perform. If the crotch gets hopelessly wrinkled maybe you need a different cut, a bigger size or different fabric.

Remember, some suits are *meant to look wrinkled* – that's their beauty. Summer-weight suits in particular are meant to look relaxed (especially modern, deconstructed styles). If this bothers you, choose one with some Lycra (just a touch) or made out of a cool wool (less than 10 oz to the square yard).

Interrogate sales people on the durability of a suit if durability is a chief concern. If you need your suits to look wonderful on a three-day business trip then ask which fabrics are best for that kind of wear. The best suit fabrics for travel are mohair, high-twist wool or wool crêpe.

GIVE 'EM A BREAK!

Your suits will look better (i.e. fab at every wearing) if you give them a rest between wearings – at least 24 hours. If you are a guy with a disposable suit mentality (this also applies to shoes) then you look a wreck most of the time. Your suits (and shoes) need recovery time to perform for longer.

If you don't own a trouser press (and you wear suits a lot) don't consider yourself grown-up. Sorry, but boys don't have trouser presses, men do. At the end of the day take out everything that you had in the pockets (to prevent damage and sagging). Hang your jacket over the moulded wooden hanger on the stand, allowing the jacket to stand like that for 24 hours – it lets it air and the fibres jump back into their normal springy state. Jamming jackets into the wardrobe, then shutting the door – after a hard day's work – is a serious offence!

Hang trousers from the cuffs allowing them to extend full length (this is after their 24 hours in the press when they have had creases restored). By the way, never put jeans in a trouser press nor iron a crease into them. If the woman in your life does this, review the relationship.

Price

This won't take long.

Simply put: you get what you pay for. Don't buy anything unless it thrills you and you look forward to wearing it. Including undies, not excluding socks. Cheap socks kill a suit – we notice them and register them. What messages do your socks send, hey? Ill-fitting underwear can also undermine (girls aren't the only ones who display VPL).

Spending good money on your clothes means you will take care of them properly. Just think of how you treat your favourite sweater, the cashmere one, as opposed to the 'bargains' you bought by the dozen.

If you care for your clothes, they will look twice what you paid for them. The converse, of course, is true.

It is smarter to invest in a £500 suit than buy two at £250. Sure, you get two suits for the price of one but you won't look, well, the business. Of course, a wardrobe full of quality suits isn't achievable overnight. But you have a long career ahead of you. Just think twice next time you might be inclined to go for the two-for-one option and spring for the one that is better quality. You won't regret it.

In summary, spend as much as you can – which is no less than you deserve!

Looking the business, going casual

OK, OK. The world's richest man has no dress sense. There has been a revolution in the last decade, driven by a geek industry, started by Chief Geek Bill Gates. With a bunch of bright kids they've changed the world. They have changed our lives with nifty, zippy technology but we still work long hours. Few of us work to live; we just work. And that's life for many of us at the start of the twenty-first century. But we're having a good time.

If work is our life (really, most of us aren't that one-dimensionally sad. It's just that with guys, I find being dramatic drives points home quicker) then we had better be comfortable and enjoy making our money. So, let's ditch the suits! Look at Bill Gates and the whole of Silicon Valley – the sartorially unconscious are running the world. So, why bother dressing up any more?

Loads of companies have jumped on the bandwagon. Not just the high-tech industries but most sectors, even some banks and law firms. They are going *smart casual* – an incongruous juxtaposition, but we get the point. Being *casual* means to be comfortable. Interpreting *smart* is the challenging bit. *Casual*, men get – it's in your genes to be in your jeans. *Smart*, now that's tricky.

FROM ONE UNIFORM TO ANOTHER

Wall Street is a good place to see smart casual in action, especially in the summer. Gone are many pin-striped and dark-suited uniforms of winter for a different uniform in the summer: chinos, blue Oxford-cloth button-down shirts, and deck shoes. Casual and comfortable, yes. Ditto tidy. But smart?

The who, what, where, when, why and how of smart casual dressing

I am going out on a limb here in laying down some guidelines on interpreting this smart casual thing. Suffice to say that I have seen it done brilliantly about 30 per cent of the time. The other 70 per cent who are dressing this way are putting no thought into their image and taking the smart casual policy as a licence to dress like a slob.

WHO

Anyone, at any level, can be professional dressed casually. Obviously, the more serious the business the more conservative we expect you to look. When coaching Barclays Bank's corporate risk managers on interpreting a new casual dress policy introduced by the bank, I told them to forget it. A business in trouble would have little confidence in a banker 'dressed-down'. They should look approachable, yes, but not *casual*. They wear their suits to meet with clients and dress casually in the office. A good compromise.

What might be a fine policy for back-room staff – e.g. telesales, operational, support teams, etc. – might not be appropriate for customer/client-facing people in certain businesses. Go back to your corporate identity. Take those values, in relation to the nature of your work, and ask yourself if your clients will have more or less or equal confidence in your abilities (and charges!) if you dress down? If in any doubt, don't risk it. Find a halfway point between being formally-suited and buttoned-up and casual dress. It does exist (see the How section).

WHAT

So what *is* smart casual? A definition won't work. See if you can visualize these guidelines:

Smart casual is . . .

- Immaculate grooming: that includes all ponytails and beards, fingernails but not toes – we don't want to see your toes
- Clean, pressed clothes
- Clothes in a genuinely viable condition – not well past their sell-by date
- Sports shirts; polo shirts and knits
- T-shirts (summer only) that are fresh, expensive and logo-free, worn out or tucked in, your choice
- Shackets – jackets with as much tailoring as a shirt – good for meetings
- Leather or suede jackets but not with matching trousers
- A jacket, when in doubt – like coming and going; meeting with the boss or clients
- Covered torsos, midriffs and armpits
- Belts (fabric, braided, casual) with trousers
- Trousers/jeans/pants that end at your shoes
- Cords, moleskins, twill, chino, woollen, linen, cotton trousers
- Socks and shoes
- Deck shoes: yes; trainers: no (unless the boss does)
- A pulled – not thrown – together look

Smart casual is not . . .

- Body piercing
- T-shirts in wintertime or with any stupid slogans, or unironed

- Anything sleeveless
- Shorts
- Torn clothes
- Sports clothes, i.e. for running, baseball, rugby, etc. gear
- Gardening clothes
- Beachwear
- Sandals: except in summertime and only if you have pedicures regularly

Ignore all of the above if you are the boss (this book is not for the boss, it's to help *you* become the boss!) or if career advancement is not a priority. But if it wasn't, I don't suppose you'd have bought this book!

WHERE AND WHEN

Smart casual is best in the office, when only colleagues and staff will see you. Think twice about dressing this way with clients. Better on your turf than on theirs; unless you know that they, too, dress down.

Dress up your smart casual look for the evening by choosing even smarter gear and possibly adding a jacket (just in case). When abroad, check to see if your version of dressing down is theirs (Americans, please note).

You'll have less luck getting an upgrade when flying if you are dressed casually. Why not wear your suit to check in then change before take-off?

Dressing down is more acceptable, and prevalent, in business in the summer months.

To influence someone who's older, show respect and dress more formally. Many over-50s just don't get it.

WHY

There are many reasons for choosing a casual style over a formal one. But my advice is to choose among the myriad of possibilities *in between the jogging suit and the power suit*. Hence, don't take full liberty and wear whatever you want. Your image is very important, even in a business culture that has a dressed-down code.

Looking relaxed is less threatening and, arguably, more creative. Without the restrictions of formal dressing you feel freer and, perhaps, act more openly. On the cerebral level, if you engage in brainstorming and problem-solving a good deal of the time, no doubt this is helped by being more comfortable. On the practical level, if you do not sit at a desk all day and get on the floor, climb things, fix things, run around generally, then more flexible clothes also make sense.

The big question mark about dressing down is if those you need to influence – perhaps, to convey capability, authority and power – will 'buy' you without any armour, i.e. the suit. Have to leave that ball in your court.

HOW

If you've been through the What section and not been too put off, here I want to give you some advice on putting together a smart casual look.

Selecting colours

You will have more liberty than you would in a formal business environment but don't take full liberties with colour. The more neutral the gear the sharper, more modern and more businesslike they will appear. Bright colours can be reserved for shirts and jumpers not for jackets, trousers or (God forbid) shoes.

A few principles on colours to look your best – healthy, approachable and professional:

DEEP COLOURING

- Dark hair; strong eyes; rich (not pale) skin tone
- e.g. Keanu Reeves, Johnny Depp, Lenny Henry, Rowan Atkinson, Ali G, Sylvester Stallone

Black, navy, charcoal and deepest (not golden) browns are great. Your white T-shirts should be as white as you can get them. For sweaters and polo shirts try rich shades like burgundy, teal, royal blue, yellow, forest or emerald green, rich purple. Chinos are best if taupe not khaki. Avoid light colours from head to toe. Dark colours are terrific.

LIGHT COLOURING

- Blond or grey hair, receding or bald; pale eyes (blue, grey or green); fair skin
- e.g. Chris Tarrant, Ade Edmonson, Duncan Goodhew, Sting, Paul Newman, Prince William, Harry Enfield

Light colours like pastels are best near your face. Tone with trousers that are a medium colour (beige, khaki, pewter, grey, denim). Very dark colours like black, navy and dark brown can look overwhelming so avoid in shirts. Medium shades of blue, soft reds, plum, aqua, turquoise, yellow, cocoa and spruce green are great in shirts and sweaters.

A caveat: if your colouring is light but you are a big bloke, you will look rather silly in light colours (especially head to toe). See Cool or Muted colouring for alternatives.

COOL COLOURING

- Ash (blond or brown), white or greying hair; blue or grey eyes; medium skin tone, no freckles

e.g. Omar Shariff, Bill Clinton, Sean Connery, George Clooney, Michael Aspel, Des Lynam

Light, medium and deep colours can be fine on you so long as they are *cool*, i.e. there isn't a hint of yellow in the undertone of the colour. All blues and greys are great. Your best browns will have pink in them, e.g. cocoa, or grey in them, e.g. pewter. Pink, plum and burgundy are your choice over peach, rust or terracotta. Avoid moss or olive greens in favour of jade or spruce.

A caveat: your grey/white hair is such an asset. Choose colours that make the most of it.

WARM COLOURING

- Hair is blond, red or auburn; any eye colour; skin has freckles or is golden brown

e.g. Charles Dance, Chris Evans, Mick Hucknall, John Hurt, Paul Gascoigne, David Letterman

Easy for you to look ill in the wrong colour. Never white, always ivory. Blue only if your eyes are blue; any shade of green or brown depending on your preference. Beige, khaki and stone are great basics. Warm types are the only ones who can wear orange, rust and terracotta successfully (if you want to, that is). Grey is less successful than brown. Choose navy if not too strong but soften with a warmer shade near your face. Black is only for funerals 'coz you'll look like death!

CLEAR COLOURING

- Medium to dark hair; bright blue, green or hazel eyes; clear skin
- e.g. Pierce Brosnan, Richard E. Grant, Prince Charles, Robbie Williams

Clear colours are your best, nothing sludgy or muddy. Your white should be crisp, never ivory; best navy: ink; best black: jet. Forget middling colours in favour of dark or light or bright shades like red, royal blue, purple, or emerald. Black denim is better than blue denim. Khaki is a non-event but stone is a good alternative.

MUTED COLOURING

- Medium brown hair; soft brown, blue or hazel eyes; skin – not light or dark
- e.g. Harrison Ford, Brad Pitt, Jay Kay, Matt Damon, Eric Clapton

Think elegant, not garish; soft not loud, when it comes to colour: rich, muted, Armani-esque colours like pewter, charcoal, khaki, berry shades, pastels that aren't insipid. Strong contrasts like black and white are horrid on you. Wear soft white not pure white. Monochromatic dressing (tone on tone) is better than bold contrasts. Patterns are best if indistinguishable.

■ Putting the look together

You are only getting safe advice in this section; basics that work every time. Once you master these and get loads of compliments, you will enter a new zone of sartorial competence. Then, it is over to you. Your job is to become fashion conscious, to watch trends, to pick up on some neat tricks others are trying and give them a go yourself. It's about going shopping when you don't *have* to just to see what's new. It means reading the occasional men's magazines. Not ones in brown wrapping or that are mainly about cars or computers or sports. Health magazines are good and some men's fashion mags are also not too scary for real guys to read. Better still, pop into quality men's stores and pick up catalogues of the new collections. These are far more practical and targeted at businessmen who are straight, mainly. We all know that gay guys have it over straights in the fashion stakes. Gays will buy this book but skip this chapter.

MIXING AND MATCHING

If your idea of a smart sports jacket is a navy blazer with brass buttons you are off the mark. OK. It's a classic and does 'take you anywhere' . . . with a yawning effect. If you are over 40 only wear a navy blazer with a smart sports shirt (never a business shirt) and jeans or chinos. Do not combine with grey flannels or you immediately become an old fart.

If you wear suits primarily, you only need two sports jackets that are viable and current: one for summer and another for the wintertime. Sure, plain colours go with more things but they can be pretty dull. Choose instead fine weaves or checks that have a variety of subtle colours in them that you can work with for shirts and trousers. The best weaves *are not discernible patterns*. If you can tell all the colours from 20 paces it is too loud. The softer and more muted the better.

Some guys like their sports jackets to work *hard* and double up as an outer jacket if and when the weather changes. If you do this, and wear sweaters underneath the jacket, remember to buy the jackets slightly larger. But you will never look chic or elegant in a loose jacket or with a bulky sweater underneath. The choice is yours.

When you buy a new jacket purchase a variety of new casual shirts and slightly dressier ones (e.g. Oxford cloth or such weaves) but never wear with a business shirt or, worse, double cuffs.

A good winter sports jacket should be able to work with trousers in fabric like wool gabardine, twill, worsted wool, moleskin, corduroy, chinos and denim. In summer, a jacket should be flexible enough to look good with: cool wool, denim, cotton, chinos and linen. If your jackets don't have this kind of flexibility then they aren't great investments; which is fine if you have money to burn. Special finishes, weird colours, new fabrics (e.g. microfibres, silk, etc.) make marginal investments in sports jackets.

KNITWEAR

Shirts made out of anything but cotton can be perplexing to men. But a smart casual wardrobe provides an opportunity to experiment with new fabrics and clothes that you, heretofore, have been oblivious to.

Fine knits and jerseys replace your shirts for a modern, relaxed look. Experiment with fit, labels and textures to find the ones that you like. If you are a sweaty sort of guy, consider wearing a vest under a knit jersey to absorb the perspiration and help on your dry-cleaning bills. Otherwise, it is important to do the whiff test whenever you attempt to wear a jersey a second or third time to be sure that you (and others) can take it. If in any doubt, wear a fresh top, and put that one in for cleaning.

Learn how to do your own hand-washing to save on dry-cleaning expenses and to help your knitwear look fresh. Most fine woollens and jersey, many knits and silks are fine when hand-washed. As this might be a new experience for you, some guidelines:

- Use a detergent made for hand-washing.
- The water should be lukewarm.
- Leave it to soak for 30–45 minutes.
- Give it a whish around.
- Drain; rinse in cold water.
- Squeeze, don't wring.
- Lay flat on a clean towel, then roll up.
- Leave it overnight to dry.
- Dry out on a clothes horse / sweater rack.
- Reshape and cool iron if needed.
- Better to fold knitwear, to keep the shape, rather than hang up.

SHOES

Your shoes are the key to turning a casual look into *smart*, so don't be casual in the choice of shoes. Quick tips:

- Leather soles are smarter than rubber soles.
- Rubber soles can be great (and practical) on quality styles. But not on trainers which are never smart, albeit, casual.
- Desert boots and suede shoes are great.
- Have both brown, black and oxblood shoes for casual.
- Espadrilles are beach, not office, shoes.
- Birkenstocks work, but flip-flops don't in the sandal department.
- Cowboy boots are unmentionable.

Accessories

It arrives with the grace of a Skoda . . . no matter how functional, it's naff. No, it is way beyond naff: it's unacceptable and if you own one take it to the scrap yard immediately for pulverizing. We're talking the ubiquitous vacuum-moulded (grey plastic!) briefcase with combination locks. Don't smirk smugly if you own the burgundy leather version. Equally naff. Carry either and you just announce your prime was 1977 and your hero is Reggie Perrin!

Accessories are tricky to get right but really important. You only need a few – a case, a good watch, and gizmos like your personal organizer, WAP cellphone and the like. Let's go through the basics and slide into the mod ones.

BRIEFCASES

Here's a minefield but it is easy to look smooth if you choose well – and a good case needn't cost the earth unless you really get one that's the business for business, like a proper black or tan stitched briefcase with brass fastenings (not combinations! Who wants your crummy files anyway?). The really traditional ones can set you back anywhere from £600 plus.

Choose a case according to the gear and according to how much you actually need to carry in the thing every day. Laptops need their own proper cases. By now, you should have upgraded to one that only weighs a couple of kilos max. or you will soon look like the Hunchback of Notre Dame. Tumi and other good luggage companies do the best versions for laptops which protect these expensive necessities better than other bags not specifically designed for the job.

Don't hesitate in getting a backpack if you commute by public transport or walk a lot. It will save your back and keep you hands-free for talking on the phone, reading the newspaper or grabbing a coffee on route. Have a smart leather file in the office to decant your papers for meetings. Lugging a backpack off to the clients doesn't make for a sleek entry. (The higher you rise the less you carry!) Black nylon cases are modern but will need replacing every 18 months as most can't take the pace.

WATCHES

Too many guys use their timepiece as a way to express their personality. Try not to deceive yourself here. Watches are for telling the time and being an elegant 'after-thought', not for showing off your deep-sea diving skills or your affinity with Daffy Duck. Gone are the days when people were impressed with a chunky Rolex. Leave them to used car salesmen.

Thankfully, elegant watches today are available for a song (£50+) so there is no excuse not to look smart with a simple timepiece.

CUFFLINKS

As discussed earlier, double-cuff shirts are both stunning and stylish. If you don't need to look so dapper every day, save them for special occasions . . . like when negotiating an overdraft (you'll look so successful that your financial problems must only be a hiccup), or for meeting with lawyers – they love them and notice them.

In fact, we all notice cufflinks, so choose well and choose your own. The coloured silk knots (£5) are sweet but make little impression. Here's where, I think, some attempt at wit is acceptable. Just avoid the Rolex equivalent in links with big gold jobbies with diamonds.

PERSONAL ORGANIZERS

Very important to have an updated organizer and to master the thing. The deciding factor is how much bulk you can handle (i.e. don't carry any Psion except for the Revo in your jacket; Palm-tops are better) and how adept you are on a mini-keyboard versus using a stylus and scribbling 'graffiti'. If adept at neither, a simple leather slimline diary that you write in (remember those) remains both dapper and practical. What looks very silly is to drag your desk diary around. They're called desk diaries because that's where they should stay!

CELLPHONES

My only advice on cellphones is two-fold:

- Choose a subtle but distinctive tone.
- Be religious in shutting the darn things off whenever you are with people that you want to impress or hope to see again soon!

Investment dressing to look the business

Back to branding yourself and how much investment might be required to look the part. It's up to you, your budget and your philosophy towards the subject of investment dressing. Suffice to say, by investing in your image you are investing in your career. Look the part before you get it so that salary increase or promotion is a foregone conclusion.

Your wardrobe is similar to your home – it keeps evolving and is never quite finished. Look at it as a journey rather than a destination and you will be more satisfied with each new sartorial sojourn along the way.

THE CODE

- £ little investment/no sweat
- ££ some investment/little sweat
- £££ serious stuff/take a deep breath

THE GEAR

£
- casual trousers £50+
- sports shirts £35+
- undies £8
- socks £5+
- wooden hangers £5+
- shoe trees £20+
- watch £50+

££

- business shirts £35+
- knitwear £50+
- casual shirts £35+
- ties £35+
- smart trousers £90+
- sports jacket £150+
- passable suits £250+
- shoes £100+
- spectacle frames £250+
- belts £35+
- pen £35+
- carry case £70+

£££

- power suits £500+
- casual suits £600
- impressive shirts £50+
- power ties £50+
- the right socks £10+
- macintosh/raincoat £250+
- the right pen £150+
- electronic organizer £250+
- watch £500, never bejewelled

▒ Grooming your brand

At the beginning of this chapter, I mentioned that many of the messages you send about your brand values are discernible through the details – like the watch that you wear, your personal organizer, pen, cufflinks or glasses. So too, can we pick up signals from your grooming – your haircut, skin condition, hands and nails. Spending time on keeping these things in condition means that you spend less time in the morning and have few worries when you meet those you want to impress.

HAIR

You have no excuse not to make the most of what you've got. Today there are plenty of terrific products and great stylists to sort you out. The women in your life are also likely to be more knowledgeable than you so ask their advice if you need to find a new salon or wonder what product might help solve a challenge.

Cut

Personal taste is the starting point. You want to look good but wonder about trying something too different from what others are used to seeing on you. If you are in the market for a new look, take it slowly, let it sneak up on you and them and you won't get comments. People will notice that you look good, but they won't know why. Beware of new hairstyles for guys as introduced by pop or film stars. They can look very funny on a man in a suit.

After taste, I rate *effort* as the next criteria in choosing a cut. If you want to roll out of bed and be off without any contact with a comb or brush (or, perish the thought, a hairdryer) then keep it close to the scalp. Do so only if you can without looking like a thug. Guys with deep colouring, a strong beard-line or heavy brows look 'thugish' in a close crop as do big blokes.

Most hair needs some stuff put into it to help it behave all day long. Hairspray should be avoided at all costs unless you want to look like you wear a wig. It makes your hair go flat. Just a dab of gel or wax rubbed on to the hands, then with your fingers *through* (not on to) the hair gives your hair texture and movement which is attractive. Alternatively, mousse helps with drying and styling (either naturally or with a blow-dryer) and can also be used after you've combed your hair to help keep it in place.

When you hair starts to recede don't try to hide the fact – even if you are only 21. Go with it, just keep the hair short. It is much cooler than the alternatives.

Long hair on a guy is acceptable in many places; but works against you in many more places. Weigh up the pros and cons of a job versus your ponytail if in any doubt about advancing in your career. Senior men, in particular, have real problems with unconventional hair lengths and styles on men. Things are changing but maybe not fast enough for you to risk it.

Hair colouring

Colouring is a big step best taken when on holiday so you can fib about it when you get back to work. But colouring requires monthly attention – hence, a major commitment in time (up to 2 hours with a cut). If you aren't prepared to do that, forget it. Roots on a chap are only acceptable in the entertainment business.

Covering grey is an option and quite easily done yourself after you've been guided by a good colourist or girlfriend (girls know about hair colouring). For brown hair, semi-permanent rinses work well if you hate the grey. Use women's products, not men's, as they are better and you have more choice.

SKINCARE

If you are still in the Dark Ages when it comes to taking care of your skin, you don't look as young, as modern or as professional as you could.

Good skin is an asset and possible for any guy should he put in a bit of effort. If you have blotches or spots, then they detract from your eyes and mouth. You don't need to have a small pharmacy at home, as many women have, only a few key products to use daily and a commitment to visiting a beauty therapist occasionally to really give the skin a boost.

Daily routine

Because you shave every day, you're exfoliating your face – i.e. getting rid of dead skin. This is what a cleanser does for women so the shaving process sorts out this step already.

While we are on shaving let's go through the basic routine. Wet-shaving is the best way to get a good shave and to have clear skin. If your skin gets aggravated from wet-shaving you need to switch your foam and always use a moisturiser afterwards.

- Shave after a shower or after warming the skin with a hot flannel.
- Use shaving soap and a brush for best results in lifting the hairs off the face. Lather the face in circular motions.
- Using the best shaver on the market (presently, the Gillette Sensor Excel). Get all the hairs off as best you can. The final shave over the face should be in downward strokes: this helps the hairs 'lie low' for as long as possible. If you shave upwards, the hairs stand up more quickly during the day.

After a shave, *always apply a light moisturiser*. If you are smart you will also apply a little sunscreen (SPF 15) to the face and neck year round to keep the wrinkles at bay. Any excess is useful on the backs of your hands (which show damage soonest). Use a heavier cream or even Vaseline (over your sunscreen) when doing outdoor sports to prevent damage from cold and harsh winds.

Never apply aftershave or cologne to the face as it will only dry out the skin and possibly cause irritation. Even scented balms can be troublesome.

An eye cream is recommended if you use a PC for several hours a day or if you want to minimize the effects of the crow's feet creeping up on you. They feel good and do make the eyes look smoother.

MAKE-UP

Don't panic. I'm not going to suggest eyeshadows and lipstick. We are talking grooming. This is a cutting-edge section. If you feel the least bit queasy, skip it. It deals with minor imperfections that you can sort easily with modern cosmetics (*and no one will know!*). Also, this is about advance grooming for presentations and TV.

Cosmetics today are light, easy to use and subtle. No one never need know that you even use them. Believe me, once you discover the wonders of concealer you will never look back.

Foundation

I recommend a light foundation for guys whose skin tone is very discoloured – light bit, dark bits. For example, there might be some ruddiness on the cheeks or burst capillaries or grey shadows, sun or age spots. Foundation can minimize these problems when used lightly; but concealer can eliminate them (well, for the day anyway).

Foundations are available in liquids, creams, compacts or sticks and have a variety of formulations. The right formulation will be dependent on your skin type. A good beautician or sales assistant can advise you best (or a girlfriend who will be empathetic).

You choose a foundation that is closest to your natural skin tone – not to create a tan. Tinted moisturisers do that. So select a colour by trying it on your jawline. If you can't see it, then it is the right colour. If it is lighter or darker, it will be too noticeable.

Apply foundation by putting a bit on the back of your hand. Grab a bit of the colour with a make-up sponge and apply (after shaving) in downward strokes. You can use it only on problem areas or all over to get a balanced look. Go lightly over the beard-line or skip it altogether concentrating on the cheeks, nose and forehead with just a gentle skim over the rest. New stick foundations you apply in strokes right on to the skin and blend – very easy and very effective.

Powder foundations

This is the ultimate level in coverage required for TV when you use a slightly darker shade than normal to look healthy under the lights (which bleach out colouring terribly). Only use for a studio and never wear out in public (please note, Mr Blair) even if a camera is likely to catch you. It is simply too sad for a man to be seen outside a TV studio with fake colouring noticeable at the chin line – brown face, white neck, yuk!

Powder foundations are applied with sponges and are of a thicker formulation than regular foundations. Have the studio make-up artist apply it for you. If one isn't available, have your own ready to do yourself. Never, but never, appear on TV without it.

Concealer

This is a great product to use instead of, or in conjunction with, foundation to really hide bags and blotches. Concealer comes in liquid form (with an applicator), cream (out of a tube), stick or in a compact. Select a colour lighter than your skin tone as you will need this to balance the blotch. A bit of testing is required to see if a yellow- or pink-based colour does the job best.

With your ring finger, dab a little on and blend so that it fades the shadows, lines or spots.

Tinted moisturiser

If you look like death, but you need to look like a million bucks, tinted moisturisers can do the trick. Better than fake tans because they are lighter and not so noticeable, tinted moisturisers have only a hint of colour. When you use it, eliminate your regular moisturiser. You will also have to train yourself not to touch or rub your face when you wear it otherwise it could look blotchy by the afternoon.

Powder

Translucent powder is good to use to take away shine if you are going to do an important presentation under lights or be filmed. If your hair is receding or you are bald, do the head as well. Apply with a powder puff for best effects, pressing the powder in. Leave it a minute or two to absorb and dust off any excess. When done properly, no one will know that you are wearing it. Promise.

Mascara

Sorry, I call a halt at using black mascara on men (unless you do cabaret) but am a fan of clear mascara which is great for keeping wild eyebrows and moustaches under control.

Lip balm

Use a lip balm if you have a problem with chap. Flaky red lips are neither nice nor necessary.

SCENT

Fragrance is not only acceptable, it is *nice* for a guy to smell fresh and pleasant. Choosing the scent is very important. Any fragrance that promises romance or virility has no place at work. Best scents for work are the old-fashioned ones that use essential oils from citrus fruit (lemons, limes) or flowers free of musk! Good labels include: Floris, Trumpers, Czech & Speak.

Apply fragrance where women do: on the pulse points: the back of the neck (behind the ear), on the wrist and lower arm, on your chest.

If people look up when you enter the room the scent is too strong.

HANDS AND NAILS

Hands take a lot of abuse at work and at home. It is important for yours to look professional and elegant when communicating your brand. Hence, some effort is needed.

Minimal hand care:

- Nails should be cleaned and trimmed Monday through Friday.
- If you can't do it yourself, get someone to help.
- The occasional manicure is a treat, not for wimps, and will guide you in taking care of your own nails.
- If you pick at your cuticles or nails, STOP. This screams *stress overload* and/or *fear.*
- Use a hand cream to keep your hands nice.
- Never polish your nails. Promise!

TEETH

Teeth, we notice. They are a focus when you communicate and can interfere with your message if they are problematic.

Dental care is basic hygiene. You need to brush *at least* twice daily; three times (i.e. after lunch) if you have an important meeting. If you brush your teeth unconscious of any methodology, it's time to invest in an electric toothbrush. These gadgets do the work for you and improve the state of your teeth as well as your gums within 2 months.

We all know that we should use floss but few of us are dedicated to the task. Put your pack of floss by the sink and then do it every time you wash. Flossing in bed, when accompanied, is not nice; nor is doing so in the car or anywhere you can be seen.

Breath fresheners and mouthwash should be kept handy for emergencies (like encounters after you've had several cups of coffee or after a spicy lunch). Bad breath makes for bad deals.

7

INFLUENCING OTHERS

Gotta get some wow!

We have all met characters who simply 'blew us away'. They've got the 'wow' factor. Just by sheer power of personality, their looks, their charisma, they influence us.

I am often told, 'It's all right for him. He was *born* that way.' I don't buy the nature over nurture argument when it comes to impact or charisma, having seen too many people develop into real stars with some advice, training, and the occasional makeover! Influential people are perpetual students – observers and learners. They are positive as well. If not just looking on the bright side of life, they are blessed with a 'can-do' spirit that enables them to turn setbacks, even defeats, into something positive – at minimum a great learning experience. Influencers don't go through life with a chip on their shoulders about what life has handed them, nor are they chronic navel-gazers. They aim to undo bad experiences by doing something positive or to ensure that the likelihood of a replica experience is slim.

Influential people also *make us feel good*. They have more than just impact – they *move us*. This ability to relate to others and to change people for the positive is something you can learn to do and incorporate into every aspect of your life. You can become more influential without a personality transplant by adopting new attitudes to yourself and others, reading situations more accurately and applying new approaches for building rapport.

Influential people come in every size, shape and age and have different communication styles. Some are very quietly persuasive, with others being more flamboyant and outgoing. I have met and worked with many different kinds of influencers in both business and politics. President Jimmy Carter was the quietly persuasive type – very influential in meetings and negotiations but ineffective in conveying determination and leadership via television or in a large public gathering. By contrast, President Reagan (while charming personally) I felt was more impressive via television than in real life. But what all influencers share in common is an ability to make us feel good about ourselves as well as good about knowing them.

SELF-FULFILLING PROPHECY

Think of the times when you were very satisfied with the influence you had over people. Perhaps it was an important meeting at work, going for a new job interview or asking someone out for the first time. Think of something that happened recently to help you dissect how you might have 'willed' the result. Before the event, you probably reflected about what you wanted to achieve and were well-prepared. For the meeting, you did all your homework and prepared an effective presentation. You also made sure that you had back-up material to handle unplanned questions as well as provided a report for all present summarizing your work. For the job interview, your CV was concise and impressive, you brought examples of your work, and had referees to hand to endorse your abilities. For that hot date, you planned the perfect evening you knew would appeal to that special person.

But in addition to the preparation, you imagined the meeting. You thought about how it would go as well as what you would say. You visualized how the audience would be interested and agree with your findings at the end (maybe with the boss adding, 'Well, done. Terrific work!'). For the job interview, you could imagine how the personnel director would give signals that you were right for the job. For the date, you could *see* and *hear* her/him warm to you because both you and the suggested date appealed to each other very much. And those dreams continued . . . !

If you have *self-belief* that you can achieve something and *visualize your success* you are more likely to achieve the results you want than if you 'talk yourself down'. I have seen this work innumerable times with people terrified of public speaking, demoralized by losing a promotion or a job, convinced that they couldn't turn around a relationship. If we tell ourselves that we are going to fail, we dream the disaster in living colour (day and night) and end up almost experiencing the horror or our worst nightmares because we are just fulfilling what we prophesied would happen.

CHANGE THE PROGRAMME, CHANGE THE RESULT

Install new software (behaviour) into your hardware (the brain) and programme yourself into having the influence that you want.

Reflect back a few years. Remember the ogres in your life then? If they were human, did you overcome them? If so, how? Top athletes break world records after they have *programmed the possibility*. The most successful slimmers achieve their goals not just because they diet and exercise but because they *visualize* the 'new me' when they would reach their goal. They can *see* how differently – better – they will look and *imagine feeling* better about themselves. These visualizations are powerful motivating tools that anyone can use, for any challenge – great or small.

I *CAN'T* DO IT

An experience many of us share when we feel out of control, incompetent and stressed is learning to ski as an adult. You head down the slope knowing that you will fall and before long, of course you do. Up you get and down you go again with the same thing playing over and over in your head: *I'm gonna faaaaaall!*

Many readers will remember their fear of mastering new technology. The initial attempts were very stressful, often humiliating. 'Kids can do this stuff (as well as ski without falling over!). Why can't I?' But you persevered and mastered it. Last year you hooked into the Net in absolute awe. Today you maintain your own web site and have thrown away your fax machine and do much of your work, shopping and recreation online. OK, those computer manuals are well-thumbed and you feel like you've earned a degree in computers considering all the time you have spent studying the damn things. But you were determined to succeed. You *visualized* it ('I've just gotta get it!') and did it. And you should realize that you can do the same thing in most situations to influence people.

True Confessions

I coach people in visualization because I have used it successfully most of my life. Reading Dr Norman Vincent Peale, Mr *Power of Positive Thinking* (and arguably the inventor of the self-help book genre), convinced me in my early twenties that 'you can if you think you can'. When I was up against tough competition to get accepted into graduate school at Harvard University (arguably America's finest), I could only imagine that I would succeed. My undergraduate degree was a modest *cum laude*, not top of the class, but I was determined to get in. And I not only succeeded in doing so, against great competition, but won a fellowship as well.

Later when I first set up Color Me Beautiful, I assumed that I could just run the business side of things and leave the marketing to others. But it became increasingly clear that unless I went out and fronted the business we wouldn't get the opportunities or media coverage that we needed. However, I seriously doubted my abilities to front something as awesome as 'Image Consulting'. I was an entrepreneur without much of a business plan, new to marketing and selling a totally new concept. On top of it, I am not a stunner, was a fledgling in the beauty and fashion industries and a novice to the British media.

Every day, when I went running, I started to imagine how I would like others to believe in me and my business. I played Steven Spielberg in my head, directing a movie about how things would go before an important meeting or interview. I would set the scene, imagine meeting the characters and visualize 'blowing them away' with a great pitch. Of course, it didn't always work the way I wanted but I was able to make it happen a lot of the time by thinking that *I could do it*.

I began to *see* opportunities for my business everywhere because I was *visualizing* my success. When TV was installed in the British Parliament, I wrote to all the MPs and the political parties about smartening up and almost overnight I became *the* leading image advisor to politicians. They came from every political party, including prime ministers and cabinet members. TV programmes from around the world were tripping over themselves to get my views on political image, not just in Britain but in other countries as well.

I have had a life and a career that has exceeded my expectations – academic achievements, being a successful mother, happily married, a competitive marathoner, author and businesswoman. All accomplished in no small measure by visualizing those results. Seeing is believing.

VISUALIZING YOUR INFLUENCE

Think of a situation you face or dilemma you are trying to sort. Find a quiet place, free from distractions and machines (especially the telephone).

- Sit comfortably and close your eyes.
- Relax. Try breathing more slowly and deeply. Put your thumbs over your navel and lay both your hands over your belly. Feel your tummy move in and out slowly. When you are breathing down here you are using your full lung capacity.
- Clear your mind of everything except the one situation or dilemma at hand.

- Imagine the situation in detail, as if you are watching a movie.
  - *Where are you?* What is in the room? How much space is there?
  - *Who's there?* Visualize everyone who will be there. What are they wearing?
  - *How do you want them to greet you?* What expressions do you want them to have? Do they touch you? Are you all sitting or standing?
- The movie is running – what's happening? What do you want to say? How do you want them to react? What do they say to you? Imagine their expressions. Do they find you amusing, attractive, kind, profound, etc. Keep the scene going for as long as you can. Create the dialogue and interactions that you want. Then close the scene. Get the result that you want. They are impressed and you feel darn pleased with yourself.
- Open your eyes. How do you feel? Is this how you *want to feel?* If so, tell yourself that is exactly how you will feel when the situation actually occurs.

WHAT'S YOUR EMOTIONAL QUOTIENT?

Seminars on 'Influence and Impact' are today among the most popular that I run, particularly at higher levels in business. Two powerful words – influence and impact – convey so much of what we all want – to be memorable, to have an effect, to make a difference.

This interest in learning how to project influence and impact confirms a growing body of research (Daniel Goleman, Robert Cooper, John Mayer, Peter Salovey among others) that *states* what we know is less important than *how* we work – specifically our level of *emotional intelligence*. Our 'EQ' needs to be higher than our IQ to handle ourselves and others successfully *and* to achieve more.

We all work with people far more intelligent than ourselves. When in doubt, we seek their input for knowledge and how to do things. But sometimes these brilliant characters are not so adept in handling other people. They shoot themselves in the foot frequently by being arrogant or off-putting or submissive and unable to project themselves beyond their zone of close colleagues who admire or love them warts and all.

The competencies required to be emotionally intelligent as determined by Goleman et al. include: *self-awareness* (self-confidence / inner resources); *self-regulations* (self-control, adaptability, trustworthiness); *motivation*; *empathy* and *social skills*. Many terrific books (especially Goleman's *Working with Emotional Intelligence*) are available to guide you through a process of personal self-development that is as inspiring as it can be life-changing. I have worked with Goleman's material, in addition to Neurolinguistic Programming, and share here workable suggestions based on 15 years of experience and study.

IT'S NOT ABOUT *YOU*, IT'S ABOUT *THEM*

In work, we can get preoccupied with the job at hand – achieving objectives, meeting deadlines, hitting targets. We are reminded of goals and told to keep focused – that forces us to concentrate on our own agendas rather than those of others. But we can't influence others without bringing people along with us. Developing a perspective on *what's in it for them* is the first step in influencing others.

CULTURAL CONSIDERATIONS

To be effective in influencing others you also must accept that your view of the world, your notion of how things should go or the 'right approach' is *wrong* to many others. We all suffer from cultural bias no matter how well travelled or well educated we are and must appreciate that what works for us most of the time in our own culture most likely won't work in dealing with other cultures.

Much of the advice in this chapter, as well as the rest of the book, is biased towards an American/north-west European perspective. OK, the American way has tried to dominate business for the last 50 years with US business schools and management gurus spouting the 'best' way of doing things. Peter Drucker, Mike Hammer, Fred Waterman, Tom Peters, Steve Covey et al. have tried, bless 'em, to tell the world how to organize its businesses and run things. But the American approach is anathema to many cultures as has been proven time and again. Ask the human resources director of any global company about the havoc caused by introducing performance-related pay in Latin countries or management by objectives in Africa. No, most companies know that at best you need to 'think global' but 'work local' in order to operate, which means when you respect the local differences and adapt accordingly you are more likely to do business successfully.

When needing to influence someone in a different culture learn the rules of *their* game rather than try to operate on your own terms. Even the Americans are learning this. How often have American companies dashed into a country and tried to dazzle a prospective customer with a whiz-bang presentation. Sorry, but US companies win, hands-down, on the knock 'em dead sales presentation. Their product can have better bells and whistles than any competitor and Americans really know how to screw down the sell-in price to grab a contract. But sometimes, even often in some cases, Americans lose out to 'inferior' offers by Europeans and Asians who take more time in building a relationship before hitting with the hard sell. The 'time is money' American ethos doesn't pay dividends in cultures where time is relative.

Many of the suggestions here are applicable in other cultures but remember to do your homework ahead of time to appreciate how business done *there* will be different to how you normally operate. The key things to discover will be:

- *The business culture:* is it hierarchical with clear lines of authority, communication and decision-making? Or is it more consensual with both discussion and power more diffuse?
- *The work ethos:* how are meetings conducted? What will impress people and what won't? Are decisions made at meetings or prior to (hence, lobby ahead) or afterwards (therefore, prepare for a delayed decision).
- *Communication style:* some cultures are more formal with business being dispassionate and language – both verbal and non-verbal – being measured. In other cultures, emotion is not only acceptable but it prevails – you need to raise your voice, show you care and not get ruffled when others stomp out of the room or shout.
- *Time:* how relevant or irrelevant? To an American it can convey *everything* about the person, to a Frenchman or Spaniard it is only relative.
- *Humour:* perhaps one of the most challenging aspects of cross-cultural communication. When and how to use humour can make or break relationships. While a warm-up joke in Britain is welcome, and always expected in America, if used in Germany you will be dismissed as a buffoon. But be prepared with a repertoire of funny stories for after-business hours or you'll be branded a factotum.
- *Manners:* business and social etiquette can be a minefield and undermine your effectiveness when working abroad. Do things on *their* terms when in their country and on your terms when entertaining them at home. If uncertain, read up. (See the bibliography for some guidance.)

▓ Building rapport

In Chapter 1, we discussed the importance of first impressions; simply put: mega. You may have been working flat out for a meeting but if you don't spend the first few minutes establishing rapport – reading the situation, signals from others and sense the mood and the atmosphere – you'll have a more difficult time in achieving your objectives. Many intelligent people disregard this stage, preferring, they tell me, 'just to get down to business'. But you *can't* get down to business unless you establish a relationship first. Sure, you can blather on about your subject but little will be absorbed until everyone has the time to 'scope each other out' – get a *feel* for the person, what they are about and what they are likely to contribute.

INCREASING THE CHARM QUOTIENT: NEIL

At 34, Neil was a brilliant financial controller with a leading retail group for 3 tumultuous years. He was brought in at group level having introduced new systems successfully for one of its ailing companies and spent his 3 years helping divisions achieve ambitious cost-reduction targets. Respected greatly for persistence, Neil nonetheless developed a reputation for being a 'hatchet man', driving divisional staff hard to reduce overheads mainly via staff redundancies. With the restructuring complete, Neil discussed promotional prospects with the chief executive who said that he felt Neil needed a few more years to be considered for a financial director slot despite there being an obvious vacancy in a new acquisition Neil knew he could handle better than anyone.

Neil was disappointed with the response and felt that his immediate boss, the current financial director, was able to take much of the glory for Neil's hard work without having to do the dirty work. He knew he was ready for a financial director's post within the group but felt he had been cast as the 'doer', not the director.

Neil decided to test his marketability by talking to a few head-hunters who were impressed with his track record. One leading advisor knew he could do a financial director's job but felt Neil didn't have the presence to work as a director and was wary about sending him to clients for consideration. It isn't in the interest of headhunters to waste the time of important clients with marginal candidates. Neil, although a star candidate because of his experience and track record, was marginal because of his manner. 'I'm not sure if Neil has taken on this persona of "Mr Tough Guy" through having had to fire so many people over the last few years. But he is very dour and takes a lot of effort to lighten up,' explained the headhunter. 'He was fine after a half hour or so and is great talking about what he's done. But I can't send him out until he learns how to make a better impression more quickly,' he added.

In the first few minutes of meeting Neil, it was clear that he had a problem. My session was presented to him by the headhunters to help him prepare for a forthcoming first interview with one of his target companies. Upon meeting him in reception he was brusque, mumbled some sort of greeting, barely looked me in the eye then dashed for a seat in the conference room. As I shut the door behind us and offered him coffee, Neil had his hands in his face and was looking down at the table. He said nothing, aside from 'Mine's black' in reference to how he liked his coffee.

Less than a minute had elapsed and this man was sending a barrage of negative signals – arrogance, shyness, underconfidence, hostility, and boorishness. I was explaining a little about the session, who I was and the kinds of work I did for his headhunter – all the basics of breaking the ice to give him an opportunity to 'get me' – when Neil interrupted after a couple of minutes saying, 'Let's get things straight. Just tell me what to expect, what to do. That's all I want.'

My response was, 'What do you mean, that's all you want? Getting the job *you want* is about determining what *others want* from you.' Taken aback by my directness, Neil replied, 'I have found that it matters little what people want. What matters is the job that needs

to get done. I can tell XYZ exactly what they need. There are direct parallels with what I've achieved in my current job and I can prove that to them. I want you to advise me on the form of the interview.' I thought this was going to be challenging.

Neil spoke for about 45 minutes about the work that he had done, the pressure that he had felt over the last 3 to 5 years in being 'Mr Nasty' whilst others talked bold but did little. He was proud of what he'd achieved but had made a lot of enemies in the process. He also felt like an outsider, ill-at-ease in the 'executive club' as he didn't go to 'good schools' and achieved his accountancy accreditation through hard work and hard graft. His other admission was that he felt inadequate socially – he hated small talk, business lunches, even socializing with colleagues outside work. You could say that he was quite a balanced fellow – he had chips on both shoulders!

In such situations, being an American is a real asset. We have little time for the notion that you are flawed by things that happened in your past, by how you grew up, what your parents achieved, where you went to school – the whole nonsense that you still find in Britain and other 'old' societies. We believe that most problems can be sorted if you want them to be. You can learn how to do small talk, how to put others at ease, how to be more interesting, how to make a greater impression. Being the person you want to be is in your own hands as is creating and managing the impression you make on others. (Just read this book cover to cover to find out how!)

Neil conditioned himself to believe that he would never be accepted for who he was, rather only for what he achieved. The past 5 years' experience proved this to be the case. Neil had impressed his bosses all right but they didn't want him to join senior management because he didn't know how to be part of them. 'Let's put it this way,' confided the financial director to the headhunter, 'Neil is a bit of a rough diamond. He rubs people the wrong way and doesn't even know it.'

Over the next 3 hours we chipped away at Neil's sense of inadequacy on a human level – that people didn't 'like' him or didn't want to know him very well. 'Why don't you think your colleagues like you?'

I asked. 'I guess I'm not a very likeable guy,' came his honest reply. 'Well, just saying that, Neil, saying how you feel about something makes you more likeable,' I said to his bemusement. 'It's a good start.'

I filmed him entering the conference room, greeting me again and accepting coffee. He was stunned to see how I felt and interpreted his manner. We tried things again, and again. He was told to worry less about himself and saying the right thing and to concentrate more on me, or the people he was meeting. Neil lightened up, started to be funny and more natural, even *charming*! When he saw his third attempt at just meeting and greeting he was delighted. 'I'd like to have a beer with that guy,' he jested. When I replayed the first session for him to compare the two he put his head in his hands in horror. 'I will never be like that again!' Neil said this with conviction, having seen himself as others see him and heard my interpretation. He wanted to *be* someone else – the real, confident and capable Neil inside who was dying to get out – to be natural and enjoy being with other people.

Three more practice sessions with the headhunters playing the role of company directors were filmed and analysed with Neil growing in confidence and enjoyment in each session. Within four months he was offered a terrific new opportunity as financial director with double his former salary. 'The best thing that they told me is that I am a perfect fit for their team, that I *feel* like I belong there,' he reported proudly. 'I'm going to love this job!'

Whether a meeting is your first or it is a repeat, focus first on an effective *meeting and greeting*, then *match the mood*, and finally, *suss the situation*.

Step 1: Meeting and greeting

HANDSHAKES

Having influence on others requires *getting on to their wavelength first*. While you should remain aware of your own objectives you must stifle them at first and spend time reading others – what they need, are interested in, motivated by – before you can achieve what you want. Upon meeting you do this with your handshake, then 'reading' the space *they* require after you break apart. Watch what they do, where they go. And *mirror* the action. Nothing is more threatening or disconcerting than someone who behaves differently to us upon greeting.

Working or travelling internationally presents many challenges in building rapport. On a corporate cruise a few years ago, I ran a session on body language in business that became an open forum for different nationalities to say how much they disliked how others treated them.

Among the 1,000 guests were over 300 different nationalities. In a packed session of 200 people squashed into a conference room, I raised the issue of 'meeting and greeting' in different cultures. I invited the audience to shake hands with the people around them and to 'find out how it was for them'. Chaos reigned but all was in good fun. The Texan called the Filipino a 'wimp' while the latter called him a 'fascist'! The gentle handshake of many Asian cultures is often misunderstood or judged on Western standards where, indeed, a light handshake conveys an insignificant impression. For the Texan not to accommodate the small stature of his partner and persist with a strong, even hurtful, handshake was insensitive and parochial. OK, 'a man ain't a man unless he breaks a few bones upon meeting' back home, but when travelling abroad you are unlikely to win kudos for being so aggressive.

An Italian said he found his Swedish partner 'cold' simply because the Swede (when demonstrating onstage for the group) stepped back almost a metre after shaking hands. This was off-putting and unsettling to the Italian, who like many Mediterranean people, lingers closely for a minute immediately after shaking hands.

A British woman took great umbrage because a more senior Spanish gentleman kissed her hand rather than shook it. 'I hate it when men take advantage like that,' she said, clearly having a sense of humour failure. Indeed, in many northern European countries men can take advantage of the growing trend to greet women in business with a kiss rather than a handshake. But in a country like Spain, and for a man of a different generation, it is boorish to treat a woman in business as he would a man. 'I can't be aggressive to a woman!' insisted the charming señor, most upset that the woman wasn't delighted by his gesture.

Hence, it is very important to be familiar with the likely local protocols and customs before visiting a country and resist the urge to judge people by your own cultural standards. Follow their lead. Put their comfort before your own and you are more likely to break down barriers more quickly. See Suggested Reading for useful guides to cross-cultural behaviour.

Next time you meet someone for the first time note what happens while shaking hands. How would you classify the handshake? We all know when we don't like a handshake. What out of the following list do you find a turn-off when shaking someone's hands for the first time?

Bone crushers

These are disconcerting for men and women but performed by both sexes (though the fellas have the upper-hand in being better at it). A bone-crushing shake indicates an aggressive, domineering nature. Sure, you want to convey confidence but actually hurting the person you are meeting is not the way to get off to an influential start.

Weak, limp shakes

A weak handshake is common in many Eastern cultures but considered very ineffective in Western, global business where it is regularly proffered. Both men and women are victims and the signals given are equally negative. Men often tell me that they give an easy handshake out of consideration for women. But the result is that the women they are trying to influence immediately feel that they are dealing with a wimp.

Wet handshakes

Many, I stress many, people have a problem with perspiring palms. They cannot help it. When they are anxious or nervous they heat up and their palms (among other zones, often) sweat. It is stressful for them and not easy for the person on the receiving end. After a wet shake both parties make desperate, discreet attempts to sort out their sweaty palm, which takes a while to recover from.

Often, those aware of their problem try rubbing their hands on their backsides or sleeves just before an introduction which is a dead give-away about what's coming. The easiest way to sort out perspiring hands is to spray them with antiperspirant before a meeting (if you wash your hands you'll need another quick spray, so, carry a small can with you if out all day).

Nearly made it

There are people who never quite manage a complete handshake – they just grab fingers. British and some Continental men of a certain vintage tend to do this when meeting women, which might convey their gentlemanly status but can insult women who feel that they aren't getting equal treatment. Business handshakes for both sexes need to be direct, firm and the Full Monty – the whole hand, not just the fingers.

Double-grasps

These handshakes, while often very genuine and warm (e.g. when someone has been looking forward to meeting another person for a long time) can be construed as patronizing. American men sometimes try this with each other thinking that they are showing great friendliness when it really is a gentle but definite assertion of 'I'm in charge here.' Former US President George Bush, 'Mr Nice Guy', was a famed double-grasper. Not only did you get two hands but George made sure you knew who was 'on top' as he would always twist your hand so that you were underneath!

Women who use the double-clasp can be perceived as equally domineering though thinking others will find it warm and mumsy. Ha! Few feel anything but on the receiving end because of other non-verbal signals (e.g. steely eyes, stiff body movements, frozen smile, etc.) Mrs. Thatcher was the queen of the double-clasp.

KISSING

Kissing is included here as it can replace handshakes in meeting and greeting and is a very dangerous zone to both enter and escape gracefully when one of the pair is not a happy bunny.

Kissing has entered business for two reasons. First there are more women in business and it seems natural to do to women at work what you like to do to them after work. But women also are more touchy with each other, they kiss each other to show warmth and friendship. Some men seeing this just want to get in on the act. The second reason why kissing is pervasive in business is because of globalization. Seeing business abroad in cultures where men kiss women quite formally has given all men the bright idea of giving it a go themselves. 'If Juan can get away with it, why can't I?'

In cultures where kissing is a formal, accepted greeting both socially and in business it is free of gropes, slurping and full body-blows. Most Latin businessmen who kiss women do so with minimal contact, just the cheek contact, no lips. Western women who rebuff these courtesies not only offend their hosts but are dismissed either as peasants or bitches – neither of which helps the brand, women. But it is up to you to decide who you will accept a kiss from and who you won't.

When to kiss

Men: you should not even consider kissing a female colleague, client or supplier unless you are darn sure that you are liked. Admired for your business savvy is not the same as being liked as a person. Know the difference before you attempt to kiss her. So as not to risk offending women, take her lead. Many women will initiate the move from handshakes to kisses so follow her. Other indications that you might not get spat at when you attempt to kiss a female colleague:

- You've spent some time getting to know each other outside the office. This might have been a social business function where you both were more relaxed and have become better friends.
- You notice that she touches you – not excessively (when you could be in for more than you bargained for) but to show empathy or consideration.
- There is something to celebrate – the deal is done! Go for it and watch her body language in reaction. If hostile, don't attempt again. If not, you are through to the kissing realm and can do so next time you meet.

Women: when you start the kissing lark expect it to continue. Better to take the initiative with peers, suppliers/consultants, or juniors not with senior colleagues; let them try if/after you've sent some warm 'n' friendly signals (see above).

To resist unwanted overtures from men keen for a smooch, try these tips:

- Keep as much space between you as possible. In meetings, sit across the table rather than next to him.
- Greet him with a formal handshake, stiff arm then move away quickly.
- Pre-empt his strike by greeting him with a friendly 'matey' slap on his upper arm. Give it a firm grip,

then twist him around and gently aim him in the direction where you want him to go (i.e. away from you!). No matter how tempting you were at the outset you will be anything but after this rebuff.

- Keep small talk, personal chat, humour to a minimum so that he gets the message that dealing with you is all business and that's the way you want it.

One, two or three?

To kiss or not to kiss isn't the only question. Equally vexing is how many kisses.

Just knowing someone's nationality is no longer an indication of how many kisses you might get. Nothing is worse than miscalculating and hanging out there in the twilight zone expecting another when the person has beaten a retreat. I'm wrong: the worst case scenario is when you both mess up and end up bumping noses or catching the lips full-on when that was the last thing you wanted.

Err on the side of caution and follow their lead. Americans and most Brits are single-kissers except for those who want to convey their worldly sophistication and mimic the French with the double-whammy. Only the Swiss, Dutch and Belgians are legitimate with the triple-kiss, all others are impostors.

Keep body contact to a minimum and only kiss cheeks unless you want to really start problems for yourself.

Hand-kissing

Fewer things are more likely to make women weak at the knees than to have their hands kissed. When done properly and appropriately, hand-kissing is the business. But before any of you guys think that you've got the green light to start grabbing the hands of women to have them grovelling at your feet, here are guidelines for carrying it off:

- Keep a metre apart for the hand-kiss to be elegant. Any closer is intimidating.
- It is most effective when proffered by men over 40 to women of any age.
- Younger guys should never try the hand-kiss upon meeting a woman in business. But *do* try it socially for great effect.
- Try using it for business social events especially when meeting female colleagues/associates and wanting to compliment them on how they look.
- Don't actually *kiss* the hand, just touch her fingertips with your lips for best effect.

Women: when you unexpectedly receive the hand-kiss don't pull away as you will embarrass yourself more than him. Accept gracefully yet coolly if you didn't like it. Chances are he'll get the message for next time. If you are pleasantly surprised try not to blush or giggle which are definitely uncool responses. Add an accepting nod and smile which shows that you have men kissing your hand everywhere you go.

Many women in my seminars scream 'Help! What do you do with jerks that insist on kissing you when you don't want to reciprocate?' Good question about a pervasive problem.

Men: rebuffing her

Kissing is an increasing problem for men being on the receiving end of unwanted, over-exuberant women who, just like men, use kissing as a sort of power gesture – putting the little man or woman in their place. You can either put up with her kissing you every time you meet or realign the relationship to become more professional. To achieve the latter, you will need to work on all aspects of relationship 'smartening-up', from phone calls being less chatty, using meetings solely to discuss the agenda rather than an update on your personal lives and to create physical space between you when you meet.

Women generally give you more warning that they are heading for you. Short of puckering up in anticipation, they beat a path, arms outstretched. Try grabbing her arms, being effusive in your greeting, holding her at arm's length to tell her how stunning she looks. After a cursory exchange held like this, it would be awkward to kiss and you can direct her where you want her to go – literally and figuratively!

SIZE THEIR BUBBLE

In Chapter 4, we discussed the importance of personal space – our proximity sphere which we define when we are with people. To build rapport quickly it is essential to read their personal 'bubble' – the space that they *want* around themselves – and to honour it. Your goal is not to feel comfortable yourself but to allow them to feel at ease first. If they are relaxed, they will open up more quickly.

Next time you meet someone for the first time, watch what they do after you shake their hands. If they move back, step forward. Watch their eyes, they will become fixed, rather hostile. In less than half a minute, many people will adjust themselves to find their comfort zone. If you keep the dance up, they will feel pursued and rapport will be very difficult to establish. Conversely, if you need space but those you are meeting do not, it is up to you to sweat it out, let them hang in closely until a natural break occurs. Again, if you can do this communication will flow more quickly.

FIND THE COMMON BONDS

Building rapport is about finding commonality as quickly as possible with those that we meet. No matter how different you seem, you need to find the hooks to help them understand that you are similar people, have similar interests, and are going to enjoy knowing each other. Are you both the same sex, age, share mutual contacts / friends? What do you notice about the environment (the office, meeting room) that is familiar or appeals to you? What happened on the way to the meeting; what anecdote/late-breaking news item you sense might amuse or inform?

Compliments always go a long way in establishing a bond. But only use them when you mean it. You can smell a false compliment a mile off. If you are impressed by the surroundings or the view, the décor, their 'trophies', say so.

There is always information – previously researched or observed – that enables us to 'relate' and build rapport. Don't misinterpret this as the glad-handing salesman routine whose slick, well-rehearsed greetings are transparent. Trying too hard is just as bad as not making any effort towards rapport. Think back to the last time someone tried the 'full court press' on you – they did *everything* they could to 'wow' you and failed miserably. Your reaction was the opposite of what they wanted – you got hostile, they tried harder and everything went round in circles.

Do as much homework as you can on the person ahead of time and choose the hooks for establishing bonds that are most natural for you. If you know that they recently worked in a company very much in the news, ask their opinion of the situation. If you have a mutual friend or associate use it as a link. As a mother, I find it easy to pick up on pictures of children in the office – ask their ages and names. Sometimes I'll get talking about their natures – 'Is he as mischievous as he looks?' – if appropriate.

Establishing commonality not only makes building rapport easier for you it makes it easier for them. In our highly pressured business lives the people who can make encounters easier as well as enjoyable and useful are the ones we want to know. If we want to know you, we share a fine basis for a good working relationship.

SMALL TALK

Perhaps the greatest hurdle for many in business is small talk. 'I just want to get down to business and hate that dancing around, waiting for things to happen,' said Mark, a senior corporate lawyer. Like many people who are seen to have trouble building rapport with new people, Mark is very intelligent as well as being both pleasant and warm. He is not what you would describe as antisocial, rather introvert. It takes time to get to know him and time for him to allow himself to enjoy other people. But, in business, you don't have the time that you would like to break down barriers and get to know people. Mark had to learn to *small talk* – something not covered in law school but a skill that could influence his chances of making partner one day. (I was brought in by the firm to 'make him *seem* more like a partner'!)

'I never know what to say,' explained Inge, a systems analyst with an online consultancy. 'I leave all that preliminary nonsense to our project director who can talk drivel to anyone, even inanimate objects!' she said with a laugh. Shortly, Inge is expressing concern about having marginal impact in meetings. 'I feel frozen out. It takes so much courage to jump in that I just don't sometimes. Then Steve and the others berate me later for not participating. I fear that they will start to exclude me which could jeopardize my chances for promotion.'

Like Mark, Inge had yet to learn that influence starts with the small talk. Get comfortable with that and you are a player from the start. Hold off, allowing others to do the work *and make a mark*, and you have to work twice as hard to make an impression because you are starting off *cold*. Small talk is the warm-up to the main event.

Clever chat, great stories, good jokes do not make small talk although all of these make for good conversation eventually. Small talk is not about *you being interesting* it is about tuning in to the other person's interests – no matter what they might be! Prior to a meeting, you do your homework. You get a company brief and background on who you are meeting. Go beyond the obvious and find out what is *hot* for the people that you are meeting. What was in the news this weekend that might be on their agenda today? Has the boss been in the limelight which might provide a hook to get them talking? What are they trying to achieve? If you haven't had the time to do your homework, observe your surroundings (their office, the hotel) and comment. 'Super location. How long have you been here?' 'Things have changed since I was last here. Have you reorganized the layout?' 'You didn't waste time getting your award up in reception. Well done! What's the feedback been like?'

You start with questions around something that will make *them* spark. Once you've lit them up, you react, which allows them to come back with more information. You draw upon your own experience (privately and professionally) that gives you material for your responses. *The goal is not to try to impress but to try to build rapport.*

Small talk is not about performing, it's about jamming – as in a good jazz session. You improvize off each other and generate something interesting. You don't need to know where the conversation is going because it is up to the both of you to bring it to a natural close.

Step 2: Match the mood

You are bursting to tell the boss about clinching a deal which means you've achieved your sales target 3 months early. You've been working on this contract for weeks and finally got the go-ahead today. You only need 2 minutes of his time, you tell him. In you charge, full of excitement (and pride) going on and on (because you are so amusing). You've now taken up 17 minutes. Your boss isn't responding and looks irritated. What's happened?

No matter what you need to discuss with others (at work, at home, with friends) take a few seconds to suss the mood. Our ebullient sales manager above didn't take the time to ask how his boss was before launching into his announcement. If he had he would have learned that his boss just had some worrying personal news. He was preoccupied and couldn't respond due to the overwhelming concern for a friend. The sales manager was so excited he didn't bother to *read his boss's mood* – his boss who looked burdened, preoccupied, worried. If the manager had read the boss's mood, and matched his announcement accordingly, he could have had much greater impact. In the 2 minutes allotted he could have said, 'I don't even need 2 minutes to give some great news. Here it is. We can discuss it in more detail on Wednesday.' Sensing that all was not normal, an effective influencer would add 'Are you all right?' That might open up the chance to build a more personal relationship.

EMOTIONAL EFFECTIVENESS

Effective influencers have an innate barometer in assessing others' moods and knowing when it is right to change the mood. We've done it ourselves to cheer up those who are down; to convince others of how serious a situation really is; to motivate a team into working together for intangible benefits. But the emotionally adept are constantly reading others and either matching their mood when appropriate or changing the mood to startle people into feeling and behaving differently.

Psychologist Howard Friedman at the University of California has done extensive research into the impact of tuning one's emotions for influencing others. He states, 'The essence of eloquent, passionate, spirited communication seems to involve the use of facial expressions, voice, gestures and body movements to transmit emotions.' Those skilled in adjusting their emotions to suit or change moods are better equipped to inspire and motivate others.

Because we involve so many non-verbal messages in conveying our real emotions it is easy to spot the fakers. The eyes have to *believe* in order to convey genuine emotions. When we are faking emotions our gestures, body movements and expressions start to send signals conflicting with what we are saying. I have worked with people who wouldn't, sometimes couldn't, express their feelings appropriately. Although a great handicap, it is not insurmountable, should you *want* to be a better communicator. The challenge is to realize – no, believe! – that others want to know what you feel. When they do, they can feel with you. You will grow as an influencer exponentially.

Step 3: Suss the situation

The third step in establishing rapport, of course, doesn't occur sequentially post introductions and once you have a feel for the mood of the people. It happens simultaneously with the other two. Your focus should, initially, be on meeting and greeting, then matching the mood and finally on sussing the situation where you will be building beyond initial rapport into establishing a relationship, hopefully, at the end of the meeting.

If in an office, what is the room like? Will it be conducive to the style of presentation or discussion you planned? Should adjustments be made for you to be more effective or others to be more comfortable? If there are people present that you didn't expect, you need to spend more time finding out their roles, their agendas, because their presence means that they, too, must be influenced as they will have a say after you've gone about what they thought of you. By all means focus on the principals but you ignore ancillary participants at your peril.

When the physical situation is challenging and not what you had hoped for *it is up to you to sort it out* as much as you can. You will show both confidence and consideration for others if you suggest ways to improve the conditions for a meeting, e.g. open the windows if it's too warm; suggest a break if the meeting has been going on for a long time; or rearrange seats if people won't be able to see the screen. If you find the situation is too formal for the sensitive one-on-one chat you had planned, suggest going somewhere else. 'Let's get a decent cup of latte across the road.'

If the physical situation is such a barrier for what you want to discuss it is preferable to defer the meeting to another time, if possible, rather than try to be influential in adverse conditions.

Integrity is integral to being influential and being truthful is at the heart of integrity. In life and in business we are faced with many imponderables, those sticky patches, grey areas that challenge us in telling the truth. When others skirt the truth (and we know it) we feel anything from irritation to disgust at their deceit.

From my experience in coaching others, I know that telling the truth about someone's blind spots or challenges is the fastest track to winning their confidence. As difficult as it can be, honesty is the most stress-free option. Think of the last time you either told a real porker, didn't own up to doing something or held back from telling someone something that you should. How did you feel afterwards? Great? 'Ha, got away with it!' Even if you could gloat about getting away with something the satisfaction was likely as superficial as it was fleeting.

'But the truth can hurt,' I am often told. Indeed it can. The challenge is to find the language to deliver the message in the least harmful, albeit most sympathetic way. Sometimes we are well aware of when we are being lied to but often we are not. But even in dire situations when we know that the person is being truthful, despite the deed, we have admiration for their courage under pressure.

There are as many examples of people in the public eye being courageous in telling the truth as there are of liars who are eventually found out. With the latter, no matter how much fancy footwork is employed, they only lose their influence and our respect for trying to rationalize their actions after having the chance to come clean. We only have to think back to US President Clinton's handling of the Lewinsky affair to be reminded of how deception leads to a dented image and loss of influence.

Still, being truthful is difficult. Think of something you want to tell someone else that you know will be painful. Write it down, the honest to goodness truth. The message is there. Now just think how you can change the wording to make it a positive learning experience for the person on the receiving end.

SHOWING AND TAKING INITIATIVE

The pace at which work is changing feels meteoric. We are part of the technological age. We read about it and watch really mind-blowing events happening in many businesses but at each of our own desks (ahem, work stations) we *feel* the evolution of work as we knew it. Change is no longer an option – it's the name of the game.

The majority of people are change-adverse, they don't feel they are, of course, or admit to it but they are. The change-adverse are the ones who rarely volunteer a new idea and less frequently put themselves forward for something out of their spec, i.e. above and beyond the call of duty.

Influencers don't wear their job specs on their sleeves; they are moulding and shaping their jobs daily by looking beyond the horizon, seeing potential and taking initiatives. They will have the confidence to challenge authority and, if done professionally and without arrogance, are highly valued, well rewarded and gain influence both inside and outside their organizations.

Initiative, like many aspects of influence, is dependent on positive thinking and an optimistic nature as mentioned earlier in the chapter. So in completing my list of key ingredients for gaining and having more influence – as a person and a brand – my advice is to decide if your self-esteem is up to scratch. If you are feeling low, unfulfilled and incomplete, you must work to resolve the reasons why and reverse the negativity in your mind and spirit. Self-esteem provides the necessary energy, enthusiasm and leadership to influence others. Without it you can't influence, only survive.

I hope that by working through the exercises and quizzes in this book along with reflecting on some of the ideas raised, you determine how you can – no, must – value yourself more.

8

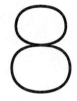

PRESENTING . . .
YOURSELF

We've covered your behaviour, manners, voice and appearance and now turn to how you can make the best impact when communicating in business.

You are both the message and the medium. No matter what the occasion, the subject or the audience, you are projecting your brand and yourself. As someone committed to being the best you can be, you must work at improving how you communicate and learn new techniques for getting others to listen to you for longer so they come away remembering you as well as your message.

YOU CAN'T *NOT* COMMUNICATE

How you communicate with others is inextricably linked to your image and how you brand yourself. Look the business, comport yourself well, sound OK and you get over the 30-second hurdle of the first impression. But after the first few minutes, if you are a poor communicator, your impact unravels.

I am often asked to coach a newly-appointed CEO on his/her image and personal presentation. Generally the call comes because of my reputation for transforming the *look* of many leading figures in business. In the majority of cases of new CEOs who have never held a top job before, it's actually their communication techniques which need more work. Just because someone was a good enough communicator to get appointed as MD or CEO doesn't mean that they always have the skills to be effective communicators at the top. The same is true for everyone as you climb the corporate ladder or switch sectors or gears in new jobs.

The main job of every managing director or CEO is to lead; and every leader's main job must be to communicate. They must convince staff, clients, investors, suppliers, distributors and the media that business is fine, it's doing just swell. Or when it's not fine, explain why and how they are going to put things right. Leaders have to galvanize, not just inform. The power brokers in business use information to move others and garner their support. They take information and make it matter to people.

No matter where you are in business, if you don't master good communication skills you risk being held back in your career. A survey of the CEOs of Fortune 1,000 companies found that communication skills are *key – the most important asset* – in advancing your career. Leadership guru Tom Peters says, 'If you aren't getting seen, you won't get on.' Well, mastering presentation skills is the greatest way to get seen and get on!

Good communicators know that every audience, every situation, requires a new strategy. The better prepared you are ahead of time the more likely the presentation or meeting will go well. But equally important is to be able to think on your feet, to read your audience and to adapt both your message and style accordingly.

How professional a presenter are you?

Hands up if you've done some presentation skills training. Well done! How long ago? You're kidding! So you've mastered Powerpoint and you think that you are in the Big League. Powerpoint is today's equivalent of the overhead projector – as equally tedious, predictable and too often badly used. Powerpoint ensures that your presentation is Prozac – it lulls audiences to sleep. The meretricious use of technology can never replace the art of good speaking.

Good communicators get coaching every year. This doesn't mean going on yet another course but it does mean getting feedback from people who can critique you objectively and help you improve. Use your next meeting or presentation as an opportunity to find out how good you are as a communicator or presenter and where you need to pay more attention or do things differently. Have someone who is a good communicator themselves critique your performance. Some of the areas you'll want some feedback on include these:

PRESENTATION FEEDBACK

1. How well did I grab their attention at the beginning?

   ❏ Not at all   ❏ Fairly well   ❏ Well   ❏ Outstanding

2. Describe how I looked at the start:

   ❏ Confident   ❏ Relaxed   ❏ Open   ❏ Nervous

   ❏ Uneasy   ❏ Serious   ❏ Fearful

3. How clearly did I explain what I was going to talk about and how things would run?

   ❏ Not effective   ❏ Fairly well   ❏ Well   ❏ Excellent

4 How well did I engage them and convey why this is important to them and get their agreement?

❏ Not at all ❏ To some extent

❏ Adequately ❏ Superbly

5 How well did I use eye contact?

❏ On everyone ❏ On a select few

❏ Too fleeting to be effective ❏ Inconsistent

❏ Natural and effective

6 Regarding my voice, describe how effective it was in delivering the message. Where is improvement needed?

. . . .
. . . .
. . . .
. . . .

7 Use of visual aids

❏ Overdone ❏ Not enough ❏ Boring ❏ Good

❏ Very interesting/balanced

Additional comments

. . . .
. . . .
. . . .

Suggestions for my being more effective next time:

. . . .
. . . .
. . . .

8   Interaction with the audience. Depending on the subject, setting and numbers how would you evaluate how effectively I engaged them?

❑   You didn't   ❑   Sporadic   ❑   Not enough

❑   Handled well   ❑   Excellent

Additional comments

....
....

9   Use of language. Evaluate what I said in terms of interest and clarity.

❑   Poor/muddled   ❑   Not bad   ❑   Good   ❑   Excellent

Specific comments on what you liked and didn't like with recommendations for improvement.

....
....

10   How effective was my closing?

❑   Ineffective   ❑   Efficient

❑   Good, but not memorable   ❑   Terrific

11   What was most memorable about what I said?

....
....

12   Comments on my appearance, please. Overall impression? What would you change? Any distractions?

....
....
....
....

Good communicators welcome – no, they relish – feedback. But some-times it can be very hard to take. You've put in the preparation time, battled with your nerves, did your damnedest! Remember that your goal is to be effective and to influence others. The only way you will know how you are doing is to bring a 'weathervane' with you who will tell you how the wind was blowing during your storming performance. Swallow hard and listen to their suggestions and you'll really knock 'em dead next time.

JUMP AT THE OPPORTUNITY TO SPEAK

There are many people who go to great lengths *not* to get up in front of others and present. 'I'm fine in meetings. I know my stuff and it's no trouble holding my own. But *presentations*, that's different.' We know. Anyone who's been in the spotlight knows just how different presentations are from speaking around a table. A platform perfor-mance can be terrifying. Public speaking is right up there on the scale of horrors that most of us dread in life, in fact, it is the second thing most of us fear next to death. The good news is that you only die once. But as a presenter you have the opportunity to die a thousand deaths!

Having died a few deaths (how else do you learn!) and resurrected myself, as well as countless others acting as their weathervane, I can assure you that once mastered always enjoyed. Once you get the basics down, put in the necessary planning and preparation, learn to think on your feet, develop a few routines that go down well, learn to enjoy *moving* people, then you will jump at the chance to give presentations.

'It's fine for you,' I am often told. 'You're a *born communicator*.' Love that . . . as if any of us pop out of the womb ready with a stand-up routine. No one is *born* to put themselves on the spot in front of an audience and entertain them. But all speakers at some point realize that if they don't grasp the nettle and master the art of public speaking they will not have the power and the influence that they want.

Effective personal branding is all about standing out of the crowd and getting noticed. No better way to get noticed than to get up on a platform and say, 'I've got less than an hour to change your life' or some such opening hook! (That's one of mine, by the way.)

OK, if that doesn't convince you to jump at the opportunity to speak, how about this: in a 30-minute presentation to 10 people you have had the equivalent of 5 hours of influence time. In an hour's presentation to 100 people you've got 2 weeks' worth of working flat out trying to influence the same number of people. Time is money, right? Just think how much more of both you can save by becoming a good presenter.

MAKE A DIFFERENCE, NOT JUST A SPEECH

But don't just jump at the opportunity to present unless you are prepared to put in some work to *make a difference*. You've seen enough presenters yourself who are deluded in thinking that just doing it or getting through it is enough. Most conferences are filled with people appointed to 'speak' about their side of the business. Often they are just descriptive reports or 'me and my team' focused presentations with little concern about getting under the skin of the audience and making it meaningful *for them*. It's a scandalous waste of everyone's time and money.

TO SCRIPT OR NOT TO SCRIPT

Moving on nicely from saving time, you, like most busy people, never have enough time. Preparing for meetings or a presentation *takes time*, often considerable time, if it is very important. What takes the most time is the staring at the blank word document or piece of paper screaming to yourself, 'OK, OK where do I begin?'

You begin with *purpose*. Why have you been asked to speak or why have you volunteered to speak about something? The 'topic' is not necessarily the 'purpose', i.e. speaking about something doesn't mean you will hit *why* something is interesting to your audience unless you uncover the purpose of the session.

Your purpose for speaking should be clear. What do I want them to know, feel, do, buy, etc? But make sure that *your* purpose doesn't conflict with *theirs*. If you are there to inform them of the quarterly results, maybe they want to know the implications of the company's performance on them and their work. Do they really want guidelines and ideas from you on how to improve their performance? If so, are you the right one to do this? If you know that they will want more than just information (and you are not the one with the solutions), team your presentation with a colleague who can jointly ensure that you give them what they want.

Once your purpose is clear, you set about writing it up. Sadly, too many people spend time *writing a document* rather than *preparing a conversation*. The former is what you hand out, summarized and bullet-pointed, for your audience's reference *after you speak*. The latter is what you need for a presentation. A script is not conversational and is better read than spoken. You'll probably agree that the only time it is fun to be read to is when you are 6 years old and not yet a great reader or when you're 96 and can't do so well any longer yourself! Reading to adults is at best boring and at worst patronizing.

A golden rule in presenting is if you don't know your subject well enough to speak without a script you shouldn't be speaking at all. All you need is a simple outline, like the Kubalek form on page 303, with bullet points to keep you on track.

If you have to 'do speeches' that are prepared for you by others, you must take time to redo the speech in your own conversation. Get the disk, edit it to your style, adding in your pauses or anecdotes. Nothing is more obvious then someone delivering someone else's speech, or more boring for you. Just think of the Queen!

So, forget a script whenever you can. You will, however, learn that crafting a good opening and closing is recommended. But all the stuff in between should be conversational, as if you are presenting an idea to a group of people around a dinner table. Tell yourself that you aren't *talking to them* rather you are *speaking with them*.

BEING MEMORABLE: ELISABETH MURDOCH

Elisabeth Murdoch, the daughter of global media magnate Rupert Murdoch, gave her first major speech after taking on the general manager's job at Sky TV at the Edinburgh Television Festival in August 1998. Preceding her was a cast of leading media moguls who spoke glued to a set, staged format – nailed to a lectern, reading speeches only alleviated with intermittent video clips flashed on an array of screens behind. Slick enough, but not what anyone would call memorable.

Petite, blonde and only 29, Elisabeth caught the audience's attention from the moment she took to the stage wearing blue jeans and a black leather jacket following the succession of 'suits'. Freeing herself from the restrictions of the lectern, she grabbed a radio mic and spoke without notes for almost an hour on the imminent reality of the digital era. She strode up and down the stage as she challenged the smugness of the TV industry saying things like, 'It's your viewers who will destroy you if you fail to meet their increased demands.' She went on to challenge the 'feeding frenzy' in the industry about the impending convergence of TV and the Internet, deemed a marriage that will live happily ever after. 'Well, I'm sorry to be the bearer of bad news, but there's been a divorce. No, not the first time I've had to talk about this subject in the last few months' (a reference to her own, very public divorce).

Murdoch's message was modern, direct and ambitious and all the more powerful because of her honest, confident delivery, which made other speakers look like dinosaurs of broadcasting rather than futurists like herself. While the content of her speech wasn't original, her unconventional delivery made it seem so. And judging by the buzz that followed, Elisabeth Murdoch was a woman few would forget as a result.

WHEN A SCRIPT IS REQUIRED

Despite what I say about throwing away the script, sometimes you simply can't. The information is so important that you can't get it wrong. Or, perhaps you are asked to stand in at short notice and deliver someone else's presentation. Then there are the learned conferences where 'papers are delivered'. If you were to free-wheel you might risk your reputation. Another reason why some people insist on a script is that they present so infrequently that they would be lost without the *security of the script*.

Accepting that you *have* to go by the script you do not have to make it tedious for the audience like the majority of 'readers' do. Here are some tips on being effective.

Make it readable

The written word makes tedious listening as I have said previously. If the material is yours, see how you can make it more compelling verbally. Generally the answer is to edit like a demon and change passive words to more active ones. If the material isn't yours, *make it yours*. Rephrase things so they flow off your tongue more naturally. Keep the important stuff that requires verbatim delivery but preface and wrap-up with your own interpretation. Your message will be more effective as a result.

Practise

Most scripts that are read are tedious because the speaker is raw to the material. She/he might have read it a few times but they didn't practise saying it. So they stumble, mispronounce words, use the wrong emphasis. The more you practise the more confident and competent your delivery.

Top 'n' tail without notes

The more you practise the more you will find opportunities to deliver parts of the text away from it. Get your introduction and closing down pat, so that you can speak them away from the dreaded lectern which turns you into an inanimate object. If you can add to your text with anecdotes or examples, again, step away from the lectern and do so.

Script it as you want to say it

There are a few key tips for preparing your script so that it is both easily read as well as highlighted with pauses and key points for emphasis. Here are the most useful:

- The text should be in a large font (minimum 18 point) for easy reading. Double-spaced, printed single-sided and on numbered pages.
- Highlight, use caps or print in **bold** the important words (but not whole sentences).
- Use a / or . . . or – to indicate where to pause.
- Never carry a sentence over to the next page.
- Use a wide margin for extra notes (written clearly).

Distribution

Only allow your *final* edited version of a speech to be distributed to conference delegates or the media after you have delivered it. Often meeting planners will ask for your speech weeks in advance when you might not have had time to really hone it to your likening. Also, late-breaking news might influence what you are talking about and make the speech seem dated.

▓ Getting organized

A good presentation takes time to develop. My rule of thumb is a 3 to 1 ratio – for every minute you will be speaking you need to spend 3 in development. And this does not include your visual aids.

By now, you may have discovered a wonderful technique for organizing your thoughts before an important presentation. I favour two different approaches to preparing and delivering a presentation. Both involve one A4 (US 8 ½ by 11 inches) piece of paper which is far preferable to shuffling index cards, reading an autocue or the dreaded script. The first – the Kubalek form – is for the linear/logical types who like to build ideas sequentially or present a problem and solution; the second – the Buzan Mind Map – is for the verbal/symbolic types who prefer to explore an idea more creatively. I use the linear approach for outlining and organizing and the Mind Map for brainstorming and developing new material. Let's see which is more natural for you.

THE KUBALEK FORM

The dynamo American communications coach Jay Kubalek developed a simple visual outline which aids the organization of any talk, be it a 10-minute meeting, an hour's presentation or a full-day seminar. I have used it effectively myself for countless meetings as well as with Members of Parliament to organize their thoughts for a debate and with teachers in developing their lesson plans.

The boxes are based on the well-proven approach for presenting. You:

> *Tell 'em what you are going to tell 'em.*
> *You tell 'em.*
> *Then tell 'em what you've told 'em.*

Sadly, too many people – having learned this approach in their Basic Presentation Techniques – take it literally. They will start with, 'Today I am going to tell you about the impact of Europe's integration on the global economy.' Then launch into it and wrap up with 'So, today I discussed Europe's integration on the global economy. Thank you.' Sure. It was well organized. We knew what she/he was talking about. But being well organized isn't enough to be remembered.

Be careful, however. The 'Tell 'em . . . Tell 'em . . . Tell 'em approach can be devoid of 'music' when it doesn't tune into WIIFM (What's In It For Me). Audiences couldn't care less about *your* objective. They want to know *why they* should be interested. So, no matter how organized and systematic you are (which is a valid approach in communication), you've got to hook 'em with *what's in it for them*. Using the Kubalek method and cognisant of its easy, logical organization, it is up to you to bring in the surprises – the startling introduction, a great story, apt analogies, helpful visual aids, jokes, etc.

The structure allows you to headline and bullet-point key issues and topics. The bullets/key words are simple triggers for you to discuss the issue. The format keeps you organized.

Here's an example of how I have used Kubalek with my own scribbled notations to make it seem less organized than it really is.

Branding Yourself

1 hr/change
your life
Define/project who
& what you see

Why	How	Looking it
You & your product Work not careers Portfolio branding Corporate vs personal Visibility	1st impressions 55% 38% 7% Image audit Priorities Sound of brand Act of Brand	We get it Looking the values Image matters Image strategy Now not yesterday Slides
Synergy required Do it	Focus & Influence	Be more than expected

? !

Many readers will be familiar with the inspirational Tony Buzan. Brain-man: inventor of Mind Maps, President of the Brain Foundation, lecturer and author. Mind Maps are used in business and education as an approach for accelerating your ability to learn, remember and record information. I find it magic for creative brainstorming as well

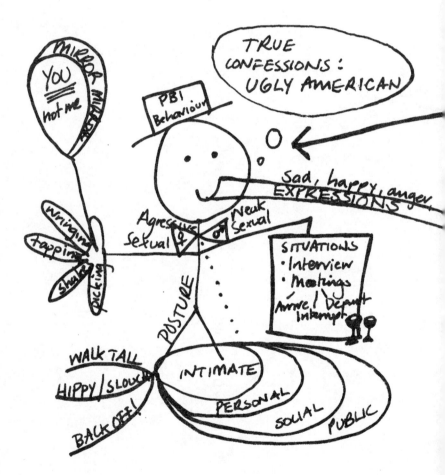

as for developing ideas for visual presentations and for writing books.

Mind-mapping involves the use of shapes, colours and dimensions as visual stimulants to the brain to help you both remember information and develop and connect ideas. Mind-mapping is not just useful, it is also fun. You play with coloured pens, draw pictures (badly) and giggle a lot. What better way to take the stress out of planning a presentation?

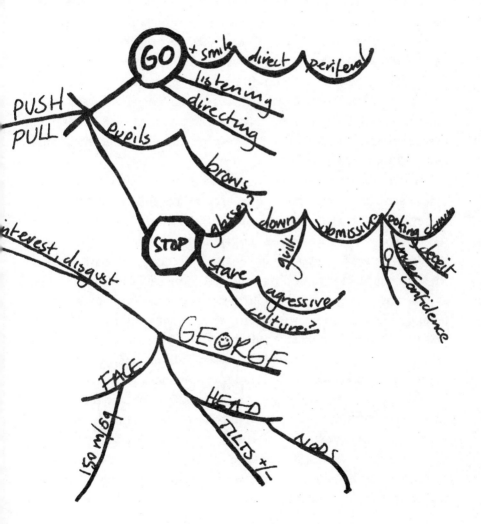

▨ No need to be nervous ever again!

You're not alone in suffering some nerves, perhaps the occasional terror, before speaking. Everyone does and everyone *should* (suffer nerves that is, not terror!). Being nervous means that you are alert, all systems are fired. (OK, you could do with a few of them being less fired up when you need 6 pit stops to the restroom before you begin!)

Over the years, I have heard any number of both dumb and dangerous suggestions for coping with pre-presentation nerves. *Why not have a drink to steady you?* Once asked to help out at a product launch with the media, when I arrived most of the presenters were all drinking beforehand – at 11 a.m.! The worst thing about alcohol is that you can tell when someone has had a drink. The slur is very slight but it is discernible to the sober. So, on the evening news these senior executives sounded like they had just left the pub when they were talking about their wonderful new car.

Mood-elevating drugs or tranquillisers of the Valium variety do relieve anxiety but are addictive and should never be tried before the big event. Everyone responds differently and you must make sure the dosage is right for you. I despair at the number of times that I've met a speaker who has taken 'something' given to him by a friend! Beta blockers like Propranol are non-addictive and effective at quashing nerves but still require a prescription. The risk you run in taking a relaxant is that you get so relaxed that you lose dynamism. OK, you might feel nice and calm but your audience might be lulled into oblivion as a result. The best prescription for nerves is practice, the more prepared you are the cooler you will feel. Promise.

Take great care if you are on any medication as it might have adverse effects under the pressure of an important presentation. I had a dreadful experience once travelling to a conference with a terrible head cold. (I am so obsessed with not letting clients down that I have presented after being hit by a car, the day before delivering a baby and with a broken arm.) I chugged away at cold remedies on the journey to the conference and when I got there I felt very strange. My mouth dried up and I started shaking all over. As a result, I just looked like a nervous twit. Simply great for a communications consultant!

So what really works? I *know* these techniques work because I use them myself and have seen them work hundreds of times for others.

10 sure-fire ways to beat pre-presentation jitters:

1   Prepare! Simply put: if you know your stuff, you've got everything organized and timed things pretty well, *it will go swimmingly*!

2   Visualize how you want it to go. Imagine them loving you, paying attention with a great round of applause at the end.

3   Don't eat for up to 3 hours beforehand. A big meal makes you sluggish and might disagree with you when the 'excitement' starts! This one's tough if you are an after lunch or dinner speaker. In which case, eat light. A lettuce leaf or two.

4   Release the adrenaline that's pumping through your system with a swift walk around the block, down some corridors, up the stairs, whatever you need to get it out of your system.

5   Don't waste your energy with useless small talk prior to a big presentation. It saps your energy and you are likely to talk about what you are going to speak about so that when you begin your presentation you'll panic and think, 'Did I already say that?'

6   Do say something just before you go on so that your voice doesn't crack at the start.

7   Lubricate the throat with sips of room-temperature still water. Have some handy.

8   If you forget water (silly) and you dry up (now that *really* can make you crazy), bite the sides of your tongue so the saliva starts flowing.

9   Make a great entrance. Your impact starts when your name is announced. Walk at an energetic pace to a predetermined spot. (This also sorts out the adrenaline rush when you hear your name.) Look at the audience and smile. Hey! They are smiling back. A positive entrance puts the audience in a positive frame of mind.

10 Your hands need sorting. The nervous wrecks never know what to do with their hands. Don't hold notes or stand behind a lectern. Both are image killers. *Expose yourself* (figuratively) to the audience. You have three options for what to do with your hands.
    – Bend them at the elbow. This ensures that you will gesture naturally when you speak.
    – Hold on to a pen to prevent yourself from holding your hands in some pathetic, undermining gesture. *As soon as you feel in control* get rid of the pen. You can keep it for 5 minutes max.
    – Keep your hands at your sides (the *most* confident starting position) but still *in touch with yourself* because you have the tips of your index finger and thumb on each hand in contact. Try it. You will feel the energy flow and *feel connected*. It works a treat and no one knows what you are up to.

▨ It's showtime

Each and every interview, meeting and presentation is a performance. If you never thought that to be the case then you have either failed in being as effective as you could or have had to work in overdrive to get the job done. When you meet with others to exchange ideas you are competing with many internal and external distractions for their attention. Everyone has a million things on their minds – the pressures of their in-trays, personal worries, and the desire to be anywhere else but here. Your job, no matter what your role or position, is to make the time with you worth *their* while. If it is, then it has been well worth *yours*.

According to research by Sam Deep and Lyle Sussman (authors of *What to Ask When you Don't Know What to Say*), the average business person speaks at 120 w.p.m. But the brain can process almost 600 w.p.m. That makes for some fairly bored brain cells in between. How you fill that gap is part of your performance. Your words had better be compelling and delivered in a way that both grabs and holds our attention. In 1992, according to *Business Week*, the average business person had an attention span of 6 minutes. That was in the good old days before most of us worked via the Net with its cryptic jargon and flashing Web imagery. Today our attention spans must be half that, on average 3 minutes!

To grab our attention and to hold it you need a power *visual aid* – the most powerful being yourself. We are visual junkies and are bombarded with messages visually every day via billboards, the television and the Net. If a brand today can't sell to us in 3 seconds or less they don't stand a chance of us perusing their web sites. If you don't grab us by how you look and how you perform when you communicate then you will also lose us. We'll give you those 3 minutes and then we're off on holiday or back to the in-tray or musing about something even better!

TECHNICAL TIPS

Make yourself easy to listen to by linking up with a sound system for groups of over 50 people. Using a radio lapel mic enables you to move around and interact more naturally with the audience. Always do a sound check and do more than just stand on the spot saying, 'Testing, testing, 1, 2, 3, 4.' Test the beginning of your presentation to ensure that nothing interferes with the mic – for example, a noisy necklace or earrings on women. Use words that begin with 'P' and 'B' to ensure that you don't get minor booms that are hard on the audience. Once the mic is set, leave it alone. If, for any reason, things don't go according to plan, summon the technician and tell him to sort it before going further. You will appear more confident as well as considerate of the audience.

GETTING PRESENTED

Nothing is worse than starting a presentation on your own – no introduction, no warm-up. There you are cold, having to explain why you are there, why the audience should listen to you, how you are going to help them. None of us do ourselves justice. When we do, people think we are arrogant. So, do yourself and your message justice by getting someone to introduce you.

Make it easy for them

It is better for you to write your own introduction than to rely on others. People often don't have enough time and are very grateful if you give them an easy introduction to familiarize themselves with before you go on.

In no more than half a page (double-spaced/18 point) prepare a brief background on yourself highlighting information that will be of interest to this audience. If you need to impress them, include degrees and publications or anything that will grab their attention.

After your biog, write a line, *We've asked Jane to speak with us today because* . . . suggesting that they ad lib why they have asked you to speak. Then a final line or two to summarize what you will be speaking about.

While you are being introduced don't stand or sit up front next to the person introducing you, if possible. It is much more effective to walk to the front of the group or up on to the stage. This way you are more likely to get a warm greeting from the audience (APPLAUSE) which makes them and you feel much more positive.

PRESENTING OTHERS

A wonderful way to get exposure as a presenter yourself is by presenting other people well. If you think of how badly this is done most of the time you will understand how easy it is to shine in front of an audience of your peers without the pressure of actually making a full-blown presentation.

Reflect on how you feel at the beginning of any presentation. On the occasion that you have been introduced effectively what did you like about how the person handled it? They, no doubt, were very flattering but in a way that you almost believed so you felt good about yourself. But also, the audience was responsive to their remarks. Good introductions, unlike the prescribed ones outlined above in case others don't do you justice, are sincere. The person expresses their personal interest and enthusiasm to listen so the audience buys in as a result.

An introduction is a mini-presentation and should be planned and crafted with the same amount of care. Do your homework on the person. Get them to provide their background details, any articles that they have written or publicity material. From here you can glean the highlights that you think will appeal to the audience.

Try to meet the person ahead of time, not 10 minutes before the speech but for a leisurely drink or coffee to pick up an anecdote or two that you can incorporate into your introduction to make it really personal. If it is appropriate to be witty, and you are humorous, try a light approach to add to your warm-up.

Get everyone's attention before you start. If there is a clamour, quieten them down. Pause. Then have a great one-liner to get their attention. 'Are you prepared to be challenged?' Or, 'I haven't had a decent night's sleep since meeting our speaker last week.' It is much better to grab them with a hook and personal anecdote as to why you think the speaker will be interesting than to launch into their CV. Look at the speaker occasionally but remember that while you are presenting him/her to the audience you are warming *them* up.

Finally, it is your job to lead a warm welcome of applause – music to every presenter's ears – at the beginning and end of a talk.

▨ Bang beginnings

Most audiences are not braced to be bored, rather they are eager to be informed and entertained. You must reward them immediately. Let them know that their attention is appreciated and that you won't disappoint them.

We remember openings and closings of presentations far more than all the palaver in between. Craft your openings to grab attention, to get people to sit up and notice and be hooked into listening.

HOW NOT TO BEGIN

Many people start so ineffectively that we switch off before they really get going. They apologize for something or other. 'Sorry about the Powerpoint not working today. I should have brought acetates as a back-up but didn't. Well, you all have copies of the presentation so, let's go through them together.' Dud!

Another way to turn off an audience before you begin is with obsequious pandering to bigwigs. 'I would like to thank Mr Chairman for his kind introduction. How can I follow someone held in such high regard, a proverbial titan amongst the actuary profession! I remember when I first met you, sir . . .' Give us a break!

But, perhaps the worst openings are those that repeat the title of their speech or regurgitate what's already been said. 'As the slide says today I am going to talk about the federation's accounts for last year. You have already heard from Sandy about the new headquarters and how much they overran the budget. I'll give you more details on that. And Dave announced the increase in subscriptions and declining membership so I will talk about that too . . .' No wonder a number from the audience slip out surreptitiously.

SURPRISE, STARTLE, ENTICE – SPECIAL EFFECTS

Surprise, startle, entice us at the beginning. Some show-offs love to create real theatre at the beginning with sound and visual effects that create excitement. I use this occasionally in small groups of very senior people because nothing is more out of place in a company boardroom than music or sound effects. The key is not to let them know that it's coming. I programme a CD player to a particular track then with a flick of a button, right on cue, on comes the music or sound effect with devastating impact.

Often I will use the sound of a helicopter (first shown to me by the Master Trainer John Townsend in Geneva) and with the whirling sounds of the chopper shout:

'Fasten your seatbelts, we are taking off.' The chopper gets louder. 'Today we are going to take a bird's eye view of how you perform. You will learn how others see you and discover things about yourself that you never knew before.'

It works a treat in grabbing attention.

THE WARM-UP

You need to warm up an audience when you are the first or only speaker. This is also true of business meetings in the role of the chairperson at the beginning of the meeting or, for example, when you call others in for a briefing. Even if you have been introduced, the audience isn't prepared for listening yet. They need to get to know you. It's like two dogs who meet in a park. They sniff each other to get a sense of how much fun they are or if they are hostile. The warm-up gives you the same opportunity and allows your audience to size you up. It's best to make your warm-up relevant to both you and the group and/or your subject.

I sometimes cue a story with the time or setting. For a graveyard slot after lunch, after being introduced, I might walk around the room looking at the audience very carefully and say, 'Yes, they are right . . . you are all brain-dead! Scientists have confirmed that after lunch our brain cells are stalled. All the blood that they need to work is diverted to our stomachs for digestion and after that lovely lunch yours is really pumping. So, it's a good thing that I'm here to talk about image because we use our guts before our brains in making judgements about people. I wonder how many of you are already churning away at me disapprovingly?' Then moving closely towards someone I'll tilt my head towards them as if listening to their stomachs and say, 'No, I promise. You've got me all wrong!' It's a pretty good ice-breaker for the graveyard slot.

FIND A BOND

You may have to speak with many disparate groups that require you to do some homework to link your material to them. When on new and uncertain territory, it is good to establish a bond upfront that conveys that you understand them and are one of them. If there are no substantive bonds between your profession/sector and theirs try making a personal link to their work.

Politicians have to do this all the time with many becoming masters at establishing links. Former US President Ronald Reagan, dubbed the 'Great communicator', was so effective at cosy openers that CDs of his presentations and jokes are hot sellers with business people (*Well . . . there you go again*). Here's an example in an address to the American Medical Association: *'I'm delighted to address this annual meeting of the AMA House of Delegates, and I want to congratulate Dr Jirka and Dr Boyle on their new positions. I can't help but think what a great place this would be and what a great moment to have a low back pain.'*

TELL A STORY

We all remember presentations that open with a compelling or funny story. You can use others' stories as a guide to develop your own but it is important that it becomes *your story*. Nothing is more obvious or boring than 'Have you heard the one about . . . ?' Of course, we've all heard it and it wasn't even funny the first time round.

You are a rich source of potentially wonderful stories. Your background, life experiences and what happens to you daily provides you with plenty of material. Dig deeply into your past, your childhood, school, sports experiences. Lessons from friendships and relationships. Lessons from what you've learned from making a fool of yourself when you got things hopelessly wrong. Nothing is more compelling to an audience than to expose your own vulnerability. People don't care how much you know, they care how much you care. The best chief executives show their staff how much their business means to them and why it should mean so much to them. Some of the best motivators, like Anthony Robbins and Steven Covey, are thus because of overcoming their own failures and lack of confidence.

Always *tell* your story, never read it. And practise telling it aloud until it works. Get the timing perfect, the punchline succinct. Try it out on as many people as you can ahead of time, especially kids. If you grip a child you've got a good story.

I like to use a story about someone who might not be dissimilar to my audience, who when I first met them was very hostile to being sent for coaching on their image. I set the scene, helping them to visualize it by using words like 'imagine' and describing a situation that they could identify with. By telling such a story, you can voice preconceived objections that some of the audience might also share and deal with them upfront in a sort of 'clear the air' exercise before you get to your presentation. I advise this approach for politicians to disarm a tough audience or boards when facing a difficult AGM. You can't expect the hostility to vanish completely but you will be given a fairer chance of getting your points across because you've been open about your vulnerability.

BRANDING HERSELF: KAREN

One of the best presentations I heard lasted only 5 minutes. I was asked to speak to a group of high-school students about image and was to share the platform with an alumna who was anorexic. The principal and PTA were concerned that many girls were overly conscious about their weight and wanted to warn students of the insidious nature of the disease. I knew she was to follow me, but the kids didn't.

The school principal introduced Karen to the audience without them seeing her. Flashed on the screen was a picture of a beautiful, healthy 17-year-old girl – just like many in the audience. The principal said, 'We are so proud to have with us today Karen Avery from the class of '87. She graduated with a 3.8 average and went on to study communications at Boston University. Like many of you seniors, Karen had dreams. But sadly, most of them have evaporated due to an illness that she developed here at our school.'

Karen came on to the stage in a wheelchair, attached to a drip. Her voice was so weak even with a microphone. 'Look at the person sitting next to you,' she said to the surprise of the students. They obliged. 'I looked just like you girls 10 years ago. Now look at me. This is what obsession can do to you. When I was your age, I started to become obsessed with my weight. Many of my friends were slimmer than I was and I wanted to be more like them. We used to take our measurements every week. Do any of you do that? WI's (weigh-ins) and MI's (measure-ins) we called them. The thinnest were the ones most applauded and envied. So, I started dieting, then bingeing, then making myself sick, then starving. There were five of us who really became obsessed with our weight. One got counselling early and recovered before getting too ill. The rest of us have been in and out of hospitals for 10 years.'

Up on the screen flashed pictures of today's celebrity 'role models' Calista Flockhart, Courtney Cox and Kate Moss. Karen continued, 'Hey, who doesn't want to look like them? They are gorgeous, aren't they? Well, I worked hard and looked just like them. I was so excited and proud when my waist was 21 inches.' Up came another slide of Karen looking 'glamorously' slim. 'But I couldn't stay that way. That's what anorexia does. You think you are in control of your life, your figure, your health, but you aren't. The disease controls you. Now I am in its grip. I've gone from being "perfect" to being next to nothing.

'Yes, I am very ill. You see this drip and the prognosis for my recovery is not good. I want to convince you all – girls and boys – that anorexia is no joke.' Another slide came up of Karen at 17 again, laughing. 'I thought it was a joke then, when I was here at school. I thought I could control it but I can't. I hope you get my message. If your weight gets out of control, you aren't the size of these TV icons or the supermodels, thank your lucky stars. Because if you become that size – that unreal, unattainable, *wrong* ideal – you could end up like me. Try and remember that.'

Indeed, I will never forget Karen nor her message and judging by the stunned audience of young people neither will the 500 or so of them.

Karen put herself on the line. She exposed her vulnerability and related it to her audience in one of the most powerful ways imaginable. Take a lesson from her. When in doubt, 'expose yourself' if you really care about getting a message across.

Be interactive or die

We all learn in basic presentation skills training that we've got to consider the audience – know who they are, what they are interested in – to influence them. In business, we do this to a much lesser degree unless we are in proper 'delivering a presentation' mode. And then we still tend to forget it and focus on *what we want to say* rather than *what they want to listen to*.

Just think of all the meetings that you attended this week. Some will have been briefings or project discussions, others brainstorming sessions with interviews and one-on-ones peppered throughout. Business *is* meetings, the day-to-day rituals with most trying to pass themselves off as useful experiences. Arguably, 75 per cent of them are a waste of time. Meetings are supposed to be about communication, where you, me and everyone else learns something, thinks and feels differently, or is charged up to do something as a result. But most don't, which is why we can only remember about 10 per cent of what was said a day later. Because you weren't involved, what happened didn't matter all that much to you. You could have done with a salient briefing document rather than getting pins and needles in your butt for all those hours.

Hence, every time you do communicate you've got to do more than just talk. The talking is important but so too is the involvement of others. The more involved, the more memorable you will be.

Out of the 3 scenarios below, which one would be the most memorable?

Let me set the scene. You are about to leave London by train to Manchester. You settle into your seat prepared to do a bit of work when you discover you have a talkative neighbour sharing your table with her flask of tea and sandwiches unpacked.

- *Scenario 1.* The woman starts chattering away about the Paddington Rail disaster. She was there on the day, saw the rescue operation, the chaos, the screaming. It was awful. Her friend was on the train (and, thankfully, survived). She knows all the details and shares them with you. Being a disaster that moved and worried everyone, you listen attentively but then return to your paper work and she gets the message that you've had enough.

- *Scenario 2*. Same situation, same woman obsessed with the Paddington Rail disaster. But now she pulls out of her case a copy of the *Daily Mail* that covered the story. It brings it all back to you, remembering how it must have felt to be in one of those carriages. The panic and fear. The woman eventually folds the paper away and starts on about of the weather. You return to your paperwork.

- *Scenario 3*. Same situation, same train and female passenger with you. All of a sudden you feel a jolt and are knocked sideways. Tea splatters, papers fly. The train stops but now seems to be on an angle. Something has happened.

OK, it's pretty obvious which scenario was more memorable. In Scenario 1, the 'presentation' was totally verbal. You were being talked at and, although marginally interested, you switched off as soon as you could.

In Scenario 2, you were more engaged because of seeing the news-paper clippings of the railway disaster. Just by using that visual aid you are 10 times more likely to remember that conversation.

But in Scenario 3 both you and your companion will remember just about everything that happened: the feel of the jolt, the sounds (breaks screeching, the thud of your briefcase on to the floor, the surprise and anxiety of the passengers), what you saw (papers and cups flying). You will never forget it because you were involved.

Unless you involve your audience, whether it be on a one-to-one, small group meeting or with an audience of 500, you risk your impact and message evaporating as quickly as their polite applause at the end. How you involve your audience can be simple. Here are a few suggestions.

ASK QUESTIONS

Dead simple, genuine and helpful. If you buy my principle of making your presentation conversational it is only natural that as part of the conversation you sometimes ask for clarity or agreement or new information. 'Hands up those of you who agree that we should scrap weekly meetings?' 'Someone from the communications team can remind us of some of the headlines that resulted from that announcement.' 'Do you all agree that we've done enough analysis and that now we need action?'

LET THE AUDIENCE INTERACT

Give your audience a brief break to talk to the person next to them or to people around them. This can be as brief as suggesting that they meet everyone around them or for them to discuss an idea or to come up with questions. Sitting and listening for any period of time can be deadly. We all love to talk and to get involved so give your audience ways to do this and you will find them more attentive as a result.

For example, 'We've been discussing the importance of leadership to our company for about a half hour and why I believe you are all potential leaders. For 5 minutes talk with the person sitting next to you about how leadership is possible in their job.' Then you identify people to share what they discussed.

COMPLIMENT THE AUDIENCE

The key to this working is sincerity. But when you compliment the entire gathering everyone glows with the recognition. 'I always have such a good time when I come to Scotland and Glasgow, in particular. Glaswegians are so demonstrative – you smile, laugh out loud and applaud very well. In Edinburgh, I have to watch eyebrows very carefully. For the only way I know that I am going down well is if they raise them after a punchline!' It's fun to 'exploit' regional rivalry; guys like to do this with sports teams. For example, if referring to a competitor you can dismiss their likely threat with 'What would you expect from a xxxx supporter.'

You can also use comparative/competitive inside information effectively if you are sure that everyone will get the point. Before the merger of Glaxo and Smith Kline-Beecham, I worked for both companies and was well aware of their competitive rivalry and would make jokes about the negative side effects of the other's anti-depressants which the staff would love. I could use the same gags with both audiences by just replacing the different brands when making my point. (Now that you are merged, guys, I figured I'd come clean!)

STARTLE THEM

The flip-side of complimenting your audience is to startle them with a challenge. The bolder the better provided you never hurt anyone's feelings. You can imagine that I have more than a few ways to be a bit challenging with my work. 'Thank you so much for having me along today and for providing me with enough potential work for the next 5 years.' Or, at the beginning of a course on 'Impact and Influence', I ask them to check what they are doing the morning after the seminar. I tell them to make a note next to their first meeting saying, 'Prepared to be blown away!'

USE PERSONAL ANECDOTES THEY'LL IDENTIFY WITH

The easiest and most effective stories are ones to which your audience will relate. When you tell the story, they get involved, nod their heads and smile in recognition. You, like me, might do some charity work. I have personal favourites that I am delighted to help out with fundraising by being an after-dinner speaker (usually to fat-cat philanthropists). However, when I can, I link a personal story with the work of the charity as part of my presentation.

At a dinner in aid of Childline (the children's telephone support line) I told them how I had mixed feelings about speaking on behalf of the charity. 'I, like all parents, supported their laudable work but must confess to being reported to Childline. Yes. Here stands before you someone who doesn't seem all that she appears. Just what you might expect from an *image consultant*! My daughter Lucy, at the age of 8, called Childline to report that she was the victim of child labour. Her mother only paid her £1 to clean up her room and it took 2 hours!'

Every parent laughed, having been subjected to similar threats from their kids. I took the judgement that I could get away with this anecdote without causing offence considering the genuinely serious subject of child abuse and went on to highlight the importance of Childline's work in light of recent harrowing scandals around abuse in state children's homes.

A ROUND OF APPLAUSE!

This is easy, effective and has the added benefit of waking up the audience. If you ask someone to make a contribution or someone volunteers a useful point ask the audience to applaud the person. I often bring up people from the audience and use them to demonstrate points. For example, I will have two people come up and describe their corporate values next to a flip chart. Then I will ask the audience how well they both project those values by how they are dressed! Can you imagine the stress those people feel? I use fun banter to take the edge off what could be a difficult situation and compliment them while also making informative observations as to how they could project the brand values even better. When they are done, I ask the audience to give them a round of applause for being such good sports. The place will generally erupt since everyone is so glad not to have been chosen as a guinea pig!

By asking for a round of applause you also humble yourself. You are in the spotlight, the expert for a few minutes. But you take an opportunity to share the spotlight and the applause with others. I always find that being generous breeds generosity in others.

▨ Visual aids

Everyone who has ever had presentation skills training has been told, 'You gotta have visuals! Otherwise your talk is just that, talk!'

Anyone who has attended a conference where every presenter used visual aids knows that nothing kills a presentation faster than endless slides the audience reads while the presenter reads them aloud. And as we can read the slide in milliseconds we have to endure the presenter taking a few minutes to tell us what we now already know!

Visual aids are only helpful for making complex stuff come alive and for presenting images that enhance your words. They can also help your audience remember key points but not everything. That's why slide after slide of data even if made simple with bullet points is, well, pointless. We'll never remember it all.

Visual aids are useful to the presenter because they can serve as a road map through your talk but too many people rely on them for this purpose, which makes things easy for them but tedious for the audience.

The best presenters do without visual aids. They don't need them, because they themselves are their most important visual aid. Sort this and you don't need any others.

MAKE 'EM GOOD

If you need to use visual aids you've got to make them good. Who's the competition? The guys from marketing? The boss? The competition? Nope – it's television. Your visual aids have to be slick, simple and effective with the clarity of a TV advert. That's what your audience is used to and that's what they 'buy'. If you can't produce clear, imaginative visual aids, don't use any.

I have to come clean and say that I am a great believer and user of visual aids and pepper most presentations with a variety of stuff. What I never do is give an entire presentation with visual aids, e.g. work through a stack of overheads or a complete computer presentation including the title of the presentation! That's what's humdrum, that's what most business people do (for comfort) and so here's your opportunity to break out of the mould and dare to be different. Let's review the 'obvious suspects' that are used in business and then cover other ideas for props that can enhance your message.

FLIPCHARTS

Perhaps the most derided member of the visual aid brigade is the humble flipchart. But I love them for 3 reasons:

- *Flippies are readily available.* They don't involve plugs or dimming of lights.
- *Flippies are easy to use.* If you can spell, write and draw you are away.
- *Flippies are interactive.* They help you engage the audience quickly, spontaneously and with great effect.

So, even in our high-tech/clip-art/Powerpoint world there remains a role for the humble flipchart.

I won't waste your time labouring obvious points in using flipcharts effectively like: WRITE BIG, use coloured pens (2 max per page), don't fill the page. Here are some better hints:

- *Prepare some pages* ahead of time to guide you through a section. Leave some info blank to generate interaction with your group.
- *Use prompt words written in pencil* to help you write/draw what you want to look spontaneous!

- *Keep a blank page between each sheet* otherwise prepared sheets show through.
- *Fold the bottom right corner of each page* to make turning the pages easy.
- *Create a waterfall* folding up sections of the page with different bits of information so that you can *reveal* ideas one at a time. Secure each fold with a bit of Bluetac or sellotape for you to whip open easily.
- *Blow-up illustrations/logos on the copier* and spray mount on to pages for added visual effect.
- *Don't use more than 8 pages at a go.* You then turn into the Absentminded Professor!

OVERHEAD PROJECTORS

In our computer age, these are fast becoming dinosaurs like the old 35mm slide projectors. But as many people find acetates easy to develop, interactive and more flexible than a computer presentation, the overhead still is a viable presentation tool.

There are several things that make the overhead a scourge in meetings. Nothing is more depressing than to see Herb from Accounts approach the projector with a mountain of slides. Oy, vey! We know how long this is going to take. Another bore is that overhead projectors are tedious to operate. Sure, there's an art to it but few people remember to turn the lever down to cut the light in between slides or they spend too much time fiddling nervously trying to get the slide straight. When bits of paper are used to conceal some exciting info ahead or you start writing or using a pointer we all are focusing more on how smooth you are with the gear than on what you are saying. Then there's the dilemma of *where to stand*. You know you shouldn't block the screen but then no one looks at you (so if the slides are naff your presentation bombs). Active presenters usually blind themselves by walking in front of the light, then lose their train of thought. The whole overhead thing is such a palaver I wonder why people bother. You also have to be sure that you only darken the area at the front so that the screen can be seen, but make sure that you keep yourself lit – as well as the audience, or they'll fall asleep!

If you insist on using your trusty overhead projector, here's some advice:

- *Bring an extra bulb* as the projector supplied will probably blow.
- *Bring your own extension lead.* You always need one.
- *Accept that OHP slides are very silly so don't try to dazzle.* Use cartoons, colours, stick figures, scribble on them. Computer-generated slides should be used on a computer, not on something used in most primary schools.

COMPUTER PRESENTATIONS

As most grown-up presentations today beyond primary school level are done via computers don't suffer from the delusion that your Powerpoint show will knock 'em dead. It won't if it is a long saga of charts, bullet points and statistics regardless of slick colours, clip art and fonts you've used. Powerpoint is so pervasive that it is standard, bog standard and about as mesmerizing as watching paint dry.

Unlike other old-fashioned visuals, like overhead projectors and flipcharts, computer-generated presentations are limiting in as much as they are sequential presentations. Once on, you are on! There is no way that you can alter your presentation aside from the very obvious re-tracking through slides or fast-forwarding. The key is to limit the amount and to use a computer presentation for only part of your slot, not for the entire session.

How do you slick-up a computer presentation in a way that won't cost you several thousand pounds? (AV/Design costs in presentations are the most expensive item in a conference budget beyond food and accommodation.) You remember these important points:

- Only use a computer presentation when necessary and then keep it to a minimum.
- Use more graphics, pictures and illustrations than words.
- Limit yourself to 20 words a slide and no complete sentences.
- Brand yourself and your company logo at the end, not at the beginning and only discreetly (if you must) on each slide.
- Don't give the entire presentation via the computer, only the absolutely essential stuff.
- Don't be in the dark. Get a spotlight on you.
- Ditto for the audience or they'll take a nap.
- Know how to operate an LCD projector yourself. The technician is invariably on a coffee break just when it's your turn to go on.
- Know how to reboot your computer if it decides to die on you.
- Be prepared to wing it without the computer (Murphy's Law rules most conferences). So bring acetates or, better still, use your wits instead.

VIDEO/FILM CLIPS

Since we are so used to the slickness of TV and film it can be useful to incorporate video clips into your presentation if they are relevant. Just be sure that the clip isn't too long or the audience will be disappointed when they return to little ole you up there on stage without the special effects.

If you want to incorporate TV clips, set them up and get them ready to go with a flick of the remote. Running around and fiddling with the monitor and lights destroys the flow of your presentation. Better still, have a technician (fresh from his coffee break) on hand to do the honours. Then you really can look good.

■ Be conclusive

We'll assume that the body of your talk has been good, you know your stuff, covered the key points and reinforced them with anecdotes and a bit of humour. Great. But the conclusion is vital for leaving a lasting, possibly permanent, impression about yourself. So make it clear, make it good and make 'em applaud.

TELL 'EM WHAT YOU'VE TOLD 'EM

Back to the structure. You've been so amazing and raised many interesting issues. Remind us how they are linked. Summarize your premise and how you've proved it. *But don't restate ideas the way you have already presented them!* Give your key points a new spin. But be brief.

TELL 'EM WHAT TO DO

If you want and need to get results from your presentation don't leave it for them to infer it. Tell them what you want and say so clearly. Here's what I mean: *'I hope that in the brief time that I've had with you today, you've learned that your complacency could cost you your life. You might think you are fine but, until you have the proof that I've discussed today, you are a living time bomb. If you are one of the 75 per cent of staff who haven't had a health screening in the last 3 years, do yourself a favour and book it today.'*

LINK WHAT *YOU'VE* LEARNED FROM *THEM*

If the forum is right, include a question and answer session as part of your presentation *before* you conclude. Going back to Q & As after you've finished, done your resounding wrap-up, means that you fizzle out after the last question when the moderator says time's up. Dud!

Fit in your Q & As after the main body of your text. If during the Q & As you learn that one particular issue remains unresolved or is still contentious include it in your final remarks. This gives value to the audience and makes them feel like they have been part of a conversation rather than talked at. As much as speakers like to move an audience, the reverse is also true (especially with in-house business conferences or seminars).

One of mine, which is useful for anyone pitching their wares, is: *'I can tell that today was not just a wonderful chance to visit this fantastic resort, it was also a great market opportunity judging by your questions! I am ready and willing.'*

REFER TO THE BEGINNING

When speaking for an hour or more you can use your conclusion to dramatic effect by referring to the beginning. *'When started I told you that we spend 70 per cent of our time in meetings and that almost half of you consider them to be a total waste of time. If you try nothing else from my suggestions on managing your time better at least review your forthcoming schedule and cancel any meeting that you know will be unproductive. For those of you who consider all of them a waste of time, you'd better get thinking about what you are going to do for 3 ? days a week instead!'*

QUOTE SOMEONE EVEN BETTER

Apt quotes are great for peppering into your presentations and are particularly effective for creating a strong conclusion. For new CEOs it is vital to make an early impact on the troops. When coaching new appointees, I often suggest a great quote to back up their message.

Here's a great one that I suggested to a new managing partner in a law firm as a conclusion to his first talk to the firm:

> 'As you can imagine, going from being a successful lawyer into a leadership role of a world-class global practice means that I've got a bit of a learning curve ahead me. So I've been reading all sorts of books by the management gurus like Tom Peters and Steven Covey. Another lesser known author, Jim O'Toole, who wrote Leading Change, is particularly relevant to someone charged with leading his equals. He says, "In essence, the leadership challenge is to provide the glue to cohere independent units in a world characterized by forces of entropy and fragmentation. Only one element has been identified as powerful enough to overcome the centrifugal forces . . . and that is trust." All I can say is "Trust me" and I won't let you down.'

Even this group of overly-confident lawyers were moved to giving him a standing ovation.

▨ Get your image right

As much as I'd like to, I can't write a prescription about what to wear to deliver a winning presentation. You know two obvious things: look smart and look sharp. In all cases, simplicity is easier on the eyes. So even if you are quite a flamboyant character let your personality wow them rather than your clothes.

Some important pointers:

- *Perfect fit.* If your clothes don't quite fit, that's what we'll remember afterwards. Women: watch straining buttons, irregular hemlines and sleeve lengths. Men: be able to breathe and move with your jacket buttoned (if you wear one). If you go without a jacket, *wear a belt* and be sure your trousers can stay on your waist without constant adjustment.
- *If wearing a suit/jacket always button up.* If you don't our eyes spend the time inspecting your waistline and environs rather than concentrate on your face. A buttoned jacket creates a V which draw the eyes to your face – where you want it!
- *Contrast with the backdrop.* It's very important to know what you will be standing in front of, what will be your backdrop. If you know the room will be darkened (e.g. for visuals) then you have to stand out. Guys need a coloured shirt or striking tie. Women benefit from wearing colour, at least in the top half.
- *Define your facial features.* Women: daytime make-up is too light. Be more definitive with everything including an extra lashing of translucent powder to minimize any shine. Men: if you shine also dust yourself down.
- *Frame your face.* Your hairstyle should be neat and not

pull any surprises (e.g. fall into your face). Use
whatever is needed to have it stay in place and off
your face.

• *No noise aside from your voice.* That means earrings,
multiple neck chains and bracelets which will be
amplified by a sound system.

After reading this chapter you should know what you need to change
to be a more effective presenter. Don't wait for the next big event.
Change now. Do it fast. Get the buzz from creating a buzz.

9

■

SEX AT WORK

Too bad. This chapter is not about how to 'get it on', rather how to *get on with* the opposite sex at work. I promise not to preach, be either pedantic or politically correct, because we have had plenty of that over the last 20 years. What we haven't had enough of is straight-talk about men and women working together and *enjoying it* in ways that are different from how we live together in our personal lives.

As a performance coach I have been sucked into the debate unwittingly for the last two decades. My women-only image seminars often evolve into how to deal with men who try to get the better of them, who make them feel uncomfortable or insignificant. 'He gets so close, I hate it.' 'He interrupts me constantly and I inevitably give in.' In the men's sessions, we discuss the perplexing challenges that both female co-workers and clients present. 'What do I do when my client comes on to me?' they'll ask. Or, 'I want to encourage my assistant but my peers think I have a hidden agenda and give me a lot of stick which is embarrassing to me and to her.'

As soon as the topic of sex and work is introduced, sparks fly as fast as the anecdotes. Many have a story about an awful experience that made them feel diminished, which is basic sexual harassment. But more are just flummoxed not knowing how on earth to deal with specific individuals who make work difficult, or how to handle situations that happen time and again that get the better of them.

We've got to figure it out

It is imperative for us to figure out how to make work *work* for the sexes because not knowing how is causing financial, recruitment and PR havoc for companies. Every week, the media reports fresh stories of sexual discrimination or harassment, which ends up costing anywhere from tens of thousands in back pay, to millions for harassment deemed to have caused an irrevocable toll on an individual. The stories range from the despicable, like the male doctor who preyed on female patients or the woman who falsely accuses her male boss of rape, to the pervasive where women lose their jobs or are drummed out of high-flying posts once they become mothers.

Then there are the ridiculous cases that end up in court because companies themselves can't find workable, intelligent guidelines to suit the changing nature of work. A good example was the female train ticket collectors who weren't allowed to wear trousers while their male colleagues weren't forced to wear skirts. The company's rationale: 'our customers prefer the women in skirts'. Or men whose jobs were threatened for wearing a ponytail or a nose stud or make-up. The company's rationale: 'it is not part of the company image to have men looking like this'.

Companies smarting from the bad press of harassment or discrimination cases usually respond with knee-jerk guidelines laying down stringent dos and don'ts which create such a tense, artificial atmosphere that staff morale plummets even deeper in the wake of a very public rebuke in the courts. Following one very public harassment case, a leading insurance company issued guidelines that included advice for male managers dealing with female secretaries:

- Never compliment your secretary on her appearance.
- If you don't like the way she dresses, raise the issue with the Human Resources department who will

deal with the complaint in light of the company dress policy.

- Do not ask your secretary to work after hours if you are likely to be alone together or without others being present at the same time in the department.
- Avoid close proximity that she might find threatening. Better to have a desk between the two of you when communicating [!].
- For performance reviews with female staff, request an observer from the Human Resources department to ensure that any misunderstandings are documented and that you have a witness to any discussions that may be misconstrued.
- Do not ask your secretary about her personal life. If she volunteers information you may respond as you see fit but never encourage her to give more details.
- Do not have any physical contact with your secretary.

It is a pretty sad state of affairs when companies have to resort to such measures. So, in she comes one day having had her long hair cut short and dyed red and you can't say 'wow!' Or, you are both under pressure to deliver on a deal but can't work overtime to get the job done because there aren't any witnesses to potential harassment. Or you come back from lunch to find her in tears, she is so upset that she can't tell you why, and you can't ask her what's happened! Another tells you her mum has just died and you can't give her a consoling hug! Madness!

As our work takes up even more of our lives (despite directives to limit working hours many sectors work *all hours*), we've got to make the workplace a more humane environment for both men and women to thrive. If we don't, companies won't be able to recruit the talent and numbers required. Recent studies (Cooper & Lybrand '98; Mintel '99) show that young graduates rank a good quality of life above salary or career prospects as their goal. Now many women wanting both a career and a family have to sacrifice one for the other or wear themselves into the ground trying to do both. And men who want to participate fully as parents are subtly coerced from doing so by inflexible work policies.

Rather than throwing in the towel when the going gets tough, men and women should join together at work to discuss mutual problems they share in juggling their personal lives and work commitments as well as how they can deal with misunderstanding between them.

HITE'S HOPEFUL

Shere Hite, the internationally acclaimed author of exhaustive studies on human relationships and sexual behaviour, surveyed leading global companies, spoke to women and men at different levels of business as well as conducted in-depth interviews of 20 CEOs of Fortune 1000 businesses for her book *Sex and Business*. As a result, Hite believes that a 'completely different emotional-psychological landscape is now trying to emerge . . . Instead of buying gender differences and being paranoid about each other, men and women can embrace their different strengths and be proud of them'.

Hite's findings concur with much of the anecdotal material from my work and personal experiences in my own career. I share her optimism about the potential for our working relationships in the twenty-first century mainly because work dominates our lives. We've just *got* to figure it out. If we don't enjoy our work – find warmth and camaraderie for most of our waking hours – we suffer. When work is crap so too is your personal life. You drag the disappointments and frustrations home with you and she/he who denies that they don't vent these feelings on their loved ones is a liar. The powerless soldier on, some with the 'aid' of anti-depressants, others taking more 'sick days', never resolving what damn-well has to be resolvable: how women and men can work together to the benefit of themselves and their organizations.

OD'D ON PC?

In the last 20 years, many men have been bruised by the inculcation of political correctness (PC) in business. OK, women needed protections in law and new codes of practice to get a fair shake in business but it has been a tedious, if necessary, process. In some companies both sexes walk on eggshells, fearful of saying the wrong thing that could be taken the wrong way.

PC has invaded business, politics, education – life. Some individuals and cultures are so attuned to what is PC behaviour and what is not that it can be puzzling for outsiders new to dealing with them. 'I couldn't believe it when I was transferred to New York,' confides Clive, the new head of global HR for a leading accounting firm. 'I have a reputation for being a champion of women in the firm both in terms of recruitment and promotion. But in the States, I have been warned that both my humour and mannerisms are inappropriate. The women just seem to be watching everything I say and misconstrue expressions as insulting when there is no such intention. It is very wearing.' It is a brave Brit who takes on political correctness American-style!

Now that there are laws against being treated wrongly we need to move beyond PC, cognisant of our protections and search for a better rapport with male colleagues. I am not alone in despairing how PC cultures are devoid of humour and natural behaviour. 'It's early days yet, but everyone seems a bit uptight compared to my last bank,' confesses a risk management advisor. 'I have to watch what I say because of these guidelines on how to deal with the female staff.'

What's required now is for men and women to experiment with new ways of working together that creates better working environments for us all. We need to discuss things through *together*. How can we talk frankly without upsetting each other? How can we show affection or concern without offending? How can we have fun together when male and female humour can be so different? How can we tell each other when we don't like their approach without sounding like Mr or Ms PC?

▓ Sex and branding

How you deal with the opposite sex is intrinsic to your brand. Just think of people who you have met who left a definite impression (positive and negative) on how they treated men or women:

- The female account manager who goes into flirt-mode with male directors and seems to compete against her female colleagues.
- The chairman (male) who ignores women in meetings and never proffers them a handshake first.
- The guy who always makes a running to kiss the 'girls' hello when he comes in for a meeting.
- The confident/dominant woman who makes others bristle, thinking she's 'just like a man'.
- The talented female middle manager who clams up in male-dominated meetings, causing some to resent her holding back with others dismissing her as a non-entity.
- The disgruntled male executive who has a female boss whom he refers to as 'the bitch'.
- The shy male systems manager who is subjected to regular dissertations on monthly periods and sexual escapades by his female colleagues.

These are just a few I've noted down in the last few months from my seminars. Think about your own office and the characters that make you or others uncomfortable. Their antics are part of their image and it can be very damaging once 'branded' as a bully, a prat, a tease, whatever.

See how good you are at stereotyping your own work colleagues and their attitudes towards working with the opposite sex. Underneath, you have a few 'role models/characters' that might describe their behaviour. If none of these do them justice, try to come up with better ones!

MALE CHARACTER 'ROLE MODELS'

Attila the Hun; Superman, Seinfeld, Inspector Morse, Mr Bean, Darth Vader, Bill Clinton, Melvyn Bragg, Harrison Ford, Frazier, Martin Clunes, Will Self, David Beckham, Angus Deayton, Oedipus, Boris Yeltsin, Sid Vicious, David Ginola, Victor Meldrew, Noel Gallagher, Cary Grant, Puff Daddy, Grant Mitchell, Tim 'Nice but Dim', Des Lynam, Eric Cantona, Jeeves, Dilbert, John Major, James Bond, Hannibal Lecter, Jeremy Paxman, Lancelot.

Male colleagues	Their 'characters'
....	....
....	....
....	....
....	....
....	....
....	....
....	....

FEMALE CHARACTER 'ROLE MODELS'

Margaret Thatcher, Carol Vorderman, Madonna, Tammy Wynette, Dorothy in *The Wizard of Oz*, Superwoman, *Ab Fab*'s Edwina, Barbie, Ally MacBeal, Dorothy Parker, Jessica Parker (Mrs Roger Rabbit), Oprah, Princess Anne, Joan Collins, Mariah Carey, Ophelia, Miss Jean Brodie, Denise van Outen, Joan of Arc, Bet Lynch, Jane Fonda, Naomi Campbell, Hilary Clinton, Mother Teresa, Doris Day, Lady Macbeth, Cinderella, Anita Roddick, Nicola Horlick, Carole Smillie, Phoebe from Friends, Cruella De Ville, Tina Turner, Ann Widdecombe.

Female colleagues	Their 'characters'
....	....
....	....
....	....
....	....
....	....
....	....
....	....

Reflect on what these stereotypes project about your colleagues' brand values. If you asked them to stereotype you, which would be your character? If you agree with their characterization, does it have a positive or negative impact on your brand? If you aspire to a James Bond characterization, how might that influence your impact on other men as well as women colleagues or clients? If friends say that you are really the in-house Doris Day character do they mean that you rely on your attractiveness and feminine wiles to score points rather than by intellectual rigour or business acumen?

Most people, if honest, don't deny that they play with the natural 'chemistry' with the opposite sex in different situations. And why not? Part of the joy, the excitement and the rewards of working in a mixed environment is that women and men get to explore and use their instincts in influencing across sexes. The only danger is when you develop a pattern of dealing with men or women that appears both predictable and manipulative. If you turn the act 'on' or 'off' so apparently you probably lose the respect of both women and men alike.

■ Vintage matters

How confident and natural we are in our dealings with the opposite sex in business has a lot to do with our vintage – when, where and how we grew up. Each generation still working has had, and is experiencing, the breakthroughs and evolution of their relationships in business. Some had much of their career in male-dominated environments while others only had all-female or all-male bosses. Others have seen the nature of work change dramatically, spending less time in the office with their colleagues and more time on their own.

So, running the risk of making sweeping generalizations and stereotyping 'generations', and well-aware of the many exceptions, here are some of my own reflections about the challenges faced by men and women of different age groups in business today.

FIFTYSOMETHINGS

Many men in their fifties who have had the support of a full-time wife seem to find dealing with senior women, i.e. their near-contemporaries, difficult. Their relationships with most women in their own age bracket are mainly social and when confronted with women in business they can find it awkward.

Two male directors when speaking about the only woman on their board (the first woman ever appointed and roughly their age) said, 'She's very good, capable and does her homework. But she's tiresome. She's forgotten that charm can work wonders in a group like ours.' Her view of them was, 'I just ignore their nonsense and really don't have time to play the games that they want. They just don't like it when I challenge them directly. They have been a closed club for a long time. I'll never be a member, really.'

When fiftysomething men have younger daughters, who are more independent and career-minded than their mums, they can find it easier to support and mentor younger female staff than women of their own vintage. They parallel the same role that they have at home with their daughters, advising them on college, making career contacts, encouraging them. The younger women who benefit from their guidance look up to them as valued mentors. Older female colleagues, whom these men can treat much differently, look *through them*.

Working women in this age bracket are well-aware of their shortening 'shelf life' and tend to 'put up and shut up' when confronted with challenges both from younger men and women. Failing to assert themselves can make them even more vulnerable than their age. If older women don't defend the value that they offer to business no one will do it for them. This is an important group to train in advanced communication skills before they just give up and 'do time' until pensioned off.

The flip side of the 'put up and shut up' brigade are the fiftysomething battleaxes. They have 'been there and done it' a hundred times before and welcome change with as much alacrity as a sheep does a shearing.

I have had these characters in my seminars and admire both their confidence and vociferousness in defending their ground. 'The chairman would disagree, I am sure. It is not appropriate for a junior ever to make small talk with his superior.' Or, 'A woman who wears trousers to work can't be taken seriously.' Bless them. They hold their ground and go to any lengths to discourage initiatives that threaten to flatten hierarchies which could jeopardize their standing within the business. Others watch them and wince and feel relief when the perfect vehicle is construed to offer them a swift exit to early retirement.

FORTYSOMETHINGS

Fortysomething men may have partners who also work and may be equally successful. This can result in competition at home causing some men to feel resentment towards other female colleagues.

Fortysomething women are sometimes accused of 'nagging' their male counterparts similarly to how they might their husbands/partners. 'I hate when she [his boss] says that I remind her of her husband. She makes snide comparisons when things go wrong or I haven't met a deadline. I can only imagine how difficult it must be for him being married to such a ball-buster.'

Other fortysomething women relaunch themselves when their children become less reliant on them. In doing so, they enter the workplace in the role of 'mum' and find themselves as the shoulder that many seek when things go wrong. Often these women are sent on 'Assertiveness Training' with the implication that their maternal natures need squashing. One manager employing many in their call centre said, 'They are lovely women but get taken advantage of. They need to say "no" more when others start on with their personal problems. I guess they need to become less emotional and more businesslike.' More's the pity as the cut and thrust of many business environments would run more smoothly if a great mother archetype were there when we (male or female) needed her.

When the fortysomething man loses the woman in his life to a new career (or a new man) he loses a tremendous support and can feel vulnerable without it. Often he tries to turn to his own female colleagues to 'fill the gap' – literally and figuratively!

Many men find the change in their partners' new careers so invigorating that they rethink and change their own approaches towards their female colleagues. 'Nigel is so different now that Caroline [his wife] is working,' explains Lucy, his PA. 'Before if I had a problem with my kids he would be very difficult, even docked my pay when I overran my quota of sick days due to my son's operation. But now he sees how tired Caroline can get and what a woman has to do to be able to work. And my situation, as a single parent, is much worse. He's almost trying to make up for being so inconsiderate for the last 5 years.'

Thirtysomething men and women suffer the equal strains of work and, possibly, a young family. She can deride that lousy turn done to women who have to put career ambitions on the back-burner or attempts to do both and ends up suffering from chronic exhaustion, with him resenting demotion on her list of priorities behind the kids, the job, and even the dog.

Men of this vintage who try to be 'proper' dads find that their own careers can suffer if they attempt to share the parenting responsibilities. Others, realizing that juggling career and parenting is a bum rap, use the 'I'm the main breadwinner' defence. They often provide their own partners supportive lip-service while taking advantage of other female colleagues caught in the same trap. He'll be 'New Man' so long as it suits him but should any key female staffer let him down because she can't manage her career and family, well, she's simply not up to the job!

This is the decade that women can pit themselves against each other with the seemingly insoluble dilemma for childless women resenting options offered to working mums that they don't share. 'It's their decision if they want to have kids and they shouldn't expect to swan back 6 months later and expect everything to be the same,' is an opinion echoed many times out of earshot of working mums. 'My career is *my* family – my whole life. If I am prepared to sacrifice what they have, I expect greater rewards at work.'

The late thirties sees the breaking-point in many careers – both for women and men – mainly caused by the stress of carrying on at the same pace whilst having another full-time job as a parent. Because many of us are working parents for a period of our careers, it only makes sense for business to develop alternative ways of working for us to manage both. Otherwise, business will continue to bear the cost of losing trained, experienced staff and having to recruit and train up younger or older replacements who might invariably hit the same crossroads. Many large firms calculate the cost of attrition (for recruitment and training) as £5k for junior staff to £50k+ for more senior staff. So, there's a strong 'business case' to be more flexible in the future. And, of course, many companies have introduced more flexible maternity and paternity programmes, job-sharing and career breaks. But if you have a 'serious' job in a 'serious' business, life is still being played by the 1960 rulebook – you are either the company's man or woman and available as the company sees fit or you are sidelined.

'If our clients expect us to be there on-call on their 24/7 schedule what can we do?' asked the human resources partner for a global consulting firm. 'The women simply can't go the distance. They have trouble with a demanding travel schedule and working long hours because of family commitments. They revert to admin jobs rather than remain at the coal face where we need them and they are better rewarded.' What he fails to add is that thirtysomething men who remain at the coal face are also stretched with their wives/partners wanting them to share parenting. This increasingly makes the men also vulnerable, unpredictable assets.

Research shows that more and more men (like women) aren't willing to continue working 'beyond the call of duty'. They want a life. The time has come for employers to think 'outside the boxes' if they want to retain good people and prosper. Focus on new ways of delivering services and goods, e.g. via teams rather than individuals or from home or online rather than on-site.

TWENTYSOMETHINGS

Twentysomethings don't know what the fuss is all about. Young women and men are mates and expect the world to be as equal and as open as it is amongst themselves. Theirs is the generation that is opting not to try to mix work and family and feeling fine about not having it all but having one or the other. They look at frazzled, fractured women and men trying to do both and say, 'Hello? Why are you bothering?'

Twentysomethings have had a different upbringing than their older colleagues with many products of a dual-career family. They are getting coached at home, at school and university and consider any working environment that is weird and silly (in terms of attitudes towards men and women or not flexible enough) as a waste of time. If they don't like how they're being treated they are out of there. They work for 'Me, Inc' and won't put in the time that their parents or colleagues have done to work it out. Long may our economies offer you options, twentysomethings! But in the meantime, if you want some advice on dealing with perplexing men and women in business, keep reading.

Men: how to deal with women at work

WHAT WOMEN WANT FROM YOU

Women want a fair deal and they still aren't getting it. This is very tedious to be discussing in the twenty-first century but women still earn 25 per cent less than men for the same job, same work, same stress. How would you like that? A 25 per cent pay cut tomorrow just because you were different, not because you were less capable?

It is also boring that it takes longer and it's harder to get to the top for women. 'I just wish I could find talented women for our top jobs,' bemoan many male chief executives. 'We believe in this *equality thing*. There just aren't enough of them out there.' This is the usual ruse when in reality many talented, capable women have thrown in the towel or had to take a major diversion due to having children, *your* children.

Companies make it hard for women to be good mums and good employees. Their brains still function, they are capable and want to work alongside you to help you be more successful as well as themselves. But they can't, since most corporations can't quite accept the idea that working in an office away from your kids for 40, 50, 60 hours a week is wrong, that there's plenty of work that women could do for and with you that doesn't require them physically to be there all the time.

Women are well-aware that men prefer to work with men – 52 per cent state outright that this is the case where only 17 per cent of women want to work just with women (Hite Research). This is not encouraging when women are assigned to your team or appointed as your boss. We recognize the value of working alongside you, enjoying your company, but you haven't felt it yet or, perhaps, feel threatened with too many women around.

Guys get guys, but women are trouble. We require a bit of effort: you've got to think differently and develop new skills to deal with us.

And that's a bit of a struggle when you've got so much on your plate already!

Well, join the club, fellas. Women work hard at figuring you out, they go on courses, read books, talk amongst themselves, seek advice from other guys. They work at it. Women want and deserve more of your time.

The good news is that time with women pays dividends. Women make terrific co-workers, just like guys but different from guys. They enjoy making others look good as well as themselves. And they don't always demand credit. Now, that's novel, hey!

Women also make great bosses. Yeah, yeah. You've heard the horror stories, seen the movie (*Disclosure*), been on the receiving end of a lashing from a sharp female tongue and, well, you don't like it. So, it's up to you to rewrite the script, prove that it can be both different and rewarding. If you don't you will be limiting your career prospects and adding 'dinosaur' to your brand.

With half the working population today being single and pursuing new 'social arrangements' outside heterosexual relationships and/or families, understanding between the sexes is just one area of new thinking required. Same sex/multiple/no relationship personal lives is forcing tolerance, new language as well as new methods of communication in work and also in society generally.

GET IN TOUCH

A gentle touch on the elbow, using eye contact and proffering a smile could be what's needed to be more influential in business, according to communications expert Allan Pease. Women are far more comfortable with human contact than men, who limit touching each other to safety zones like the football pitch or the pub.

'Touching is a form of friendship and bonding and the British are the least touching in the world, while the Europeans, especially the French and Italians, are very tactile,' says Pease, author of *Why Men*

Don't Listen and Women Can't Read Maps. 'Certain body language such as a light touch on the other person's elbow for three seconds or less, reinforced by nodding the head, can strengthen our actions, leading to a more positive outcome.' Try it for yourself, the next time you want to reinforce a 'thank you' or 'well done' to a female colleague. When done appropriately, it can pay dividends in building relationships.

DOS AND DON'TS: MEN DEALING WITH WOMEN

In 5 years' time, the advice I'm giving you here hopefully will be obsolete. You and business are changing but, perhaps, not fast enough. To be ahead of the game and a role model for others try some of these suggestions.

I am going to risk being rather arbitrary because you need *and want* guidelines (at least that's why many companies call me in). These are suggestions that I have discussed at length with both men and women over the last few years in different sized companies. The input has been from many different nationalities who work in global companies. However, remember that there is a residual American/north-west European cultural bias which still pervades many of the top global organizations. You are the final judge of what is right for you, the woman involved, and the situation. When in doubt, use *your own* best judgement as to how *you* would like to be treated if you were in her shoes.

Do:
- *Imagine having a female boss.* Conjure together a composite woman from all the women in your life that you like and admire. Imagine this wonderful person guiding and mentoring you; helping *you* to succeed. This is the attitude to approach your new female boss. She'll get the vibes (most women are

good at this) and reward you with the attention that you deserve.

- *Coach your female colleagues.* Next time one of them gets shot down, invite her for coffee or lunch and tell her how, from your perspective, she is screwing up and how she might try to handle others better. Women will be more co-operative if you help them understand how to be more effective (particularly with other men).

- *Encourage females to contribute in meetings.* Unlike men, women are inclined to hold back unless they have something useful to contribute. Men, generally, don't have this problem. Before meetings, suggest where they can get involved. Otherwise, ask their opinion when you know that they have an important perspective.

- *Orchestrate how you can share credit.* If you work on a team, send an update to the boss bearing both your names. Get her to sign off with you. For presentations, plan a team approach for each of you to shine and to convey a united front.

- *Express an interest in her interests outside work.* You know how easy it is to develop rapport and friendships with most of your male colleagues, so too is it possible with women. You don't need to commit to a close friendship to be good colleagues. The more you know about each other the more you can *understand* each other. Don't pry into intimate areas, rather get background, lifestyle and interests. Better to drip-feed your enquiries rather than hit her with a full-scale investigation!

- *Develop a collegial relationship.* This is not about dating or, as mentioned above, the need to become friends. There is a zone below friendship that is pleasant, warm and human – colleagues. If you are between meetings, have lunch together. If you are travelling and have some time on your hands, why not pop into a museum. If you both like to run, why not suggest the occasional jog around the park together? These are opportunities for you to 'bond', it can enhance your business partnership and teamwork. You will also be seen as a good man by other female colleagues and admired (despite their wisecracks) by your male counterparts for getting on with 'the women'.

- *Tell her if she makes you uncomfortable.* Women aren't averse to trying it on with men at work either with language or actions that are inappropriate. You can ignore her, which should send the message that you don't like certain language or banter. If she is smart, she'll get the message. If she is stupid or a bully, meet with her and say that you want her to knock it off. Tell her you don't like it yourself, but that her behaviour and/or language is more damaging to her than to you. (Teach her a bit about branding herself and lend her this book!)
- *Listen to her.* Try to encourage women by looking attentive (rather than at your watch or shuffling papers); lean forward and nod occasionally. If she goes on a bit, interject and say something like, 'You've covered so much already, let's sort out these points before we go further.' Or, 'I only have 10 minutes before my next meeting, so tell me what is the most important thing we need to resolve today.'
- *Resist the urge to always go first.* In meetings, urge *her* to speak first. As women find it hard to 'get entry' into many male-dominated meetings, give her the

floor at the beginning, which will encourage her participation throughout.

- *Notice change.* It is absurd not to compliment a colleague when she has a new outfit or cuts her hair. You know when a compliment crosses the line from the acceptable into the unacceptable. If in doubt, imagine your friend/partner/wife in the same situation and how you would like her male colleagues to compliment her.

Don't:

- *Flip at the first sign of emotion.* Sure, it's inappropriate to get emotional at work but sometimes there are valid reasons. Keep calm, get her to sit with you in an office (not so close in case she leans forward expecting physical support) and try to discuss the issue at hand. If she is too emotional, suggest she goes for a walk outside to calm down but comes to see you when she feels more composed to discuss things.
- *Interrupt.* Many women report that men are chronic interrupters, which makes women feel both diminished and humiliated. If particular female staff aren't effective communicators (they ramble, sound strident, or are too verbose, etc.), help them see their weaknesses and encourage them to improve. People who interrupt try to pass themselves off as highly intelligent (but bore easily). At best they are insensitive; at worst, they're bullies.
- *Judge women differently.* Sure, women *are* different to men but they are work colleagues and need to be judged with the same yardstick as male colleagues. That's what women want. Value their work as equally as the men and take them to task, as you would a man, when you are disappointed.

- *Assume your female boss will be like your mum* – telling you what to do! Teachers and your mum might be the only other 'authority' female figures that you've known thus far. When a woman boss is directive she is just being that – direct in making her mission clear and explaining what has to be done so that the company, her team and *you* succeed. Be grateful for the clarity that she gives you rather than bristle, viewing them as a demand from mum. *Go clean up your mess!*
- *Exclude her from huddles.* Notice when you guys are excluding women and make an effort to include them. Guys form huddles in reception areas, before meetings or over coffee / drinks. Your male 'pack' is physically exclusive to women. They have to hover on the edges, excluded. Try as we might, we can't get in. So, be aware that you do it. Once you have bonded with the boys, be gracious and step away and try to include your female colleagues.
- *Assume that she fancies you.* As attractive as you are, female colleagues aren't necessarily sending 'come hither' glances just because they convey that they like you. Remember the goal is to be good colleagues, possibly friends. If you cross the line assuming that she does fancy you, be sure your antenna is well-tuned and you don't ruin the working relationship.
- *Show your anger.* Male anger is very threatening and scary to many women as it is reminiscent of bad personal experiences, a disappointed father, angry lover, rejecting partner, or worse. *Assume that most women have been frightened by a man at some point in their life, because we all have.* Always confront the problem and do so behind closed doors, one to one,

i.e. without an audience. If she does merit your wrath see how you can express it without being insulting or threatening. For example, 'You didn't follow the brief and we got nailed as a result. Explain yourself.' Or, 'You misread them completely. They weren't worried about the systems until you raised them. Now we have real problems. What was your rationale?' Both of these would be preferable to 'How could you be so stupid?'

- *Assume she's a 'bitch'.* If a woman shoots you down in business, your pride can be severely dented, particularly if you've lost face in front of other male colleagues. Reflect back on the criticism and its validity and remember her language. Then imagine a male manager taking you to task the same way. Would it have been easier coming from him? If so, you just need to put in some time getting used to having women *talk and work like men* in business. Of course, women in business can be 'bitches' just as guys can be real 'bastards'. Just watch that you don't tar all strong, competent women with the same brush.

- *Shy away from singing her praises when you don't have to.* We all have opportunities to be magnanimous in business but men can find it hard to be so on behalf of women colleagues or staff among men *when they don't have to*. It is new and different for men to promote the qualities of women in business but you enhance your brand every time you do. You can do it for the guys, so try also doing it for the women.

- *Worry about women taking over.* Most women aren't interested in 'taking things over' and ruling over men in business. They want to be part of things just like they are part of your life in so many other ways.

Ambitious ones will seek out opportunities and occasionally you may lose out on a promotion to one. Don't feel castrated when it's a woman rather than a man who does better. It's only business.

Women: how to deal with men at work

WHAT MEN WANT FROM YOU

No, they are not all looking for a new girlfriend or a bit on the side. And, with a few notable exceptions, most men in business are trying to figure out how to be fair to their female colleagues. Of course, there are plenty of Neanderthals still hovering in boardrooms, salesrooms and mailrooms but most men *like having us around*.

'Jane is so different from other bosses that I've had,' explains James, a senior member of her team on a major systems project. 'She is generous and spends so much time on *me*, guiding me, helping me. Before Jane, I was just turning up, doing the job, collecting the pay. Now, I know where I'm going, have a new career plan thanks to her. I don't know any other senior directors here who do the same kind of personal coaching that Jane does. By the way, I'm not her golden boy. Talk to other people here and she's done the same for many of them.'

Hence, not everyone's experience with a female boss is negative. Like James, there are many men who welcome your different approaches to doing business and in managing them. You can be a breath of fresh air and make a real difference. The key seems to be doing it on *your* terms, not on some unisex notion of what all good managers must do. Women *are* different, we can rewrite the rules and prove to guys that we might not only be good but, often, preferable to having a male boss.

Men, like women, use their own personal experiences, previous relationships, to guide them in dealing with their female colleagues, staff and bosses. As we look to senior males as 'father figures' or troublesome junior men as 'just like my brother or son' so too do we remind them of the irritating big sister, mummy, or previous girlfriends – good, bad and indifferent.

With every change in business – mergers, down-sizing, reorganization, etc. – we witness a change in the male/female culture. Men, like women, are learning loads and getting better by the day at feeling better *in themselves* about having us around.

You've read through Vintage matters and understand the difference in male attitudes by age just from your own experience. There are other cultural, psychological and social issues that create some of the baggage that men have to contend with in figuring out how to deal with us as staff, colleagues or bosses.

Culturally, men never gained much cred from hanging out with women. They were called names as a kid for being 'tied to Mummy's apron strings' or a 'girl' because they hated sports. Women, heretofore, haven't added value to a man's positioning in his male packs at school and at work aside from as girlfriends or trophy wives. They have yet to determine how to enjoy being part of your team and be proud of you.

We enter their business domain with new language and 'instruments' to measure them – emotional barometers –which men have limited knowledge, experience or encouragement to develop. No longer do they just need to be competent and get the job done but they have to make people *feel* good about them and the company along the way. 'Emotional intelligence' really defines for men what most women do instinctively. We have had to learn how to be more analytical while the men have had to learn how to be more intuitive and communicative.

SO, WHAT DO YOU DO?

Women know how much the male ego is attached to his job title and salary. Think of any social situation and how long it takes the man in you life to make his identity known. 'Hi, I'm John. I'm with Brat Pack, Plc. What do you do?' What does it take? Minutes? Seconds? He further clarifies exactly where he is in the organization, just in case folks don't know already. Few things are more stressful than for a chap not to make his credentials known and clear to new people. It is the equivalent of dogs sniffing each other out – once done, they can relax and play together!

Although many women now share the same pride/obsession of identifying who we are with what we do, it still isn't as vital to our self-esteem as it is for men – yet. But ask any man if he would like his partner/wife to earn more than he does and the answer is: 'Hell, no!' (when he's being honest or his reply is confidential). These are the guys we live with and we *work with*. In Hite's research 20 per cent of CEOs (all male) admit that 'men just do not feel comfortable with women around' at the top of companies. This explains why losing out on a promotion to a woman can be quite painful for men. What kind of guy is second best to a *woman*? Playing second fiddle at work is as bad as playing it at home!

Men with working partners are waking up to the freedom and benefits of a second income. Our earnings give men the opportunity to chuck in dead-end jobs, play 'at-home' dads for a while, try new careers or take a welcome break from the treadmill. Recognizing these benefits, men are beginning to bask in their wife/partner's achievements and are becoming champions of their female staff, colleagues and bosses often as a result.

DOS AND DON'TS: WOMEN DEALING WITH MEN

More arbitrary suggestions that you can take or leave follow. These are validated by many of the men as genuine issues and the advice provided has been honed from working with and interviewing both men and women about what they feel are good and viable solutions.

Do:
- *Visualize yourself on their team.* Initially, it's better to become a team player, then differentiate yourself. All

that's required is some effort and a good attitude. You don't need to become 'one of the boys' to be part of their team. Just convey that you *want* to be part of it.

- *Sell your assets.* Women undersell what they are doing, and what they've achieved whilst men do this without feeling like twits or braggadocios. Take emotion out of the picture. Talk achievements – in black and white. Well done!

- *Talk money.* Know where you stand in the pecking order and exactly what you should be earning (aware that many women are underpaid for the same work they do as men). Raise money as a topic for discussion. 'I know my performance review isn't due for 3 months but I would like to discuss with you my expectations in light of the business I've delivered so far this year. I'd be interested in your views. Can we have that conversation some time soon?'

- *Talk promotion.* Don't wait for the opportunities to present themselves, rather make it known that you are interested in new areas and want to develop professionally. You don't necessarily want to appear money-grabbing or overly ambitious, rather driven by your own goals. So, get them sharpened up.

- *Be magnanimous* in your dealings with male colleagues. Share the credit, tell him of *his* contributions in front of others who matter. In doing so, you are showing your management potential to motivate and reward others.

- *Use your image to your advantage.* Women need to be told this, not the guys. I'm not talking thighs, cleavage and flowing locks here, which might get you one or two deals along the way but will make you more enemies than it is probably worth. Just make the most of your natural beauty and enjoy how you dress and present yourself. Never 'apologize' by denying your femininity and dressing unisex (unless that's your style). Besides, the men love the difference the women can lend to the team just by being women.

- *Deal with objections.* Many women regard objections raised by men as a personal slight on their capabilities. Recognize that objection is not about *rejection*, though it might feel like it. Consider an objection as an awkward request for more information. For example, your senior manager might say, 'I really don't think you've done your homework for this meeting.' Your natural reaction might be to reply, 'What the hell are you talking about! I've busted my guts over this presentation' which you can see really won't win him over to value what you've done any more. You've got to find out *why he's objected.* Get clarification; 'Tell me why you think that?' As you get more information see how you might not have fulfilled what he needed from you, then explain how you have, indeed, done what he wanted, plus some!

- *Try to be dispassionate in conflict.* Probe, probe and probe some more to really find out the underlying issue. You can deal with issues; uncertainty is what's troublesome, leading both you and them to jump to the wrong conclusions.

- *Take risks.* Men admire bravery in each other as well as other women. Calculate the downside of things going against you but show courage (they don't always expect this from women) and you will earn tremendous respect. However, don't rub their noses in it if they bottled out and you went charging in to win the day. Smirking 'I told you sos' of either sex are tiresome.

- *Touch them.* That's right. Following point 8 is a good example of how women can change the nature of the workplace. *Occasionally* and *appropriately* touch them, a pat on the back, the shoulder or upper arm. But don't do anything that you know will send the wrong messages, e.g. stroking his hair, pressing your body against his, or kissing him on the mouth.
- *Tell men when they offend you or make you uncomfortable.* You don't need an audience for this (unless he's been a real prat). Rather than let him continue to upset/annoy you, clear the air. 'I want us to get on and if ever I do anything that upsets you I want to know about it. Likewise, I need to feel that I can do the same with you. OK? I like you and enjoy working with you but it does bug me when you put your arm around me in front of people. You don't do that when we are alone and others might misread things. So, no more hugs!' Such a message has the right amount of sweetener to deliver the no-nonsense punch. I've always found the carrot and stick combo effective in dealing with either sex.

Don't:
- *Treat your colleagues as you do your partner.*
  It's easy to slide into this one and very inappropriate. Besides: it's a dead give-away as to how things are going at home!
- *Assume he can read you.* If you cry he'll know that you are upset and if you are perky that you are happy. Otherwise, you are a blank canvas. If you are concerned about anything at work, raise it clearly with him.

- *Apologize.* Apologies are only acceptable in the following instances:
  - His cat has died.
  - You forgot his birthday.
  - You've kept him waiting.
  - You've screwed up big time and have no excuse.

  Otherwise, *don't apologize.* Women do so constantly. 'Sorry, what did you say? 'Sorry, is this the file you wanted?' 'Sorry, I wrote three versions of the presentation to give you some options!'

- *Use 50 words when 10 suffice.* Women are more verbal than men which can drive them round the bend when we get into full, descriptive flow. Try to imagine yourself giving a briefing just like a news reporter: Start with your headline hook, follow by key points, add an anecdote or evidence, then conclude or suggest next steps / options / what needs discussion.

- *Hold back and wait until you are invited to contribute.* Jump in there, woman, because you will be (or have been?) bitterly disappointed if you wait for men to ask your views on things. Guys don't usually ask, they just spout forth aware that if they don't they might not get heard.

- *Wait for a break.* You spy an opportunity? Make a case for your pursuing it, then *say that you want to do it.* Don't make it hard for them to give you the opportunities you might deserve. Women nurture staff, men don't.

- *Turn down chances to socialize.* The men might enjoy drinking or sporting sessions more than you do but try to find ways to mix with your male colleagues outside the office (occasionally). 'You guys go to the Eight Bells on Friday, right? I've had a killer of a week. Can I join you for one?' Should you get rejected, dust off your CV – you are working with brutes.

- *Always believe the rumour mill.* Your intelligence might reveal that your male boss or colleague has been mouthing off about you unfairly. Assume an element of hype but some truth to the accusation. Confront him, one to one, and if he has done you wrong (and he damn well knows it), say that you expect him to put it right, in your presence.

- *Put yourself in dumb situations.* Travelling with male colleagues presents all sorts of challenges. While it is a great opportunity to get to know each other better and have some fun, you can't assume that after a long day and a few drinks things can't get 'confused'. Relax, enjoy time together, but watch the alcohol intake. Best to enjoy yourselves over dinner then make a retreat to your room afterwards, resisting a nightcap which can lead to the weird territory of 'saying goodnight'. Make your own way back to your room to avoid the awkward lonely lift and key fumbling scenario which somehow can arouse unforeseen and invariably passionate episodes.

- *Challenge if he's likely to lose face or self-esteem.* Earning a reputation as a ball-buster might be fun for a while but invariably comes back to haunt you. Humiliating others in public – male or female – is not an admirable trait and a sure-fire bet that you will be the one over next time. Men are much better than women at not getting mad and just getting even!

What about sex?

We know that it is a dangerous business mixing sex and business but it happens – at Christmas parties, over the photocopier, at trade fairs. It happens with bosses and with staff, with wives and lovers of co-workers, even with valued clients. It creates 'atmospheres' and hurt feelings. It loses contracts and good employees. Sex is always a messy business!

According to Hite Research, 42 per cent of people are in relationships with people at work and 35 per cent of those are hiding the fact from co-workers. Companies have a range of 'policies' governing office romances which range from the outright ban on relationships or others that allow only one of the pair to remain with the company, to threatening the dismissal of both if found out. The rationale, of course, is that if companies allow any flirtation in the office then it is a very slippery slope to sexual harassment – which can cost companies money, big money.

But if work is our life – realistically 50+ hours a week – and if over half of all employees are single, is it realistic that they should shut down their sexual instincts for most of their waking hours? Whether you are in a relationship or not, few of us get through a day without some fantasizing. Does a ban on relationships at work mean we will spend less time working and more time daydreaming? What happens when any of us is banned from doing something? It becomes more intriguing and desirable. Surely companies that are so heavy-handed in trying to prevent relationships between staff are only adding fuel to the fire.

Besides, where are our single colleagues going to meet eligible partners? The boom in dating agencies bears witness to how difficult it is find the time and the energy to play the field. It is only natural (and healthy) for staff to get to know each other well and, for some, to form richer personal relationships as a result.

Political correctness has a lot to answer for. Drawing up rules to govern the behaviour between men and women adds to the confusion of working together rather than clarifying things. Guidelines are needed to protect the vulnerable from the bullies of either sex. What we don't need are moralistic and unrealistic codes of practice that stifle the development of close relationships from colleagues to friends, and to lovers in some cases. Men and women need to explore further how we can be some of these things, sometimes all of these things, with each other during our careers. Both our work and our sex lives are too important to us for us not to.

Until we've got things sorted, here are some guidelines for not getting yourself into trouble at work:

- *Don't preen yourself* in front of others: run your fingers through your hair, stroke your body, and women don't put your make-up on in public. Such antics are not just inappropriate in business but can be off-putting.
- *Keep your distance.* The closer you are the greater the chance of temperatures rising, or you touching them in a way that announces your intimacy.
- *Watch the lingering eyes.* 'I only have eyes for you' is a dead give-away that you were 'at it' last night just by your ability to hold eye contact ad nauseum.
- *Avoid even 'friendly' kisses* where possible. If you are apprehensive about someone's interest avoid even their 'air kisses' (cheek to cheek) – you are still too close for comfort. Better to show 'friendliness' by touching their shoulder or upper arm. Both are safe non-erogenous zones.
- *Don't be alone with them* if you don't want to encourage them further.
- *Put them off your scent – lie!* If you aren't interested or really don't want the hassle, spread the news about the terrific new (hot!) person in your life.
- *Become mates.* If you really like them, see if you can be

friends. Do things together (with others) and see if you can find a relationship that is other than becoming lovers, something close, genuine and caring. We all need mates and, God knows, they last much longer than a love affair.

The rules of how men and women should interact at work are being written by the day. Your own experiences will certainly colour your views and either broaden or narrow your perspective. If you have had unsettling or negative past experiences with the opposite sex at work try not to be defensive about future possibilities with new colleagues. Assume sincerity first whilst not ignoring worrying danger signals discussed in this chapter. Reflect on how your own behaviour, language and humour might unwittingly offend some people some of the time.

But when you get it wrong, have enough integrity to put things right with whoever might have been on the wrong end of the stick. The man or woman courageous enough to apologize for hurting a colleague not only enhances their standing and brand within the organization but gains the satisfaction of doing the decent thing.

CONCLUSION

Whether you have ducked and dived through the various chapters and exercises in this book or been methodical in following my path from start to finish you should now have a clear idea of the person you want to project to the world. Your brand values are defined and you have a firm plan to project them through your behaviour, your voice and communication skills and by how you look and interact with others.

You might now realize that you've got some work to do if you want to be different, be more, be the person that you dream possible. What you don't have, dear reader, is time to hang about. Time is flying and with it are the opportunities for you to get what you deserve.

So, get on with it . . .

What's going on later today, at the weekend? How will you be better for that experience than you would have been before you opened this book? Visualize how you want people to react. What do you need to do *to get those reactions*? Should you try walking tall or a more impressive handshake? Are you ready for small talk? How can you improve the way you look? Yes, now! Get to the gents and run your fingers through your hair. Button your jacket, straighten your tie. On second thought, dash out and get a better one. Women: powder your face and freshen the lippy. Big, confident smile followed by a big, confident handshake. You are going to speak within the first 5 minutes of your next meeting. No, you are going to start it off with a brilliant soundbite. Not honed yet? Then get drafting and memorizing.

Don't reflect on past bloopers, when you were a complete oaf or wimped out when you should have stood the test. You've blown it before and you'd be a fool to think that you might not again.

Value your brand and everything you stand for. You owe it to yourself and to your future. Which is *now*.

FURTHER READING

General inspiration

Bradbury, Andrew, *NLP for Business Success* (Kogan Page, 1997)
Csikszentmihaligi, Mihaly, *Living Well* (Weidenfeld & Nicolson, 1997)
Buzan, Tony, *The Mind Map Book* (BBC Books, 1993)
Gleick, James, *Faster* (Little Brown & Co, 1999)
Goleman, Daniel, *Emotional Intelligence at Work* (Bloomsbury, 1998)
Peters, Tom, *The Circle of Innovation* (Hodder & Stoughton, 1997)
Ridderstråles, Nordström, *Funky Business* (FT.com, 2000)

Corporate branding

Jenkins, Nicholas, *The Business of Image* (Kogan Page, 1991)
Ollins, Wally, *Corporate Identity* (Thames & Hudson, 1991)
Pringle, Hamish and Thompson, Marjorie, *Brand Spirit* (John Wiley & Sons, 1999)

Cross-cultural communication

Lewis, Richard, *When Cultures Collide* (Brealey Publishing, 1996)
Marx, Elisabeth, *Breaking Through Culture Shock* (Nicholas Brealey Publishing, 1999)
Mole, John, *Mind Your Manners* (Brealey Publishing, 1998)
Trompenaars, Fons and Hampden-Turner, Charles, *Riding the Waves of Culture: Understanding Cultural Diversity in Business* (Nicholas Brealey, 1997)

Dress and image

Chic Simple: Women's Wardrobe (Thames & Hudson, 1996)
Griffin, Linda, *What Should I Wear? Dressing for Occasions* (Thames & Hudson, 1998)

Spillane, Mary, *The Makeover Manual* (Pan Books, 1999)
——*Look and Feel the Age You Want to Be* (Pan Books, 2001)

For men

Gross, Kim Johnston, *Men's Wardrobe* (Thames & Hudson, 1998)
Solomon, Michael, *Chic Simple: Shirt and Tie* (Thames & Hudson, 1993)

Influencing others

Bryce, Lee, *The Influential Woman* (Piatkus, 1989)
Leeds, Dorothy, *Marketing Yourself* (Piatkus, 1991)
Peale, Norman Vincent, *You Can If You Think You Can* (Heinemann, 1974)
Stone, Douglas et al., *Difficult Conversations:How to Discuss What Matters Most* (Harvard Negotiation Project, 1999)
Temporal, Dr Paul and Adler, Dr Harry, *Corporate Charisma* (Piatkus, 1998)

Voice and presentation

Brown, Lillian, *Your Public Best* (Newmarket Press, NY, 1989)
Kushner, Malcolm, *Successful Presentations for Dummies* (IDG Books, 1995)
Townsend, John, *The Great Presentation Scandal* (Mangement Pocket Books, 1999)
Urech, Elizabeth, *Speaking Globally* (Kogan Page, 1997)

Men and women

Gray, John, *Men are from Mars, Women are from Venus* (HarperCollins, 1999)
Hite, Shere, *Sex and Business* (Pearson Education, 2000)
Pease, Alan, *Why Men Don't Listen and Women Can't Read Maps* (Orion, 1999)

 INDEX

accents 81–2, 98–101

accessories 169, 170–1, 174, 189–91, 243–5, 337

alcohol 148, 150, 151, 308

Amazon 15, 17

anecdotes 325

apologizing 370

applause 325–6

approachability 109

articulation 90–2

assets 59–63

attention 311, 315

backpacks 128, 189, 243–4

bags 189–90, 199

behaviour 57, 103–52

beta-blockers 308

blind spots 33–4

body language 57, 58, 66, 105–41, 272, 356–7

boomerang effect 26

boredom 140

brand statement 64, 68, 70–1, 73, 74

Branson, Richard 16, 42

breathing 85, 263

briefcases 243–4

Brim, Orville 27

budget 175, 176, 231, 246–7

Bush, George 275

Buzan, Tony 306

Carter, Jimmy 6, 259

casual dressing 177–88, 214, 232–42

celebrities 19, 42

change 25–6, 27, 73, 287

clarity 90, 93

Clinton, Bill 91, 286

closed gestures 127

clothes 336

case studies 66, 67, 74–5

for men 205–42, 246–7

for presentations 336

for women 155–88, 202

Coca-Cola 15, 16

collarless jackets 172

colours

hair 195, 249

men 220, 223, 228, 237–9

women 182–5

commonality 279–80

compliments 324, 326, 360

computer presentations 330–1

concealer 251, 252–3

conclusions 88, 333–5

confidence 110

Conran Group 42

Conran, Terence 42

corporate culture 158, 159, 209–11

corporate identity 43, 157–8, 178, 209, 233

corporate values 209, 233, 325–6

Coupland, Douglas 28–9

If this book has inspired you to do something extra to project your personal brand more successfully we can help. ImageWorks can coach you and your team in the fine details of getting your branding right first time, every time.

Contact us at **www.imageworksuk.com**.

If you want guidance on selecting colours and styles to suit you or even be taken shopping to get the gear together, Color Me Beautiful can help.

Contact them on **www.colormebeautiful.co.uk**.